THE
ITALIAN LEFT
IN THE
TWENTIETH
CENTURY

THE
ITALIAN LEFT
IN THE
TWENTIETH
CENTURY

A History of the Socialist and
Communist Parties

ALEXANDER DE GRAND

**INDIANA
UNIVERSITY
PRESS**
Bloomington and Indianapolis

Manufactured in the United States of America

Library of Congress Cataloging-in-Publication Data
De Grand, Alexander J., 1938–
The Italian left in the twentieth
century.
Bibliography: p.
Includes index.
Partito socialista italiano—History. 2. Partito—
comunista italiano—History. I. Title.
JN5657.S6D4 1989   324.245'074   87–46371
ISBN 0–253–33107–2

1 2 3 4 5 93 92 91 90 89

To Linda, alone at last.

CONTENTS

ACKNOWLEDGMENTS

The original idea for this project grew out of research done while on a National Endowment for the Humanities Fellowship in 1980–81. Robert Mandel, now at the Wayne State University Press, offered his initial encouragement, and Lauren Bryant and the other editors at the Indiana University Press were patient and helpful in seeing the project through to its conclusion.

I also owe a special debt of gratitude to my friends and colleagues at North Carolina State University and elsewhere. Marion Miller, Alice Kelikian, Steven Vincent, Richard Drake, and James Banker read all or parts of the manuscript and were generous with their time and suggestions. In addition, David Miller, Marta Petrusewicz, Jon Kofas, and Anthony Cardoza offered useful advice along the way. They helped me to avoid errors of fact and interpretation, and to make the manuscript more readable.

INTRODUCTION

"The Red Flag will triumph!" So promised the worker anthem to generations of Italian workers and peasants. The movements of the Italian Socialist and Communist parties embodied this dream and sought to transmit it to the entire society. As with most visions, reality proved more obdurate than expected. A new Italy did emerge, in great part out of the struggle of the socialists and communists, but the results were quite unexpected. Their secular version of the "shining city on the hill" turned out to be a modern Italy of computers, traffic congestion, and supermarkets.

This book offers a parallel history of those two parties, centering on the interaction of their internal evolution and the relationships they established with each other and with the larger society. I concentrate on Italian socialism and communism because the two parties remain among the most active and interesting movements of the contemporary European left. Both parties have shown extraordinary adaptability. Until recently, Italy was led by Bettino Craxi, the head of the Italian Socialist party, who first remade his party ideologically and then attempted to displace both the Christian Democrats and the communists as the pivotal parties in Italian politics. The Italian Communist party continues to be the largest and most innovative of the European communist movements outside of the Soviet bloc. Defeated in the elections of June 1987, it is currently struggling against predictions of inevitable decline, but in the past it has consistently broken new ground with its theories of polycentrism and Eurocommunism or with its political strategies, such as the "historic compromise" with the Catholics. Until now, however, the two parties have been studied separately, despite the fact that their histories have been closely related. In the following pages I shall bring together recent scholarship on Italian socialism and communism in an attempt to understand not only how they dealt with the problem of gaining power, but also how they dealt with each other.

The Communist and Socialist parties were natural allies, bound by their common hostility to the existing capitalist society, yet they were also natural enemies, competing for the allegiance of the same workers. The rivalry between communists and socialists is part of a larger dialogue between revolutionaries and reformists within the Italian left, and between differing concepts of socialism. It was a necessary debate, but it was also destructive and debilitating. In the end, perhaps, it has been superseded by the great economic and social changes of the 1970s and 1980s that have made a violent proletarian revolution seem like a distant dream. Yet revolutionary socialism has been relegated to the attic before—most notably by the confident liberal prime minister, Giovanni Giolitti in 1911—only to return with a vengeance when the underpinnings of the capitalist system gave way during and after World War I.

The story which follows is as much about the search for a common and workable definition of socialism as it is about plans for revolution. It is also another way of looking at the history of Italy from the 1890s to 1979. The Italian left reflected the patterns of the society in which it developed. The Italian state and society have been marked by strong local and regional loyalties that date back to the Middle Ages. Not surprisingly, the left-wing parties had similar strong communal and regional structures. Italy has also had a sharp division between North and South. So it is with the Italian left, which developed much more rapidly in the North. Italy has had great difficulty integrating its rural and urban development into a satisfactory pattern of unified growth. This has been a persistent problem of the socialist movement, and was one of the primary causes for the failure of the revolution at crucial moments, such as during the "Red Years" of 1919 and 1920. The Italian ruling class has had difficulty bridging the enormous social and economic differences in the country. Thus, it should not be surprising that the Italian left was marked by a similar deep-class antagonism which blocked successful reformism and led to intransigent and violent action.

It is important to understand that many of the so-called defects of the left-wing parties merely reflected deeper problems in Italian society. As these problems changed over time, so did the Socialist and Communist parties. As long as the problems remained essentially the same, certain patterns could not easily be broken. In this regard the great turning point in Italy's modern history came not with the World Wars, or with the triumph of fascism, or with the victory of the Republic in 1946. Rather, the turning point came in the 1950s and 1960s with the occurrence of the economic miracle. This period altered Italian history more than any other, creating the basis for a new society and, arguably, for a new left.

There was a substantial degree of continuity in Italian development from the turn of the century to the post-World War II period. Breaking points—such as the start of World War I, the triumph of fascism in 1922, the fall of Mussolini in 1943, or the establishment of the Republic in 1946—brought great changes in both the national and international context within which Italy developed; but Italian society, like a river flowing through a path deeply carved by history, resumed its old course. The left-wing parties, so eager to redirect the flow of history, became prisoners within the narrow confines of Italian social and economic development. Then, when the great transformation of Italy took place in the late 1950s and 1960s, it did so without creating new political and institutional structures. Instead, society changed and enlarged the content of the republican and democratic forms that had been built after the fall of fascism.

Observers tend either to ask too much of political leaders or to accept the absolute standards that the leaders set for themselves. This is especially dangerous for Italian revolutionaries. It is not necessarily true that the leaders of the left failed because Italy avoided revolution throughout the period covered by this book. In the following chapters, many of the men and women who led the left-wing parties must be judged not on some well-defined standard of success or failure, but on the basis of the moral coherence of the ideals for which they fought and on their contribution to the long struggle of the Italian working class to obtain a substantial degree of citizenship within the state. That this came about in ways quite unexpected should not in any sense diminish the achievement of the left in helping to create this new society.

In writing this history, I have tried to avoid using today's perspective to judge how the socialists should have acted to transform their ideals into reality. Despite that caveat, I believe that reformism was the only realistic possibility for the proletarian movement during the period covered in this book. Still, reformism was never an easy or convenient option. The pessimistic, but inescapable, conclusion is that for most of the years from the turn of the century until the 1960s there was often scant hope for even a reformist policy. In Germany, where the Socialist party was dominated by reformists and followed policies quite different from those of the PSI, the results were no better until after the economic miracle of the 1950s. Similar conclusions might be reached for England until after 1945.

There were, however, three moments when an aggressive reformist program might have had some chance of success. The first came during the Giolittian era between 1903 and 1912; the second in the Red Years of 1918 through 1920; the third during the period immediately following the fall of fascism. Each represented a missed opportunity, either because the reformists did not press hard enough, or because the left was distracted by a vision of vast revolutionary change. Only once, perhaps, in 1919, were conditions ripe for revolution; but the Italian Socialist party was never organized to lead a successful assault on bourgeois power, nor were the leading revolutionary socialists in agreement on what a successful revolution might entail.

The following chapters are divided into two roughly equal parts. The first covers the years from the founding of the Italian Socialist party through the fall of fascism in 1943. Chapters 1 and 2 deal with the growth of the socialist movement before World War I, when it seemed that the economic boom from 1900 to 1907 might carry Italy on an evolutionary, not revolutionary, political course. These hopes were dashed, however, by economic crisis in 1908, by the polarization caused by the Libyan war in 1911, and by the outbreak of World War I. Chapters 3 and 4 focus on the attempt at an Italian revolution in 1919 and 1920, the emergence of the Italian Communist party in 1921, and the complete triumph of fascism between 1922 and 1926. The final chapter in part one covers the reorganization of the Italian left in exile from 1926 to 1943.

Part two picks up the story with the establishment of the Republic. Chapter 6 describes the reconstruction of the left-wing political parties in Italy after the fall of Mussolini in July 1943. The impact of the Cold War on Italy from the rupture of socialist unity in January 1947 to the Popular Front election of 1948 is dealt with in chapter 7. The chapter which follows encompasses the years of gradual thaw from 1949 to 1960. Chapters 9 and 10 carry the story to a conclusion in 1979, when both the center-left coalition between Christian Democrats and socialists and the Historic Compromise between Catholics and communists reached an impasse. Since 1980, the Italian Socialist party under Bettino Craxi has embarked on an ambitious but successful effort to make itself the fulcrum of the political system.

As with all products these days, disclaimers are necessary. This book is not a study of left-wing ideologies. Such a study would entail a very different approach. Instead, socialist theories will be discussed only as they are necessary to explain historical events. Nor is this a survey of the entire Italian left. Middle-class democrats, anarchists, and syndicalists enter the story only marginally. What follows is a political study of two parties—the Socialist and Communist—which embody the major traditions of the Italian proletarian left. It is a history of the two movements "from the top down." Little space has been given to electoral geography or to the changing nature of the parties' constituencies. In determining the size and scope of this work, I have followed the model of my earlier study of the Italian Fascist regime. I have tried to be brief, but, I hope, complete and readable. Footnotes have been eliminated; however, my substantial debts to scholars working inside and out of Italy will emerge in the extended bibliographical essay that concludes the book.

THE
ITALIAN LEFT
IN THE
TWENTIETH
CENTURY

PART ONE

The Left from the Formation of the Italian Socialist Party to the Triumph of Fascism

CHAPTER 1

The Origins of the Socialist Movement in Italy, 1860–1900

In 1892 the city of Genoa celebrated the four-hundredth anniversary of Columbus's voyage to America. The railroads offered reduced fares to encourage participation in the festivities. These reductions by the state settled the choice of location for a venture far removed from, and totally opposed to, the official ceremonies in honor of the great explorer. On August 14 and 15, 1892, delegates from various worker organizations met in Genoa to create the Partito dei Lavoratori Italiani. Those in attendance had no idea that the party they created would have lasted nearly one hundred years. So uncertain of success were they that many delegates doubted whether the venture should be undertaken at all. Orthodox marxists wondered whether Italy had reached the economic and social maturity to support a socialist movement. The anarchists, most of whom abandoned the meeting in protest, disliked the whole idea of commitment to legal political action and organization. Yet the party, renamed three years later Partito Socialista Italiano (PSI), not only survived, but became a major force in Italian politics.

The path was never easy or smooth. Like the modern Italian nation itself, the new PSI was a latecomer on the European scene. The German Social Democratic Party (SPD) dated from 1875, and was closely followed by the socialist movements of Denmark (1878), France (1881), Belgium (1885), Norway (1887), and Sweden (1889). The British Labour Party would not emerge until after the turn of the century, but the English left benefited from a long history of labor union activity.

THE ECONOMIC AND POLITICAL CONTEXT

The Italian state, created only in 1860, was the relatively fragile achievement of a narrow economic and social elite. National unification meant the destruction of the Papal States and their absorption into Italy in

1860. When Rome was also taken in 1870, Pius IX retaliated by excommunicating those who had any part in the seizure of his lands, and he forbade Catholics from serving in the new national government; but Catholic hostility was only one problem. Regionalism remained strong in the South and Center and was made worse by the decision to create a centralized state structure based on the laws and constitution of the Kingdom of Sardinia. Few Italians could vote, and fewer still participated in the political life of the new Italy.

Poverty and a huge national debt exacerbated the isolation of the national political class from the masses. The wars of unification had been financed by foreign loans. The taxes, imposed to pay this debt, fell hardest on the peasants, who composed the bulk of the population. Moreover, the new rulers of Italy had to build the roads, harbors, rail and telegraph lines, as the indispensible material bases for unity. They too were paid for by increasing the tax burden on the poor and embittered masses.

The economy was largely agrarian, but there were wide disparities within the agricultural sector. In the fertile Po Valley conditions were right for widespread capitalist agriculture. In the South, large estates, farmed inefficiently by poor tenants and sharecroppers, needed state protection in the form of tariffs to survive. In the North, there was a basis for industrialization, but the nascent industries faced enormous problems arising from a lack of raw materials and technological backwardness.

Because of the great social and economic disparities, economic development in both rural and urban Italy not only could not bridge the gap between the masses and the new state, but actually widened it. Conflict deepened between classes, between regions, between city and countryside, and between North and South. United Italy progressed, but at great cost to the peasant's and worker's standard of living. By the turn of the century, the political class had consolidated the institutions of the new state and prepared the groundwork for the take-off period of the Italian industrial revolution between 1898 and 1907. A liberal parliamentary system existed for the wealthy and educated, but very few workers in the largest cities had a voice in political affairs. Mass political parties were superfluous in a world that revolved around local and regional considerations, personal loyalties, and the rivalries and ambitions of a small elite.

Such a system carried with it the ever-present danger that other forces—hostile to the ideals and values of the national political and economic elites—would gain a foothold among the masses. The Catholic Church first took advantage of this vulnerability when it organized a network of local peasant organizations and savings banks in the regions where it conserved its greatest strength. But peasants and workers outside of the church had no way of channeling their discontents until they formed the Italian Socialist party and its affiliated labor organization, the General Confederation of Labor. When this happened, beginning in the 1890s, the existence of organized Catholic and socialist forces, holding the loyalties of large numbers of Italians, posed a challenge to the Italian political elite. The rulers of Italy feared that the power of the socialist and clerical organizations could be fatal to the new Italy.

To deal with this threat, political leaders alternated between two opposed strategies. If, somehow, either the Catholic or socialist mass movements could be brought within the institutional framework, the liberal state would gain new stability. This process could be achieved either by force or by conciliation. At times, the political leaders lashed out against the worker and peasant organizations, as they did in the late 1870s and again between 1894 and 1900. Then, between 1900 and 1914, the tactic of accommodation was tried. From 1914 to 1920 both strategies were applied inconsistently and incoherently until, finally, fascism offered a wholly novel way of creating a mass-based authoritarianism which crushed the left but came to terms with the Catholic Church and its social and economic organizations.

THE RISE OF WORKING-CLASS POLITICS, 1860–1892

Labor organizers who strove to plant the seeds of new working-class political and economic organizations did so in a hostile economic and political environment. Unlike the advanced industrialized sectors of England and Germany, Italy's industry was fragmented into small productive units. Until the rise of the automobile and metal industries in Turin after the turn of the century, few modern factories existed outside of the cotton and woolen industries. The largest concentrations of workers were in the textile mills and in the state tobacco monopoly. Traditionally dominant sectors of the economy, such as textiles, clothing, and food processing, employed large numbers of women and children who were difficult to organize. Moreover, many of those classified in census reports as workers in manufacturing were actually independent or semi-independent craftsmen. Finally, social and geographical differences complicated unionization. An enormous gap in wage levels, literacy, and political consciousness existed between the North (Turin, Genoa, Milan) and the South and Center. Italian socialist organizations were never entirely able to overcome this regionalism or to represent the diversity of interests within the working class.

Even greater obstacles stood in the way of organizing peasants. Yet, Italian socialists, unlike their counterparts in Germany, France, or England, did manage to reach large numbers of peasant laborers in the North. This was an achievement of heroic proportions. Italian landholdings varied considerably from region to region, making a national effort problematical. Agricultural labor demanded a low level of specialization and workers were easily replaced. Employment was seasonal and precarious because of persistent overpopulation on the land. A large pool of unemployed hands engendered depressed wage levels. Even regularly employed peasants, like the poor Lombard farmers, portrayed in Alberto Olmi's *Tree of the Wooden Clogs,* sharecropped precariously on short contracts and could be demoted to the mass of seasonal laborers for the slightest infraction.

Rural Italy suffered badly from the agricultural depression of the 1880s. Prices dropped for most basic commodities and lowered the peasant standard of living. Smaller farmers, unable to manage the burden of debt, fell into bankruptcy. Public policy accentuated this trend. The state intervened in favor of larger producers in 1882 with a land-reclamation law which accelerated the transformation of agriculture to modern commercial production in the rich Po Valley. In this region the existing agricultural proletariat grew with the increasing numbers of day laborers who had been cut off from the traditions of property ownership or stable sharecropping still common in other parts of Italy. Their plight was worsened by a decline in traditional crafts and domestic industry. Many peasants emigrated to America; others gravitated to the provincial centers where, out of desperation, they grasped at new ideas and new forms of organization. Extreme hardship and social disruption created an opportunity to organize the poorest of landless workers.

COMPETING IDEOLOGICAL TRADITIONS ON THE ITALIAN LEFT

Three ideologies—Mazzinianism, anarchism, and social democracy—competed for the loyalties of the Italian workers. The first worker organizations were mutual aid societies (*società di mutuo soccorso*), formed during the 1850s in Piedmont. These purely economic organizations were dominated by a cautious pragmatism. The followers of the great republican leader, Giuseppe Mazzini, first challenged this conservatism with a program of national unity, education, and republican politics. But Mazzini, a democrat who preached the reconciliation of class conflict within the unity of the nation, would go no further along the road to socialism than the cooperative movement. In the same tradition stood Giuseppe Garibaldi, the most popular Italian leader of his day. His ideology was a vague mixture of republicanism, egalitarianism, sympathy with the oppressed, and faith in direct action. While lending his name to many causes, he wavered between traditional radical democracy and socialism. The early 1870s found him politically close to the International Workingman's Association (the First International), which had been formed by Karl Marx in 1864.

Paradoxically, it was not Marx, but the anarchist Bakunin, who represented the First International in Italy and who almost succeeded in rooting an anarchist tradition in working-class politics. Bakunin arrived in Italy in 1864 and returned sporadically until the early 1870s. The Russian revolutionary's anti-statist and decentralizing positions appealed to workers who were alienated by the heavy-handed policies of the new central government. Moreover, Bakunin's stress on the importance of the peasantry, and on an alliance between urban and rural workers, naturally fit the Italian situation. Finally, his vision of the revolution as a direct and violent blow to the existing state had a natural appeal to the millennarian instincts of many Italian peasants. In 1868 he formed his own International Alliance of Socialist Democracy, which was affiliated with the First International. While Mazzini's dream of interclass cooperation faded before the harsh realities of the new Italy, Bakunin's version of revolution gained adherents.

The heyday of Italian anarchism came in the years between 1871 and 1879, in the wake of enthusiasm for the Commune of Paris. Mazzini's death in 1872, and the formation in September of 1872 of Bakunin's independent faction within the First International, furthered the anarchist cause. Marx and Engels, by now bitter opponents of Bakunin, decided to counter-attack. They chose Carlo Cafiero (1846–1892), a brilliant but unstable aristocrat, as their agent in Italy; but in 1872 Cafiero went over to the anarchist camp with two other men who would play a major role in the history of anarchism and socialism in Italy: Errico Malatesta (1853–1932) and Andrea Costa (1851–1910). Errico Malatesta, only eighteen years old when he joined the anarchist movement in 1872, came to symbolize the cause for which he plotted and struggled until his death during the Fascist dictatorship. Andrea Costa was the son of a servant in the family of Felice Orsini, the attempted assassin of Louis Napoleon. Costa, a talented and charismatic political organizer, converted from republicanism in the early 1870s to become the most important figure in the anarchist camp. His subsequent conversion to social democracy in 1879 and election to the Chamber of Deputies in 1882 squelched all hopes for the anarchists.

The seventies were hard years. A deep depression hit Europe in 1873. Its impact was magnified by the harsh economic measures of the Italian government. The state-imposed grist tax in 1868 affected the most important item in the diet of the poor and led to a series of strikes and protests. By 1874 the anarchists tried to take advantage of the discontent by organizing a revolt in alliance with the republicans, but the leaders of the plot were arrested at the Villa Ruffo near Rimini. The anarchists suffered another blow to their prestige in 1877, when an abortive revolt in the Matese Mountains outside of Naples failed miserably. Finally, in 1878, an attempt on the life of King Umberto I by Giovanni Passanante brought down the full weight of police repression on the entire subversive movement. Andrea Costa was quick to draw a political balance from this unhappy experience. On July 27, 1879, he set forth his new position in a letter "To my friends in the Romagna." He had been convinced as early as 1877 that clandestine organization and sporadic violence merely fed the reaction, and that the legal struggle was the only possible means of building a movement.

In this conviction he was joined by Anna Kuliscioff, one of the most extraordinary and attractive figures in the history of the Italian left. Kuliscioff was born in Russia in 1854 into a Jewish family which had converted to the Orthodox faith. She left Russia for Switzerland to study medicine in 1870, but soon, in the exciting atmosphere of the emigré community, converted to the revolutionary cause. In 1873 and 1874 she re-entered Russia where she attempted to work among the peasantry. Almost immediately, however, she was forced back into exile and, except for a brief visit to Russia in 1876, never returned. Kuliscioff met Andrea Costa in 1877, just as both were making the transition from anarchism to socialism. Their personal and political relationship continued until the mid-1880s, when Kuliscioff met and fell in love with the young Filippo Turati.

Costa formed his own political movement, the Partito socialista rivoluzionario, in 1881 in the Romagna, and was elected to parliament as the first official socialist the following year. In a sad but touching gesture, Carlo Cafiero gave his blessing to this legalitarian tactic in one of his last letters before a mental breakdown ended his political career. However, neither Costa's Partito socialista rivoluzionario, nor the Partito operaio which was formed in 1885 by Costantino Lazzari (1857–1927) in Lombardy, were able to establish a national base. The new social democratic movement still lacked ideological and organizational consistency. The defections of Costa and Cafiero in 1871 and 1872 had cost Marx and Engels a large part of their Italian following. Even after Costa's conversion to socialism, it was clear that the tradition to which he belonged was part of an instinctive protest against injustice rather than a full-blown ideological system. However, Costa did see two things quite clearly. First, he understood the need to break with the conspiratorial and direct action of the anarchists in favor of open and legal tactics. He also linked the socialist movement to the urban working class rather than to the peasantry. What Costa, Lazzari, and the other pioneers still needed was an ideological framework.

TOWARD THE FORMATION OF
A SOCIALIST PARTY

Despite the lack of organization and ideological preparation, by the 1890s several things began to converge in favor of a nationally based socialist party. There was a process of ideological renewal, especially within Italian marxism. Although very little of Marx and Engels had been translated into Italian—the first edition of the *Manifesto* was published only in 1891—Engels knew a number of Italian revolutionaries, like Enrico Bignami, the editor of *La plebe* of Lodi, who kept alive the socialist current during the heyday of anarchism. Moreover, the French reformist, Benoît Malon had spent much time in exile in Italy where he helped spread a version of Marx's ideas. Both Bignami and Malon argued in favor of open and legal political and economic action by the proletariat.

Of even greater importance was the influence of the German Social Democratic Party. Italian socialists, like Bignami, greatly admired Germany's socialist and syndical movement. Karl Kautsky and other German socialists visited Italy during the 1880s, and *La plebe* devoted much space to their struggle against Bismarck's antisocialist legislation during the 1880s. The strong showing of the German Social Democratic Party in 1890, after the repressive laws were lifted, provided an incentive for the Italians to form their own party. The electoral success of the SPD seemed to validate a strategy of political participation and open organization.

Marxism's slow penetration into Italy accelerated when Antonio Labriola (1843–1904) converted to the ideas of the German revolutionary. Labriola, who held the chair in philosophy at the University of Rome, took the well-traveled road from Hegel to Marx, as he moved to the left in the 1870s and 1880s. His writings on Marx's system gave academic prestige to theoretical socialism and briefly won over Benedetto Croce, who flirted with marxism in the 1890s. Labriola, however, had less to do with the development of the Italian Socialist party. He did attend the Halle congress of the German Social Democratic party in 1890 and, on his return, argued forcefully in favor of autonomous proletarian political organizations, freed from the tutelage of bourgeois parties. Yet, when the congress was called in August 1892 to form the new Socialist party, Labriola refused to attend on the grounds that the movement was premature and lacked a firm ideological base.

The individual most responsible for the creation of the Italian Socialist party was Filippo Turati, a major figure in the reformist wing of the movement. Turati was born in Canza on November 26, 1857, into a conservative family of civil servants. But the younger Turati was attracted more by the bohemian and avant-garde culture of Milan than by familial tradition. He gravitated toward positivism, atheism, and political radicalism before espousing socialism in the 1880s. In 1885 he met Anna Kuliscioff and established an intellectual and sentimental tie which lasted until her death in December 1925. Unlike Kuliscioff, Turati was never a systematic theorist, but remained throughout his life a sensible, if overly cautious, political strategist. Their review, *Critica sociale*, founded in 1891, became the leading voice for reformist and democratic socialism in Italy. The Turati-Kuliscioff apartment, near the Piazza

Duomo in Milan, was for many years the general headquarters for the PSI, and a think tank, which helped transcend some of the divisions within the movement.

Socialism for Turati was a mixture of scientific certainties and ethical imperatives. Borrowing from Marx and from Engels, with whom he was in regular correspondence during the 1890s, Turati emphasized organizational and political, even parliamentary, action as a means to the eventual liberation of the proletariat. He rejected violent revolution as a way of bringing about change, and held that socialism might be achieved by evolutionary means. A serious program of reforms would, he felt, speed the inherent contradictions in the capitalist system. Turati was also well aware that the proletariat did not form a majority of the population. To succeed with their program, the workers would have to forge alliances with peasants and middle-class democrats. Although neither Turati nor Kuliscioff abandoned the ultimate goal of a socialist society, their means were flexible and democratic. They faced an insurmountable obstacle, however, because any hope of success presupposed a willingness to negotiate on the part of the bourgeoisie. Unfortunately, Italy lacked the solid middle-class democratic tradition which existed in England and France. It was precisely the existence of a serious negotiating partner which would often be absent in the future.

During the debates leading to the congress of Genoa, Turati argued that political action within the existing parliamentary institutions would succeed. He rebuffed objections from those who wished to limit the movement only to workers, from the anarchists who refused in principle to create a legal political party, and from Antonio Labriola who argued that the whole effort was premature.

As a concession to those who believed that the party should be exclusively proletarian, membership was not allowed on an individual basis but only through constituent worker organizations. At Genoa, delegates attended from over two hundred worker societies, representing 200,000 workers. From the beginning, two different versions of what socialism meant struggled for dominance within the Italian movement. The program of the new party borrowed its call for gradual, but concrete, political and economic reforms from Turati's Milanese Lega socialista. But the other soul of Italian socialism was also present in the new party's emphasis on the fundamental incompatibility between proletarian and bourgeois interests which could only be resolved in violent revolution.

From the outset, many socialists doubted whether the legal option was possible or even desirable. Gradual reform inevitably favored the integration of the masses into the state and seemed to contradict the goal of a revolutionary overthrow of the existing society. But the Italian political class and the social and economic elites which dominated the state were equally uncertain about how to react to the new socialist movement. They showed no willingness to share power, as the reformists hoped they might. In the end, neither the Italian Socialist party nor the bourgeois liberal parties could ever determine with consistency whether they preferred confrontation or cooperation. In fact, in Italy, middle-class politicians often seemed more comfortable with a revolutionary PSI than with a moderate one. Thus, the margin for a reformist tactic varied, depending on the balance inside and outside of the party. Nor was the situation eased by prosperity and economic growth. In a society marked by such deep inequalities, expansion seemed only to exacerbate and deepen class antagonisms. Ironically, economic progress, which was a *sine qua non* for any type of reformism, tended to undermine the stability of the reformist alternative. The total economic gain was so small that any sign of progress set off a frantic scramble to participate in the prosperity, thereby augmenting class tension.

Several other characteristics of the new party emerged quite early. A gap developed between the party's general principles and their practical realization. The PSI tended to state its revolutionary message without regard to how it might be achieved. Two structural difficulties accounted for this problem. The first was horizontal or geographic. Party strength was in the North; little base existed in the South and on Sicily and Sardinia. The second was organizational or vertical. The party comprised a collection of local federations that worked independently of one another and of the national executive. Unlike the English or German parties, the PSI lacked a solid union structure that could integrate the base and the leadership. The only common bond in the party was the official newspaper, *L'Avanti!*, which was created at the 1896 congress of Florence. Its editor was far more visible and important than the secretary of the party. The importance of the editorship was reflected by the stature of the men who held it—the reformists Leonida Bissolati and Claudio Treves, and the revolutionaries Benito Mussolini, Giacinto Menotti Serrati, and Pietro Nenni. Unfortunately, the editor of the paper dealt in propaganda and not reality. He could shape the image of the party, but not control its activities. Local federations, the parliamentary deputies, cooperatives, and the labor unions all operated with varying degrees of autonomy.

The Socialist party was drawn into the turbulent politics of the decade almost immediately. At the congress of Reggio Emilia in 1893, the socialists formally organized their parliamentary party but rejected electoral alliances with bourgeois democratic parties. It was a time of confrontation and crisis, so much so that the PSI was unable even to hold a congress in 1894. A series of banking scandals brought a nationalist and authoritarian government to power under Francesco Crispi in November 1893. Almost immediately, the new prime minister was faced with labor unrest centered among the poor Sicilian peasants. A network of local groups, called *fasci*, sustained the peasant resistance and encouraged the seizure of communal lands. Crispi, a Sicilian, blamed the unrest on the newly formed PSI. He received parliamentary approval for the imposition of martial law in Sicily and for the dissolution of the Socialist party.

The socialists, led by Turati and urged on by Friedrich Engels, allied with Crispi's democratic opponents in the middle-class Radical and Republican parties. The struggle against Crispi and his successors, Antonio Di Rudinì and General Luigi Pelloux, lasted from 1894 to 1899. Crispi fell from power in 1896 after an abortive attempt to conquer Ethiopia. Economic crisis spread political unrest at home, culminating in May 1898 in Milan when unarmed demonstrators were raked by cannon fire from the military. King Umberto called on General Pelloux to restore order. After initial efforts to compromise, Pelloux reverted to a heavy-handed attack on parliamentary authority and freedom of the press. The opposition retaliated with overt obstructionism to block the repressive legislation. When the courts rejected the government's power to legislate by royal decree, it was forced to call an election that it lost in 1900.

During these years the PSI's principled resistance to repression came to symbolize opposition to the corruption and banality of the post-Risorgimento Italian state. This willingness to oppose the government at whatever cost attracted broad support from many prominent writers and intellectuals, such as the poet and dramatist Gabriele D'Annunzio, who had little to do with socialism or democracy, but who temporarily lent the party a kind of symbolic prestige. With typical bombast, D'Annunzio announced, as he crossed over from the extreme right to the left, that he was moving toward life. But Turati and the reformists within the PSI drew quite another lesson from the experience. They were convinced that the preservation of democratic liberties was the basis for any political action. Like the great French reformist socialist, Jean Jaurès, who rallied to the defense of the Third Republic during the Dreyfus affair, the Italian reformists took as their cause the preservation of the parliamentary system. But Turati envisaged this as only a first step. The heterogeneous coalition which formed between 1896 and 1900 included socialists, Catholics, and bourgeois democrats. Even some industrialists doubted the wisdom of embarking on colonial expansion at the cost of repressive government at home. Turati believed that the progressive bourgeoisie might accept reform as a step to a modern social and economic system. His perspective was not of an Italy rigidly divided into social blocs with irreconcilable interests. Northern industry might be willing to buy social peace in the name of economic growth. An alliance of the advanced sectors of industry and of the working class could be based on lower agricultural tariffs, cheaper food, and stabilized labor costs. In return, the employers would recognize trade unions and collective bargaining. The victory of the parliamentary forces after years of struggle from 1894 to 1900 held out the promise of an understanding with at least part of the bourgeoisie.

The PSI never fully endorsed Turati's policies at party congresses during the 1890s. Instead, it wavered between acceptance of and hostility to the idea of interclass alliances. At the Congress of Parma in 1895 the party embraced the tactic of allowing socialists to vote for bourgeois democrats as a temporary expedient. But, recognizing the hostility of the bulk of the ruling class, the PSI shifted to membership on an individual basis to avoid having all its constituent organizations dissolved, as happened when the party was outlawed briefly in 1894. The party also took its permanent designation of Partito Socialista Italiano and established a directorate to run the party's affairs between congresses. A year later, at the Congress of Florence, the PSI again reverted to a more intransigent line on electoral alliances with bourgeois democrats. In seeming contradiction with this reversion to revolutionary principles, the party put its newly established daily newspaper, *L'Avanti!*, under the control of Leonida Bissolati (1857–1920), who represented the PSI's more moderate wing. Bissolati, one of the most principled and attractive figures in the Italian socialist movement, converted to socialism as a result of his legal work on behalf of the peasants in his home region of Cremona. His political beliefs were more an extension of classical democratic and humanitarian ideals than they were a product of marxism. After an initial radical phase in the 1890s, he became unabashedly reformist. He believed that the PSI had to adopt an unequivocal democratic and parliamentary strategy with a party structure modeled on the socialist movements of England or Germany. In Bissolati's movement control should rest in the hands of the moderate and practical union and cooperative movement.

Bissolati and his allies on the right wing of the PSI —Ivanoe Bonomi (1873–1951) and Angiolo Cabrini (1869–1937)—differed from Turati in two important ways. They wanted to tie the party to a largely economic agenda and were willing to abandon the goal of integral socialism in favor of the full realization of a modern democratic state. The line between Turati and Bissolati marked a deep split within Italian reformism. Both Kuliscioff and Turati remained convinced that capitalist society could not survive its internal contradictions. Reforms were designed, not to modernize the bourgeois state, but to transform it. These different perspectives were not apparent in the 1890s, but would eventually divide Turati from Bissolati. They help explain the reluctance of Turati and the other left reformists to cut their ties to the PSI's revolutionary wing which emerged as a rival faction after 1900.

Between 1896 and 1900 the PSI's flexible tactics seemed to be rewarded by modest gains. In the elections of 1895 the socialists won twelve seats in the 500-member parliament and over 76,000 votes; they increased their representation in 1897 to sixteen seats with over 135,000 votes. In working-class Milan, Turati engineered socialist support for victorious local democratic lists in the communal elections of 1899. The arrest of many of the PSI's leaders, including Turati in 1898 and 1899, added to the party's moral prestige. The crucial elections of 1900 which became a referendum on Pelloux's decrees restricting civil and parliamentary rights, saw the PSI jump from sixteen to thirty-three seats and from 135,000 votes to 215,000. Turati, backed by radicals and republicans, won a special election to parliament in November 1899.

A clear path had been traced for the party, and it led in a reformist direction. In return for concrete political and economic benefits, Turati seemed willing to bring part of the organized working class into a temporary alliance with the bourgeois democrats. Two fatal flaws, however, undermined this strategy. First, the success of the PSI depended on bringing larger numbers of unskilled and radicalized workers into the fold. Turati and his allies counted on their ability to control the pressures from within the party for a faster pace of change. But, to mobilize these new recruits, the PSI had to offer the prospect of immediate and direct benefits. Thus, hope of change, dangled before those who had been oppressed for so long, unleashed enormous pressure for more rapid and sweeping transformations. Second, a successful reformist program needed bourgeois politicians who could deliver a program of benefits without losing the support of the middle class. The boom years immediately following the turn of the century revealed the potential and the limits of this reformist alternative.

CHAPTER 2

The Heyday of Reformism and the Challenge of Revolutionary Socialism, 1900–1917

Around the turn of the century Italy entered a prolonged period of sustained growth. Even before the end of the political crisis of 1898–1900, economic indicators had turned up and showed steady growth until 1907. Manufacturing production increased by 60 percent between 1900 and 1913, but still provided only a quarter of the total gross national product. The capital goods sector, led by steel and automobiles, advanced despite a lack of raw materials, limited domestic markets, and problems in absorbing new, high-cost technologies. Traditional industries, such as food processing, textiles, and tobacco, which had comprised almost three-quarters of the industrial product in the early 1890s, declined to 60 percent by 1915. Economic growth in the most advanced sectors led to greater concentration of capital and to an increasingly skewed geographical distribution which favored the northern triangle of Genoa–Milan–Turin over the South and Center.

A degree of political stability also returned. In 1901 Giuseppe Zanardelli, an elderly progressive liberal from Brescia, became prime minister. However, the most powerful minister in the government was Giovanni Giolitti, who would succeed Zanardelli in 1903 and dominate the political scene until 1914. Giolitti was an instinctively tolerant, antirhetorical, pragmatic liberal. Convinced of the need to broaden the base of the political system through reform, he tried to anchor his program on the enlightened self-interest of the entrepreneurial class. Under his direction the government favored heavy industrial development through tariffs and guaranteed state purchases. In return, he wanted the economic elites to support a series of moderate, piecemeal reforms to the benefit of the organized workers of northern Italy.

The working class reflected the changes in the larger society. Italy was still an agrarian economy poised on the brink of its industrial revolution. Workers in manufacturing made up only about four million or approximately 25 percent of the active population, as against 59 percent in agriculture. However, these workers were often not true industrial laborers, but rather artisans, small shop-owners, independent home-weavers, or workers in the clothing, building, textile, food, and wood processing industries. The important textile and clothing industries also employed large numbers of women and children. Many industrial workers still labored part time in agriculture; almost a half-million peasants worked some time in industry. Swollen by recent migrants to the cities, the work force lacked the discipline and organization achieved by highly skilled workers. Labor relations were hierarchical and patriarchal in the numerous small shops and factories. Wages remained extremely low and the laboring day averaged around twelve hours for most semi-skilled workers. Harsh working conditions, persistent unemployment, and geographically uneven economic growth spurred massive emigration. Between 1900 and 1910 between 550,000 and 650,000 Italians left their homeland each year in search of better opportunities.

The capacity of this system to accept real reform had yet to be tested. No one knew how far the economic system could bend before the lack of raw materials and limited domestic markets would put a clamp on the ability of industry and the government to make concessions, or how long the patience of the workers would last once they glimpsed the possibility of a better life and a fairer distribution of wealth.

A first test of the new possibilities inherent in economic growth came, not in industry as might be expected, but on the land. The shift to modernized capitalist agriculture in the Po Valley had been accelerated by the economic crisis of the 1880s. Extensive land-reclamation projects further concentrated land holdings and formed a large agricultural proletariat, known as *braccianti*. The misery of peasant Italy attracted the attention of reformers such as Camillo Prampolini (1857–1930), Nullo Baldini (1862–1945), and Leonida Bissolati, three pioneers of rural socialism, who used their legal and organizational skills to promote and defend the nascent peasant movement. The *braccianti* succeeded in unionizing despite the use of violence and mass dismissals by the landowners. The culmination of this unionization drive came in 1901 in Bologna with the formation of the Federazione dei Lavoratori della Terra or Federterra. The Federterra primarily represented landless workers in the Po Valley; it had little support in the South and Center. At the first congress the latter two regions had only 23 peasant leagues with 10,000 members, whereas in the North some 795 leagues enrolled almost 150,000 members. Even in its bastion in the Po Valley, the Federterra did not reach small farmers, sharecroppers, or renters to any great degree. In the Catholic areas of Lombardy and the Veneto, these farmers often gravitated to the Catholic or "white" peasant leagues which became serious rivals to the socialist organizations in those areas. The Federterra's program of socialization of the land offered little to other categories of peasant labor, even though the Federterra approached the problem cautiously in order not to alienate potential allies. The creation of the Federterra pushed labor militancy to new levels. The landowners were completely unprepared for the wave of strikes which hit in 1901 and continued during the following three years. But their increasingly bitter resistance to the Federterra, which cost forty lives and over two hundred wounded, boded ill for political and economic reform in a key economic sector.

REFORMISM AND THE SECOND INTERNATIONAL

The reformist strategy during the 1898 crisis paid immediate benefits with the formation of the liberal Zanardelli government in 1901. Similar developments in France and Germany had already opened a broad debate within the Second International over reformist tactics. Within the German Social Democratic party, Eduard Bernstein's denial of a trend toward greater class polarization or toward inevitable violent revolution initiated bitter polemics. In France the decisions by Jean Jaurès to support the Dreyfusard cause, and by the reformist Alexandre Millerand to join the government headed by the moderate René Waldeck-Rousseau in 1899, sparked a full-scale debate within French socialism and the International over how far the socialists might go in working with bourgeois democrats.

In Italy, the dominant reformists in the PSI were tempted by, but refused Giolitti's offer to include Turati in his new government in 1903. Turati had no desire to become the Italian Millerand. Until 1900 the Italians had not cast their debates in theoretical terms. With the exception of Antonio Labriola, who played little role in the party, no one in socialist leadership was a major socialist thinker. The financial inability of the Italians to send large delegations to the congresses of the Second International muted the impact on the PSI of the debates within the International.

THE SYNDICALIST REVIVAL

All of this was to change rapidly, however. The moderating influence of German socialist thought, so important up to the 1890s, began to decline in Italy. Its place was taken by revolutionary syndicalist thinkers, like the maverick Georges Sorel. In September 1900 at the party Congress in Rome, Turati and his allies still won a vote allowing the PSI to make alliances with other parties on all levels with the sole proviso that these alliances remain compatible with the aims of the party. Emphasis on the minimal program of reforms provoked a reaction from a new syndicalist opposition led by Arturo Labriola (1873–1959, no relation to Antonio), Enrico Leone (1875–1940), Angelo Oliviero Olivetti (1874–1931), Ernesto Cesare Longobardi (1877–1943), and the ex-anarchist, Francesco Saverio Merlino (1856–1930).

The syndicalists attacked the reformists on several fronts. First, they argued that the revolutionary content in marxism had been abandoned by the reformists without any corresponding gain for the workers. Turati, Bissolati, and their allies, the syndicalists argued, built their strategy on only a small sector of the total working class. Recalling sentiments that had won Bakunin many followers, Arturo Labriola, the Neapolitan revolutonary, proposed a program that would unite North and South, peasants and factory workers. The Socialist party had to adopt a militant strategy to avoid being co-opted by illusory reforms promised by the ruling class. The proletariat needed no help from the bourgeosie, but could draw on its own resources to make a revolution. Rejected were interclass political alliances and political tactics of any kind outside of proletarian organizations like the unions. Moreover, the syndicalist F. S. Merlino, whose background was anarchism, saw in worker syndicates a way of reorganizing and decentralizing the state and the economy. The wave of strikes which followed the formation of the Federterra in 1901 seemed to confirm the syndicalists' belief that a revolutionary tide was flowing in their direction. Finally, the syndicalists pointed out that the socialist movement under reformist leadership had lost the élan which had drawn intellectuals and young people to its ranks in the 1890s. Benedetto Croce, who led an idealist philosophical resurgence, heaped scorn on the pseudo-scientific positivism and optimism of many Italian reformists. Syndicalism was more in tune with the new emphasis on will and force as determining factors in history. The theories put forward in Merlino's *Rivista critica del socialismo* and in Arturo Labriola's *Avanguardia socialista* seriously challenged reformist intellectual hegemony within the PSI. By 1903 Turati had even lost control of his own Milanese federation to the syndicalists.

THE LIMITS OF REFORMISM

How justified were the syndicalist attacks? Were the gains made in the years from 1901 to 1914 purely illusory? Such a blanket statement would certainly be unfair. A contrast with the years from 1894 to 1900 would make this clear. During the earlier period, unions and labor chambers were dissolved and police were used to break up worker resistance. Under Giolitti greater leeway was given to socialist unions to organize in the private sector (although public employee strikes were still severely repressed), and to cooperatives to win a share of local contracts. Most important, from the standpoint of spreading socialist ideas, Giolitti allowed much more latitude to the PSI press. In terms of concrete gains, we see from those years limited accident and disability insurance and regulation of female and child labor; the Italian Labor Office was created in 1902 to gather statistics and coordinate programs. A state monopoly over the insurance industry was instituted in 1911, and universal male suffrage was in effect the following year.

But the reformist strategy suffered from major defects. Very few of the new laws provided the structural alterations promised by the reformists. Organizational gains were mainly limited to the North. The factors which reinforced the culture of poverty, especially in the South, such as unfair taxation, poor schools, and inequitable land distribution remained intractable. Two reforms in particular were never achieved: a shift of the tax burden away from consumption toward incomes, and reduction of the military budget, which in some years before World War I, fully absorbed one-quarter of state expenditures. Only universal male suffrage could be called a profound structural change.

Related to the failure to achieve basic changes was a question of trust. The relationship between Giolitti and Turati never became one of true equality. Giolitti used all his considerable powers to avoid establishing any institutional framework for his dealings with the PSI. He merely wanted to insert the party into the existing system, rather than make fundamental alterations in that system. As a result, when Giolitti fell from power in 1914, the reformists had no base from which to fight against a new, hostile right wing government headed by Antonio Salandra.

Despite the introduction of universal suffrage for the elections of 1913, Italy had not advanced to a modern party democracy, nor had the socialists achieved any measure of control over the levers of power within the state. The reformists themselves were partly to blame. Twice Giolitti made serious overtures to include them in his government. In 1903 the offer was made to Turati who refused. In 1911 Leonida Bissolati also backed off under pressure from Turati and the other reformists. Formal participation in a government might not have made a significant difference, but it would have tested the possibilities of reform to the limit. On the other hand, the reformists in the parliamentary party had offered all but formal participation without gaining the basic changes that would have altered the structure of power. Whether the mere presence of one or more socialist ministers would have countered the pressure from the employers, who moved to the right in the years after 1913, is a question that can never be answered.

The syndicalists were undoubtedly correct in their judgment that the reforms achieved by Turati, Treves, and Kuliscioff would never advance the proletariat toward revolution or even toward major structural change under capitalism. But the syndicalists offered no viable alternative. In an Italy where the working class had barely begun to organize, the chances for successful revolution seemed slim. The party's left wing could only mount a verbal attack against the state and against the reformists. They were able to provoke repression but little else.

This hopeless dialogue compounded the serious organizational problems of the PSI between 1900 and 1914. The formal leadership of the party acted and debated in a vacuum. In theory, the PSI was led by a directorate of eleven members (five elected by the congress, five from the parliamentary group, plus the editor of *Avanti!*) and a four- member executive. The real life of the party stayed in its local sections or in the parliamentary group which was always controlled by the reformists, even when the revolutionaries had nominal control of the directorate. On the local level the socialists exercised real power over housing, health, city services, and contracts. The link between the communal administration and the national scene was not through the party directorate but through the parliamentary deputy in Rome. Thus, the local unions, peasant leagues, cooperatives, and labor chambers lived in their own world. They waged local strikes and concentrated on gains that affected the immediate area. The labor chambers coordinated the various worker and peasant organizations within a given city or province. At the PSI's 1901 congress the party recognized the importance of controlling these organizations, but, even when the socialists dominated, little interaction existed between one province and another. In Rome the parliamentary group worked to extract pork-barrel concessions for cooperatives and municipalities. Only the newspaper acted as a bridge between various local party organizations. But the editor of *Avanti!* was accountable for his actions only to a party congress. The newspaper was free to maintain the ideals of the party without having to confront daily political reality in parliament or in the local sections. The Italian socialist party was only a unified national political formation in the context of the Italian system which had not developed modern and centralized mass parties. In fact, it was a loose confederation of local and regional organizations.

The history of the party between 1900 and 1914 confirmed this lack of coordination. A wave of strikes over which the reformists had no control began in 1902. By 1903, stiffer resistance from the landowners and industrialists decreased the number of successful strikes and increased disillusionment with the reformists who ran the party directorate. At the Congress of Bologna in April 1903, an alliance of PSI syndicalists and centrists ousted Turati and his allies. The new leader of the party was Enrico Ferri (1856–1929), a professor and noted criminologist whose marxism was decidedly of the outmoded positivistic and deterministic variety. Ferri also edited the *Avanti!* between 1903 and 1907. His verbal intransigence appealed to the syndicalists, while not entirely rupturing ties with the reformists on the issue of short term gains. His was the sort of solution that had perennial appeal within the PSI because it offered an illusory best of both worlds by combining the worst in both arguments. Yet it somehow befitted a man who avoided the ignominy of becoming a Fascist senator, only by dying days before his installation.

Spurred on by the syndicalists, Ferri mindlessly backed Italy's first general strike in 1904, which was called in protest against harsh police measures taken against peasant organizations at Buggerru in Sardinia and Casteluzzo in Sicily in September 1904. In backing the general strike Ferri inaugurated another tradition within the PSI, that of recklessly acting without preparation or thought of consequences. The 1904 strike was purely a symbolic gesture of protest. However, it revealed both a revolutionary mood among the masses, which boded ill for gradualism, and the total isolation of the workers and their political party. Giolitti responded to the strike by calling general elections that resulted in a setback for the PSI and widened the gap between the reformist parliamentary party and the party directorate under control of Ferri and the syndicalist Arturo Labriola.

The 1904 electoral defeat made the reformists acutely aware that suffrage extension was a precondition for change. Leading the call for broadening the electorate was the historian Gaetano Salvemini (1873–1957), whose socialism was inspired by a passionate interest in the problem of the South. Salvemini argued forcefully that modern democracy would break the power of southern landlords and their clienteles, which Giolitti used to win his parliamentary majorities. In so doing, it would raise the level of political culture in the entire country, not just in the advanced North, as Turati seemed to envision. In these prewar years Salvemini became the leading PSI spokesman for a balanced worker-peasant agenda to overcome historic problems of regionalism and separatism.

THE FORMATION OF THE GENERAL CONFEDERATION OF LABOR

In 1905 the government proposed the mandatory arbitration of labor disputes and a ban on strikes in the rail industry. The failure of the unions to defeat the bill made them aware of the need to act effectively on the national level. Until 1905 these unions had acted within a loose coordinating body, the Segretariato Nazionale della Resistenza, but it broke up as a result of disputes between the rival syndicalist and reformist railway unions.

A number of national craft federations already existed in printing, textiles, building trades, and rails. The most important of these was formed in the steel industry in 1901. The metal workers' Federazione impiegati e operai metalmeccanici (FIOM) led a successful strike in 1906, which imposed on management a factory commission to supervise adherence to contract provisions. The reformist-dominated unions formed the General Confederation of Labor (Confederazione Generale del Lavoro—CGL) on October 1, 1906. The much weaker syndicalist federations organized their own Comitato di Resistenza in 1907 under the leadership of Alceste De Ambris, the fiery head of the labor movement in Parma.

Under reformist leadership, the CGL worked in alliance with the PSI to lobby for favorable legislation from the government. Inevitably, it became another power center within the PSI. Through the CGL and the Federterra, which continued to grow after the round of peasant agitation and repression from 1902 to 1906, the labor movement had consolidated a precarious foothold in the working class, although the pace of organization in manufacturing was well behind that in England or Germany. Moreover, the hostility of the employers was unrelenting. Successful strikes in 1906 conducted by the FIOM and by the textile workers union sparked management to form the Turin Industrial League and to pool resources in an antistrike fund in 1907. By 1910, sixty-nine industrial associations had grouped into the Confederazione Italiana dell'Industria.

THE REFORMIST REVIVAL, 1908–1912

The reformists within the PSI, spurred by the failure of the political general strike of 1904 and backed by the union movement, managed to shift the party's balance of power back in their favor at the Congress of 1906. A new formulation—integralism—was hammered together by Oddino Morgari (1865–1944) to reconcile the conflicting reformist and revolutionary programs. Now, however, the compromise substantially accepted the reformist position and by the time of the Congress of Florence in 1908 they were back in full control of the party.

The reformists' victory proved to be fragile. The economic crisis of 1907 had already begun to undermine the basis of their policy, and factional disputes threatened to undermine the reformist majority from within. Two issues were at the root of the problem. The party's ultra reformists, headed by Leonida Bissolati and Ivanoe Bonomi, pushed in 1909 and 1910 for the creation of a labor party that would be controlled by the pragmatic union leaders. The main body of reformists, led by Turati, Kuliscioff, and Claudio Treves (1869–1933), insisted that the party, not the unions, set the political agenda for the working class. The fact that the CGL represented less than 10 percent of all workers was an additional argument against the idea of a labor party, but Bissolati and his allies on the right wing of the PSI played on a growing mood of resistance within the CGL against dictation by the PSI.

The second issue involves the essential meaning of reformism. Turati, Treves and Kuliscioff had always remained true to the long-term objective of socialism. Bissolati, Bonomi, and Salvemini viewed the Socialist party as an instrument in the political democratization and modernization of Italy. They cared little about marxist theory. Salvemini believed that the PSI had to press aggressively for a series of radical reforms such as universal suffrage, changes in education, and a fundamental restructuring of the southern social and economic system. He broke with Turati and the other reformists over what he took to be a northern strategy of political and economic development which counted on the most advanced industrial workers. Salvemini's inability to make the PSI into a democratic and modernizing political force for the entire country drove him out of the party in 1910.

The ultra-reformists, Bissolati and Bonomi, pressed for an ever-closer alliance with the bourgeois Radical and Republican parties. Their willingness to compromise reflected the fundamental shift in Italian politics that had taken taken place since the general strike of 1904. During the subsequent elections greater numbers of Catholics entered the political arena with the Pope's blessing to vote against the "subversive" (socialist) candidates. This policy continued during the elections of 1909. In order to combat a potential shift of the political axis to the right, the anti-clerical and democratic left-wing parties, joined by the Freemasons, forged electoral blocs to which the socialists were invited to adhere. The mutual support strategy seemed to work in 1909, as the PSI went from twenty-six to forty-two seats while the Radicals moved forward from thirty-six to forty-eight seats and the Republicans from twenty to twenty-three. But by 1910 the reformists were divided over how far to cooperate with the bourgeois and masonic democratic bloc. At the party Congress of 1910 Bissolati favored the complete abandonment of any revolutionary pretensions; Salvemini insisted on a policy of moral intransigence which would break with Giolitti's system of piece-meal, limited change; Turati opted for a middle position which left open the possibility of continued bargaining with Giolitti, but rejected making the PSI an appendage of the bourgeois system by casting off its socialist program.

THE RESURGENCE OF MAXIMALISM

Although Turati's compromise held in 1910, the issues came to a head in 1911 and 1912. The scorn of the reformists for the revolutionary ideology of the PSI was all too evident. At the Congress of 1910 Bissolati referred to it as a "dead branch" and, in a parliamentary debate, Giolitti confidently boasted that Marx had been relegated to the attic with all the other useless baggage. As it turned out, the news of marxism's demise was decidedly premature.

Two things combined to alter the political system to favor a revival of revolutionary socialism. In March 1911, Giolitti, after two years out of office, returned as prime minister with an ambitious program (i.e., nationalization of the insurance industry and universal male suffrage), directed at winning left-wing support. He also asked Bissolati to join his government, and with great reluctance the reformist leader refused. Bissolati's hesitation outraged the revolutionary wing of the party.

Foreign policy was a second disruptive factor. Almost immediately after taking office, Giolitti was confronted by a rapidly changing situation in North Africa where France intended to consolidate its hold over Morocco. Italy's international agreements guaranteed Libya as a *quid pro quo* for any fundamental alteration in the North African power balance. The war against the Ottoman Empire over Libya, which began in September, 1911, ruptured the already fragile reformist majority within the PSI. Bissolati and Bonomi had made it clear during the 1908 war scare over Austria's annexation of Bosnia that they stood ready to defend their country. In 1911 they broke with Turati by supporting credits for the Libyan war. The bulk of the party firmly came out against the war. The alienation of the PSI from the patriotic fervor, which swept Italy in 1911, pointed to the growing polarization of political life. The Libyan war bolstered the right wing by integrating more Catholics into political life, and it left the socialists isolated in bitter opposition to the policies of the government.

From the moment of its recapture of the PSI, conflicts within the reformist camp invited a revival of the party's left wing. Hostility to Bissolati provided the catalyst for the discontents of the revolutionaries. They forced him to relinquish the editorship of *Avanti!* to Claudio Treves in 1910. On May 1, 1911 Giovanni Lerda (1853–1927), Costantino Lazzari, Alceste Della Seta, and Arturo Vella (1886–1943), responded to Giolitti's disparaging remark about the demise of marxism by publishing *La soffitta* (*The Attic*), as a forum for the party's revolutionary faction. The left demanded a return to the spirit of revolutionary intransigence and idealism that marked the l892 program. Bissolati's rebellion against party discipline, stagnation of membership, and loss of enthusiasm and dynamism provided immediate issues for the left. At the party Congress of Modena in 1911 the reformists lost their majority, but remained in control because the left and center could not yet muster a clear alternative. Then the Libyan war provided the impetus for change. Bissolati's rejection of party discipline over Libya led to calls for the expulsion of the right reformists.

Splits within the reformist faction before the congress of Reggio Emilia in 1912 allowed the maximalists to triumph by default, and to set the future course of the PSI in the political system. The victory of the revolutionary left meant that the PSI rejected the option of becoming a modern party of opposition within the framework of the existing institutions, as outlined in the reformist alternatives of Salvemini or of

Bissolati and Bonomi. Nonetheless, any reformist option faced major obstacles both outside of and within the party. Giolitti never wanted to deal with the PSI as a political equal, nor could Turati overcome his own ambivalence about the role that the PSI ought to play.

After 1912, whatever slim chance existed for an understanding between the socialists and Giolitti was lost. The reformists never regained control of the party. Bissolati, Bonomi, and their allies were formally expelled through a motion proposed by Benito Mussolini (1883–1945), a charismatic young revolutionary from the Romagna. The right-wing reformists, led by Bissolati, eventually formed the Partito Socialista Riformista Italiano; but this effort, despite gaining twenty deputies and 196,000 votes as against fifty-two deputies and 883,000 votes for the PSI in the elections of 1913, was doomed from the start. Its natural constituency of labor leaders stayed within the PSI. The most prestigious figures of reformism—Turati, Treves, and Kuliscioff—refused to follow Bissolati's lead. They correctly calculated that the mass of workers, alienated as they were from the liberal state, would remain loyal to the old party. Awareness by the left reformists that they would lose much of their influence over the workers kept them within the party from 1912 to 1922 despite countless disappointments and defeats.

Leadership of the PSI passed into the hands of those who stressed the revolutionary or maximalist part of the 1892 program. The leaders of this "maximalist" current were Giacinto Menotti Serrati (1872–1926), Costantino Lazzari, Arturo Vella, Angelica Balabanoff (1869–1965), and Benito Mussolini. The faction united around three issues. First, its followers believed that the party had to return to a position of absolute revolutionary intransigence. Unfortunately, the maximalists had no way of bridging the gap between theory and practice. The party structure, which was to be the motor of the revolution, remained as inefficient and geographically fragmented as ever. Second, the maximalists demanded that the parliamentary party cease positive collaboration with the government. In fact, they were convinced that cooperation between the bourgeoisie and the proletariat on any level was impossible. There could be no repeat of Bissolati's dalliance with Giolitti's government. Relations between the directorate and the reformists in the parliamentary group became marked by tension and suspicion because the maximalists could assign no clear positive role to the parliamentary deputies. Finally, the maximalists made antimilitarism a dogma. Opposition to the Libyan war gave the faction control of the PSI and made the reputation of Benito Mussolini, one of its prominent leaders.

The new maximalist majority, against the better judgment of its more moderate members, offered the editorship of the *Avanti!* to Mussolini, on the principle that, in the land of the deaf, the one with the loudest voice might be king. Initially, at least, the shift from reformist to maximalist control galvanized the party. Mussolini's mixture of Marx and Sorel, a veneer of rationalism masking an emphasis on force and will, was more in tune with Italian youth culture between the turn of the century and World War I. By opening the pages of the *Avanti!* to unorthodox syndicalist and socialist writers, he won a new readership and gained enormous popularity among the rising generation in the Socialist Youth Federation (FGSI).

This success, however, had an ugly side. It meant that the established leadership of the PSI had lost control. Even within the maximalist majority, new and unproven men, like egocentric Mussolini and the demented Nicola Bombacci, competed with sincere socialists like Serrati and Lazzari, who had solid ties to the working class, and who had been founders of the PSI. The permanent stalemate between the maximalist leadership in the directorate, and the reformists in the parliamentary group and in the CGL, blocked the emergence of any positive program.

A deteriorating economy further darkened the horizon of the worker movement in the years before World War I. By 1913 a major business slump hardened management's bargaining positions and led to a particularly bitter strike in Turin between the FIOM and the Turinese Industrial League. As a result, many businessmen soured on the conciliatory policies of Giolitti. The new suffrage law also altered the political map. The liberals had never organized to bring out a mass electorate. Their elitist associations needed Catholic assistance to reach the new voters. The problem was immediately apparent when the election results came in. The liberal monarchist bloc was reduced from 370 to 318 seats and even many of these were elected with clerical support. The PSI received fifty-eight seats and twenty went to the new Partito Socialista Riformista.

In March 1914 Giolitti resigned and Antonio Salandra, his successor, represented the most conservative wing of the liberal political class. Salandra sought to take advantage of the isolation of the PSI to forge a large, antisocialist bourgeois coalition. At its congress of Ancona in April 1914, the PSI eagerly assumed the challenge. The maximalists hurled their revolutionary and antimilitarist message back at the bourgeoisie.

Ancona was the center of a vast strike wave which paralyzed much of northern Italy in June 1914, after troops fired on an antimilitary demonstration. *Avanti!* pledged its full support for the subsequent general strike. The Romagna, Mussolini's region, led the way by proclaiming a republic. But it soon became clear that the maximalists had never organized the PSI to take advantage of any mass rising. Faced with a growing right-wing reaction and no direction from the PSI, the CGL's reformist leadership, amidst much recrimination, called an end to the strike.

THE CRISIS OVER ITALIAN INTERVENTION
IN WORLD WAR I

The Red Week of June 1914 was the last major event before the outbreak of World War I in July. The coming of the war caught all Italian
parties by surprise and provoked a unanimous reaction on the part of
the left. Socialists, syndicalists, republicans, and radicals were of one
voice in rejecting Italy's commitment to Germany and Austria under
the terms of the Triple Alliance. The whole gamut of left-wing opinion,
from bourgeois democrats to the maximalists, favored England and
France over the authoritarian Central Powers. As long as it remained
a question of keeping the country from sliding into war on the side of
the Triple Alliance powers, this unity held up. Within the PSI, feeling
against Germany and Austria was especially strong. The PSI had also
been one of the leading parties of the Second International to favor an
unequivocal stand against support for war. At the PSI congresses of
1908 and 1910, antimilitarist resolutions were regularly passed by large
majorities, even before the party threw itself wholeheartedly against the
Libyan adventure. Then, in late July 1914, the PSI was one of the parties
which attempted to hold the International together, as the Socialist parties
of the other major powers deserted the cause of proletarian solidarity.

No one in the PSI knew how to translate the party's declaration against
war into effective action, however. The short-term strategy was to block
an immediate declaration of war by Italy on the side of Austria and
Germany. On August 5, a meeting of various worker parties and unions
confirmed the united stand of the left by proclaiming that the proletariat
was best served by Italian neutrality. In fact, the Salandra government
had already opted for neutrality on August 3 on the grounds that Austria failed to fulfill the terms of the Triple Alliance by not consulting
with Italy before the attack on Serbia. Once this decision was made, it
turned out to be irrevocable and completely transformed the nature of
the debate. Henceforth, Italy faced a choice between continued neutrality, which began to favor Austria and Germany, or intervention on
the side of the Triple Entente.

Mussolini's editorials in the *Avanti!* fully supported the neutrality proclamation. But his pacifism was not absolute. He made it clear that in
the event of Austrian reprisals against Italy for not honoring its alliance
commitment, the proletariat would defend the nation. On this issue the
party supported Mussolini, so deep was the feeling against Austria and
Germany. Thus, contrary to conventional wisdom, the PSI's position
was not absolute neutrality under all conditions; rather, it was an instinctive reaction against the Triple Alliance that left the door open to
a possible defensive war under certain circumstances.

The PSI's position became less ambiguous when the nonsocialist democratic left, backed by Bissolati, came out for intervention on the side of the Entente. In October, Mussolini attempted to push the PSI to follow suit. This action finally put him out of step with his party. The break came when Mussolini became convinced that the PSI could only avoid isolation and remain politically effective by joining the movement for war. Strangely, Turati and Mussolini, at opposite extremes within the PSI, had not initially differed on the issue of war. Both had been flexible on the question of neutrality. When, on October 18, Mussolini wrote an article, "For Active and Effective Neutrality," in which he called for a change of line, he hoped that the pervasive anti-German feelings within the PSI and his own popularity would carry the day. Whatever his calculations, Mussolini was completely mistaken. The party directorate, between October 18 and 21, voted to condemn Mussolini, to oust him from the editorship of *Avanti!*, and to expel him from the PSI. Serrati, who took over as editor, promptly reaffirmed the hard-line position of the PSI against intervention. Mussolini's ouster must have given pause to Turati, who did not conceal his own fears about the potential isolation of the party in the event of any patriotic revival that would accompany the outbreak of war.

The crisis over Mussolini's defection to the prowar ranks foreclosed one option for the PSI. There was no longer any possibility that the party might join the bourgeois democratic left in favor of the war. But a second alternative was also blocked. The orthodox maximalists could never bring themselves to coordinate their antiwar position with Giovanni Giolitti, who also favored continued neutrality. Only by allying with Giolitti might the PSI have defeated the war party. But Giolitti and the revolutionary maximalists had nothing in common. Turati and Treves, both traditional pacifists, had no problem, in principle, dealing with Giolitti, but they did not control the party. To keep Italy neutral, the PSI would have had to work in conjunction with other groups. Nothing was more alien to the spirit of maximalism, which really only believed in politics by proclamation.

A mood of passivity and resignation in the working class weighed against the PSI in 1914 and 1915. High unemployment had put the workers on the defensive. Although antimilitarism was strong, the socialists fought against the war in highly personal terms. They focused on the leading defectors from the socialist camp, like Mussolini, but found it extremely difficult to mobilize the masses to defend what amounted to the status quo. An ominous sign for the future was the PSI's loss of control of the streets in 1914 and 1915 to the militant prowar parties, who found it much easier to mobilize their followers than did the socialists. When the government decided to join the Entente powers in May 1915, the Socialist party had no effective response. Only the youth federation called openly for a general strike at its congress in May 1915, but this appeal went unheeded. The party fell back on Lazzari's comfortable slogan, "neither adhere, nor sabotage," which meant, in practice, that each power center within the PSI could make its own arrangements. In May 1915, Turati and Treves privately offered their support to the Salandra government, but the prime minister preferred to use the war to isolate further the PSI and ignored the reformists' offer. The CGL and the socialist-controlled town administrations did their best to help the families of soldiers and to organize war relief. In so doing, they rendered an enormous contribution to the Italian war effort.

The maximalists had fewer options. Lazzari's contribution was to coin the "neither adhere, nor sabotage" slogan, which held the party together. Serrati called for full legal opposition to the war, but police measures and censorship effectively muted his appeal. The most positive steps were taken on the international level. On July 11, 1915, Swiss, Russian, Polish, and Italian delegates (Balabanoff and Morgari) met in Berne to organize a formal meeting of the antiwar parties. On September 5 the Italian and Swiss parties sponsored the Zimmerwald Conference where Lenin and Trotsky put forth their revolutionary defeatist views, which urged the proletarian soldiers to turn their weapons against their country. The Italian delegation, however, was divided between traditional pacifists (Morgari and G.E. Modigliani) and those who were more receptive to the Leninist appeal (Serrati and Balabanoff). At the next meeting, held at Kienthal, Switzerland on April 24, Serrati and Balabanoff moved even closer to a Leninist position. As editor of the *Avanti!*, Serrati was the most visible spokesman of the PSI. Emotionally, he was drawn to an extreme antiwar stand, but he also put tremendous importance on party unity. He believed firmly that the reformists had a role in the party. Moreover, he was well aware of the inability of the PSI to create a revolution. Until 1917, then, Serrati offered no real opposition to the pragmatic cooperation which the reformists offered the government. Nor did he seem to oppose Turati's efforts to win the party over to positive collaboration with other democrats on the issue of postwar reconstruction.

In early 1917 the reformists within the PSI mounted a campaign to recapture the party. A joint meeting of the parliamentary group, the directorate, and the CGL, called for the establishment of a republic, abolition of the appointed Senate, progressive taxation, socialization of land, and the eight-hour day. Such a program would have served as a bridge to cooperation with bourgeois democratic parties. The PSI seemed ready to rethink its choice of 1912. Its revolutionary vision had not yet crystalized; nor had the amorphous maximalist majority found any real issue around which to mobilize. Under these circumstances, the pragmatic realism of Turati and Treves made effective headway. Yet, just as it seemed that the reformist revival might be possible, these hopes were dashed. Major food riots in Turin in August, the Bolshevik revolution in October, and the near collapse of the Italian front at Caporetto in November, turned the PSI to a quixotic search for the Italian road to revolution.

CHAPTER 3

The Left between Revolution and Reaction, 1917–1920

World War I drastically changed the context within which both the reformist and maximalist factions of the PSI operated. It accelerated industrialization and encouraged a concentration of larger and larger units of production. With a close dependence on the government, war industries made enormous profits. In 1915 the Salandra government proclaimed an industrial mobilization and set up a special cabinet office to oversee war production. Initially, this move benefited the working class. Strikes and political demonstrations were banned, but the government assured internal peace in war industries through wage concessions. By 1916, however, the fruits of labor's collaboration had largely been washed away by inflation and shortages of all consumer goods. What remained were harsher working conditions and a system of political censorship and police surveillance of socialist and union activity that became more burdensome as the war dragged on into 1917.

The war also enlarged the role of the state. Not only did state regulatory powers proliferate, but public and private bureaucracies also expanded to meet their new responsibilities. Yet, if the state in general emerged strengthened, the parliamentary institution was greatly diminished. Parliament proved too cumbersome to control the operations of the war. Moreover, it contained a substantial minority which followed Giolitti in opposition to the decision to intervene in the conflict. The various wartime governments—Salandra until June 1916, Paolo Boselli until October 1917, and then Vittorio Emanuele Orlando—faced a deeply divided liberal majority. The crisis within the political class had been delayed by the wartime political truce and by Giolitti's inability to take control of the government without provoking a constitutional crisis with the prowar monarch. Ironically, as the state became larger and stronger, the political class became weaker and less rooted in the new reality created by the war. To remedy these deficiencies, some on the extreme right hoped to apply the wartime experience of a hierarchical militarization of society to deal with the problem of postwar social cohesion.

By 1918 it was clear that the war would drastically alter class relations. Most of the army was made up of peasants, while many workers in the war industries received deferments. Although both peasants and workers shared a common dislike for the war, the conclusions which they drew from the experience were quite different. The number of small farmers, already on the increase before 1914, accelerated during the war. The peasant soldiers translated the promises made to the troops during the war to mean a piece of land. While it brought great suffering, the war also came to mean, to some peasants, the possibility of betterment.

The industrial proletariat and the *braccianti* nurtured hopes which differed significantly from those of the peasant proprietors and stable tenants. The war greatly increased the proletariat's alienation from the state. It received the maximalists' appeals for a violent break with the existing order as an immediate call to arms. The leaders of the PSI awoke to the fact that their party's mass base was far more radicalized than they thought. From late 1917 to the end of 1920 their concern was to not be outstripped by the masses. The reformists within the PSI were preoccupied by the national, rather than the party, mood. They hoped to use the democratic potential of the war to press for a series of fundamental reforms. Seldom had the perspectives of the two wings of the socialist movement been so divergent.

By 1917 the fragile consensus over the war had been stretched to the limit. The entry of the United States into the war in April offered hope to the reformists that the war might end. In July, Claudio Treves called for a peace without annexations and proclaimed, "next winter, no longer in the trenches." The strikes and food riots of August, 1917 in Turin had to be put down with force. The fate of Italy hung by a thread after the defeat at Caporetto, when the Austrians and Germans smashed through the Italian lines in late October and November, 1917. Although the reformists immediately rallied to the defense of the nation, conservative Italy blamed socialist agitation for the collapse of Italian morale, and the basic class conflict deepened.

More than anything else, the Bolshevik revolution opened a deep fissure within the PSI and alienated the socialists from the other political movements. The inability of the maximalists to act politically during the early years of the war had given new hope to the reformists. In May 1917 they convinced the party to support a program of concrete reforms that could be coordinated with the aims of other democratic parties. Subsequent events of the summer and fall, however, overtook these plans. Angelica Balabanoff, a Russian exile and prominent maximalist, returned to her homeland in May and began to send back to Italy extremely favorable reports on the Bolsheviks. Serrati, who had been impressed by Lenin at Zimmerwald and Kienthal, declared himself in favor of the Bolsheviks in August 1917, and the news of the Bolshevik revolution pushed him even further to the left. From this point on, Serrati searched only for a way to transfer the Bolshevik experience into Italy.

Even the arrest of the major maximalist leaders of the PSI in early 1918 did not strengthen the reformist position. In April 1918 the Orlando government appointed Turati, Treves, and a number of other reformists to a commission to study postwar problems. The PSI directorate demanded that they resign. A split in the party was barely avoided when Turati reluctantly accepted this ultimatum. At the Congress of Rome, held in August 1918, the PSI abandoned its moderate 1917 position and rejected any reformist solution to the postwar crisis. It simply declared war on the capitalist state with no preparation and no weapons except for the uncoordinated determination of millions of workers and peasants for a better life.

ITALY'S MUTILATED VICTORY

The crisis of 1918–1920 exploded with unprecedented force. The strike wave in Italy and the demands of the revolutionary left were more extensive than in the other victorious countries. The involvement of peasants on a massive scale was also unique to Italy. This enormous wave of discontent hit institutional structures already weakened during the war. In France or England the war ended with electoral victories for the nationalist right, but not in Italy. The liberal political class failed to organize for modern political competition. Instead, it made do with loosely organized local constitutional or liberal monarchical associations. Clearly, there was little hope that such organizations would be adequate after the introduction of universal manhood suffrage. New movements emerged to challenge the traditional elites. A veterans' movement, led by young officers, threatened to become a force in the South. Catholics, given a green light by the Vatican, formed the Partito Popolare Italiano (PPI) in December 1918, under the leadership of a Sicilian priest, Don Luigi Sturzo. On all sides there was agreement that things had to change. At the end of 1918 many of these demands centered on the convocation of a constitutional assembly to propose new, possibly republican, institutions for the country.

Both the political class and powerful industrial interests stood ready to accept limited reform with the hope of avoiding a more serious challenge to their interests. The impact of inflation and military demobilization did not hit immediately. For several months after the end of the war, there seemed to be an opportunity to make some economic and political concessions in exchange for a return to labor peace and cooperation during the transition to a peacetime economy. An agreement was signed in February 1919 between the Industrialists' Confederation and the FIOM that exchanged the eight-hour day for a no-strike policy.

The PSI faced two reformist options short of a Bolshevik-style revolution. It could pursue democratic reform through the convocation of a constituent assembly or work for change within the existing constitutional structures. In both cases, the support of the Socialist party for constructive change was vital. The reformists understood this fact, but were divided on whether to back the constituent assembly movement in alliance with veterans and Catholics or to work for precise political reforms by entering a government headed by Giolitti, or the more liberal Francesco Saverio Nitti, who became prime minister in June 1919. In either case, the socialists would have lent their support to a broad, interclass movement to reform the old liberal state. Basic changes, such as tax reform, land redistribution (partially attained as the result of peasant land occupations in 1919), the vote for women (almost won in 1919), and reform of the Senate, might have had a significant impact as part of a systematic program. The moment for the long-awaited structural reforms had come. Claudio Treves favored the idea of a constitutional assembly, while Turati felt that more could be gained by working within the existing framework. As it turned out, the reformists did nothing. Rather than risk losing their hold over the base of the party by pushing for a moderate policy at the cost of rupture with the maximalists, they temporized in the hope that revolutionary illusions would dissipate.

Again, the opportunity for reform disappeared. The maximalists, swept up by the militancy of the working class, scoffed at any reforms as too little, too late. Instead, they staked out an extreme revolutionary position that precluded anything short of a total, violent overthrow of the existing order. On December 7–11, 1918 the directorate of the PSI rejected the call for a constituent assembly and demanded the creation of a socialist republic. At a joint meeting on December 22 of the parliamentary group, the directorate, socialist local government officials, and the CGL, Turati failed to win a reversal of this decision.

The essence of maximalism between 1918 and 1920 was expressed in five propositions: total and firm opposition to the Great War and to those who had supported it; loyalty to socialist internationalism; support for the Bolshevik revolution; confidence that violent revolution was the only outcome of the postwar crisis; and, finally, rejection of any interclass alliances. They wanted no cooperation with Catholics, veterans, or liberal politicians who did not share the revolutionary vision. Having proclaimed the need for revolution, the maximalists believed that they had merely to ride the wave of history. They were to be destiny's children, agents of the inevitable. Little wonder that they soon became history's orphans. Rhetoric could not be substituted for reality. For all their sincerity and dedication, Costantino Lazzari, Giacinto Menotti Serrati, and the other maximalists did not lead the workers. They were the tail on the kite of the protest movement, buffeted and out of control in the turbulence of the Red Years.

The extreme left, represented by the future leaders of the Communist party, Amadeo Bordiga and Antonio Gramsci, was little better. They differed from the majority of maximalists in their certainty that they could break successfully with the bourgeois order and in their willingness to purge the party of its reformist wing. They devoted almost all their attention to transposing the Bolshevik experience directly into Italian practice. Bordiga emphasized the seizure of political power above all else, and argued that the key to revolution could be found in the Leninist idea of the disciplined and elitist party; Gramsci sought the counterpart of the soviet in the factory councils that the workers were creating in Turin in 1919 and 1920. Neither man grasped the concrete possibilities for change in postwar Italy.

The PSI was quite unsuited for revolutionary action, and a new party could not be created in time to take advantage of the moment of greatest weakness in the bourgeois order. The PSI had grown enormously in 1919 and 1920. In 1914 membership in the party was 58,000. By August 1918 it had slumped to only 24,000, yet two years later it had increased to 216,000. In the elections of November 1919 the PSI received 1,840,000 votes and 156 of 508 seats in the parliament. The CGL went from 600,000 members in May 1919 to 1,200,000 in October and to over two million in 1920. The Federterra had almost 850,000 members. These impressive statistics conceal the reality that the PSI still remained a series of cooperatives, peasant leagues, unions, local federations, municipal officials, parliamentary deputies, and frustrated Lenins. The party had never accepted strong leadership, and the unfortunate experience with the charismatic Mussolini only reinforced this distrust.

The key figure in these years was Serrati. He had forged his socialist commitment in the Italian and North American labor movement and had been one of the first generation of party members. The maximalists turned to Serrati, an able and agile journalist, to replace Mussolini during the 1914 crisis. The solidity of his principles and dedication to the cause were unquestioned, but in 1919 and 1920 he was torn between his realistic understanding that there was little hope for immediate revolution and a visceral desire to bring down the system. He wanted to follow Lenin's example but knew that Italy could never reproduce an exact duplicate of the Bolshevik success. The result was paralysis. He would neither support the reformists nor expel them. He favored Lenin's program but refused to apply it to Italy. Tragically, after 1920, Serrati would have little idea of the true nature of fascism or how to combat it. He was not the best possible leader for the PSI, but he embodied perfectly the virtues (generosity and humanitarianism) and the defects (a penchant for verbal extremism and posturing) of maximalism. For better or worse, he would be the party's choice to lead it in troubled times.

The maximalists were totally caught up with the *idea* of action, even if it involved merely spinning their wheels. In March 1919 the directorate ended the PSI's relationship with the old Second International and announced that it would join the new Communist International. The decision was made with no idea what such a choice entailed. The embattled Bolsheviks, delighted by the unexpected support, and recalling Serrati's positions at the antiwar Zimmerwald and Kienthal conferences, immediately hailed him as the Italian Lenin. The Bolsheviks went a step further in 1920 by making Serrati a member of the executive commission of the new Third International. This was an endorsement that they would soon regret.

Meanwhile, the workers took matters into their own hands in a series of massive protests. During the first half of 1919, 200,000 metal workers, a quarter million peasants, and countless textile, dock, and railroad workers went out on strike against the high cost of living. Municipal services were disrupted and store owners forced to close. In early 1919, the Federterra proclaimed the goal to socialize the land, and by the summer and fall peasants in central Italy began to occupy vacant and ill-used land. In July a major national general strike was called in solidarity with the struggling revolutions of Hungary and Russia.

The socialist agitation had certain common characteristics. It was largely spontaneous or locally controlled. Little coordination existed between one series of demands and another. Violence was aimed at property, not people; but there was also extensive intimidation of soldiers and veterans, small shopkeepers, and in rural areas, sharecroppers, tenants, and small landowners who did not share the day-laborer's enthusiasm for collectivization. Neither the PSI nor the CGL did much on a national level to direct the wave of strikes in early 1919. The maximalists concentrated their efforts on the symbolic July general strike but without identifying a strategy other than Lazzari's idea of "throwing sand in the machinery."

In the country there were some signs of possible reaction. In April 1919 veterans of special combat units (*arditi*) destroyed the presses of the *Avanti!* in Milan. Then, in September, the poet Gabriele D'Annunzio, riding a wave of nationalist fervor, successfully led a band of volunteers to seize the disputed Adriatic port of Fiume to keep it from the Yugoslavs. Yet the maximalists viewed these signs of nationalist direct action as an indication of the collapse of the bourgeois state. The revolutionaries optimistically confused a crisis in parliamentary government with a crisis in the state itself.

THE CONGRESS OF BOLOGNA, OCTOBER 1919

At the Congress of Bologna the PSI formally set its postwar agenda. The four most urgent items were: to choose between a reformist or revolutionary strategy; to decide whether to expel the reformists; to consider conditions for adherence to the Third International; and to discuss participation in the national elections which were to be held in November.

On the first issue there was no doubt. The party declared itself in favor of a violent revolution; it sought to establish the dictatorship of the proletariat on the Bolshevik model. Ignored was Turati's sarcastic comment that a party unable to defend its own newspaper presses from attack could hardly make a revolution. Yet, as if to prove that decisions do not necessarily have consequences, the reformists neither withdrew, nor were they expelled, as Bordiga demanded. So convinced were Serrati and Lazzari of the inevitability of revolution that they refused to back expulsion. The reformists, by unwisely remaining in the party, were blocked from collaboration with the governments of Nitti and Giolitti in 1919 and 1920. Absolutely nothing was achieved except total paralysis.

Relations with the Third International were resolved when the PSI overwhelmingly declared itself willing to open negotiations with Moscow. Unfortunately, the directorate failed to realize that expulsion of the reformists and acceptance of democratic centralism were preconditions for membership in Lenin's new International. If these two decisions were not contradictory enough, the decision to participate in the electoral process was a recipe for total confusion. The introduction of proportional representation held out the promise of great gains for the PSI. The maximalists also understood that many workers were excited about voting for the first time, so they were willing to go through the motions of electioneering on the condition that the elected representatives in parliament would under no circumstances be used as an instrument for change.

THE ELECTIONS OF NOVEMBER 1919

The national elections of November brought home the full extent of the crisis in the political system. The collapse of the old political elites had been delayed by the political truce during the war. Then the size of the socialist victory sent shock waves through the system. Of the PSI's 156 deputies, 131 came from the North, the Po Valley, and Tuscany. The South produced only ten, of which five came from Puglia. No socialists were elected from Sicily or Sardinia. In parliament as a whole, over sixty percent of the deputies were newcomers. The Catholic Partito Popolare received one hundred seats and, together with the PSI, held a majority. But this paper majority did not translate into effective control. Although the liberals, dominant in all prewar parliaments, emerged as big losers, these results were somewhat misleading. The victories of the socialists and Catholics were as much the product of division and confusion in conservative Italy as an indication of the real strength of the new forces. Superimposed on the prewar division of Giolitti and his enemies was the new demarcation between supporters and opponents of the decision to enter the war. Moreover, the liberals were not geared for the system of proportional representation favoring nationally organized parties over local clienteles.

The most unlikely outcome of the November election would be for the PSI to join in the formation of a democratic government with the Catholic and bourgeois parties. Both the maximalists and the Vatican opposed PSI–PPI cooperation. Many of the 156 socialist deputies never bothered to attend parliament—so convinced were they of the imminent revolution. The directorate viewed the party's parliamentary strength merely as another sign of the disintegration of the state.

In the short run, the most probable result of the elections would be a government headed by one of the established liberal leaders. Most likely to succeed was Giolitti, who returned to power in May 1920. However, the Piedmontese leader no longer dominated parliament as he did before 1914. When he failed to create a stable majority in 1920–21, the gap between parliament and society widened, but certainly not to the advantage of the revolutionaries.

BORDIGA AND GRAMSCI

By early 1920 the PSI had split into three wings. The reformists, led by Turati and Treves, still intended to stay within the PSI. The centers of reformist strength remained in the CGL and in the parliamentary delegation. The various maximalist currents, headed by Serrati and Lazzari, dominated the center-left of the party. The maximalists remained torn between the rhetoric of a violent overthrow of capitalism and the realization that revolution was impossible. The maximalists controlled numerous local governments, but they had no way of enforcing that strength on the national level. Instead, it was frittered away in uncoordinated strikes and protests.

The party's left was made up of two groups. The first was led by Amadeo Bordiga (1889–1970), a charismatic engineer from Naples, soon to be Serrati's successor as the "Italian Lenin." Bordiga's strength was in the clarity of his positions. He opposed participation in elections, called for a purge of the reformists, and demanded the reorganization of the PSI into a select, militant revolutionary force. Whether this would have advanced the prospect of revolution is unclear, but at least it cut through maximalist confusion.

The Turin group, which edited the review *Ordine nuovo* and formed the other major faction on the extreme left, was led by Antonio Gramsci (1891–1937), Angelo Tasca (1892–1960), Umberto Terracini (1895–1985), and Palmiro Togliatti (1893–1964). Gramsci and Tasca founded *Ordine nuovo* on May 1, 1919, creating a link between the avant-garde culture and the revolutionary worker movement. The *Ordine nuovo* group placed great emphasis on the the development of an autonomous worker consciousness through cultural as well as economic and political means. They modeled their movement after *Clarté*, the revolutionary and culturally avant-garde French review, edited by Romain Rolland and Henri Barbusse.

Gramsci stood out as the most original thinker of the Turin group. Born on January 21, 1891 at Ales on the island of Sardinia, Gramsci was forced to make his way through the University of Turin as a poor scholarship student after his father, a minor bureaucrat, lost position and status in a financial scandal. In Turin he met Tasca, Togliatti, and Terracini, and was drawn into socialist politics. The socialism of the Turin group combined Marx and the new idealist culture inspired by Benedetto Croce. Briefly, in 1914 Gramsci was even attracted by the charismatic Benito Mussolini and almost supported the *Avanti!* editor's stance, in October 1914, over the issue of intervention in World War I. However, Gramsci soon returned to an orthodox neutralist position. Excused from wartime service for medical reasons, he emerged as a leader in the local party and the major force behind its newspaper, *Il grido del popolo*. The war, especially the food riots of August and the Bolshevik Revolution of October 1917, further radicalized Gramsci.

By 1919, as the *Ordine nuovo* group searched for a way to translate the Bolshevik experience into Italian terms, the auto workers' union, FIOM, solidified its position as Italy's most progressive and aggressive labor organization. Before the war, the FIOM had won recognition of "internal commissions" to supervise the working of the collective contract within the factory. In 1919 and 1920 the union sought to expand the role of the internal commissions beyond purely contractual matters and encouraged them to share in the control of production. As they were further elaborated by Gramsci and others, the internal commissions became councils where workers from each unit in the factory could be represented. The representatives might be unionized or unorganized workers. A new framework of power would develop from the single factory to whole sectors and regions. Gramsci saw the factory council as the Italian counterpart to the Soviet of the Bolshevik experience. The workers created a new instrument by which they could seize control of the productive apparatus. Thus, they would merge the struggle for political liberation with the creation of the post-revolutionary economic system. Unfortunately, the council movement was limited to a few areas in the North like Turin and Milan and, even in the areas of greatest strength, it still met the opposition of both the PSI and of the CGL, which feared that a new and untested experiment might dilute worker energies.

THE STRIKE OF THE HOUR HANDS

The decisive moment for the Turinese workers came in March 1920. The year began with major rail and postal strikes and factory occupations at the Mazzonis textile works near Turin, and at the Ansaldo steel complex in Liguria. Then, in March, the Federterra called a major strike of Piedmontese agricultural workers. As peasants battled police throughout the province, the autoworkers challenged the auto industry over the issue of daylight savings time in what came to be known as the "hour hands strike." This relatively minor concern was a pretext for a struggle over the issue of the factory councils. Although the strike was called by the shop stewards at a moment of peak agitation, there had been little effort at coordination with the Federterra or with the CGL. The management of the auto giant, Fiat, dug in its heels, promising a long battle. If good fortune is a child with a thousand godparents, then disaster surely is an orphan. At the meeting of the PSI's National Council in April, the Turinese vainly appealed for help. As the revolutionary offensive became mired in the mud of the failed Turin strike, all the tragic defects of the Socialist movement came to the fore. Serrati and the other party leaders bitterly criticized the Piedmontese provincial federation for acting alone, while the Turinese argued that the party had a duty to come to the aid of its most militant vanguard. The reformist leaders of the CGL sought to regain control over the factory council movement by backing their maximalist enemies against the upstart leaders of the council movement. Turati pointed out that unplanned local initiatives would never advance the cause of revolution. But he also wondered whether the party could think of no better use for 156 parliamentary deputies than obstructionism and passivity.

THE PSI AND THE THIRD INTERNATIONAL

By mid-1920 another one of the decisions made by the PSI in 1919 proved more complicated than originally estimated. The party recklessly passed the resolution to join the Third International. Quickly, two issues emerged as central to success: the continued role of the reformists within the PSI, and the application of the Bolshevik experience to Italian conditions. Serrati, a leader shaped in the traditions of the old pre-1914 socialist Second International, had little understanding of Lenin. Moreover, he was convinced that the bourgeoisie was getting stronger rather than weaker. To the exasperation of the leaders of the Third International, the more Serrati became convinced that revolution was no longer imminent, the more he believed that the unity of the PSI was essential to face the growing reaction.

The Second Congress of the Communist or Third International (Comintern), held in July and August 1920, should have dispelled these illusions. As if to force the hand of the reluctant Italian socialists, the International insisted that the conditions for immediate revolution in Italy were present. The only impediment was the PSI's hesitancy and refusal to expel the reformist wing of the party. Serrati, faced with the International's demands, temporized. In theory, the PSI accepted the decisions of the Second Congress, including the twenty-one conditions for membership, but reserved the right to apply the conditions in its own way. The Italian leadership held firmly to the autonomist traditions of the old Second International in applying the directives. But Lenin had set up his new Communist International precisely to limit this independence which he saw as a major weakness in the old Socialist movement. Moreover, two of the twenty-one conditions struck at the PSI's self-image. The Italians were proud that they never had an overtly pro-war faction. Support for the war had been one of the grounds used in other parties to expel the reformists, although a notorious social patriot, Marcel Cachin, emerged as one of the leaders of the French Communist party. Then came the vexing demand that the PSI abandon its name and accept the new designation of Communist Party of Italy. Many of the old-line maximalists, like Lazzari, resisted for sentimental reasons. But all of these points merely masked the PSI's failure to understand how and why the Moscow International was created.

THE WANING OF THE REVOLUTIONARY MOVEMENT: THE FACTORY OCCUPATIONS OF SEPTEMBER 1920

Even at the peak of revolutionary disturbance in 1919 and 1920, the PSI was never sufficiently organized to mount a threat to the existing order. Several factors combined to limit the party's revolutionary potential. Little coordination existed in the PSI between its regional and national organizations, between region and region, and between rural and urban areas. Even when gains were made on the provincial level, they seldom went beyond what Angelo Tasca defined ironically as "socialism in a single province." Major strikes, led by Federterra, in Ferrara and in Bologna had given the peasant leagues enormous local power without advancing the cause of revolution on the national level. The army and the police were unshaken. The Catholic Church retained its hold over millions of Italians. Moreover, the Church had its own labor unions that managed to enroll 1,182,000 members, of which almost a million were peasant sharecroppers, small proprietors, and renters. Finally, the local elites, especially in the South, were still quite strong. The socialist party leaders used local victories to build the myth of an invincible national movement. They ignored the fact that their gains were initially as much the result of temporary disorganization and confusion on the part of the bourgeoisie as of anything positive done by the socialists.

The end of the revolutionary drama occurred in the fall of 1920. In Emilia, the peasants of the Federterra won a long and bitter strike that allowed them to control the hiring of workers through their union halls, and to create fixed quotas. In the new master contract, owners lost many of their traditional prerogatives. Reacting to the defeat, a substantial number of agrarian entrepreneurs turned to self-protection. They recruited squads of veterans, students, and small holders, headed by former army officers, to launch a counterattack, first in Bologna and Ferrara, then throughout the Po Valley. They aimed to wipe out the infrastructure of rural socialism by physically destroying the peasant leagues and the Socialist party.

The second crisis came in September in Milan and in Turin where the auto workers, now on the defensive but still suffering from the March defeat, decided to occupy the factories in order to force the companies into good-faith negotiations. The occupation was largely to prevent management from forcing union concessions through a company lockout. The outcome was a tactical success but a strategic failure. The workers maintained production and, after the intervention of the government and of the CGL, the auto industry conceded a relatively favorable contract. In a larger sense, the factory occupations were a defeat. The exhausted workers proved, once again, that limited victories do not open the way for revolution. The factory occupations, often viewed as a turning point in the fortunes of the left, widened the gap between the reformists and revolutionaries within the PSI. They had little incentive to work together now that the chances of revolution were lost. Finally, the factory occupations convinced many small and middle-sized industrialists to abandon Giolitti's moderation and to support the growing Fascist movement as the best means to retaliate against the working class.

THE RISE OF FASCISM

Although the rise of fascism is not the subject of this work, it is important to understand that the Fascist movement developed in Italy for several interconnected reasons. The first was the thwarting of the movement for reform in late 1918 and early 1919. Much of the fault for limiting the possibility for change lies with the maximalist wing of the PSI which rejected concrete, attainable goals in favor of a Bolshevik-style revolution. But there was, in fascism, a strong element of revenge. Those threatened by revolution were determined to destroy the very base of the movement that menaced them. A second reason for the rise of fascism involved the fragmented and antiquated nature of bourgeois politics.

The first two postwar prime ministers, Francesco Saverio Nitti (from June 1919 to May 1920) and Giovanni Giolitti (from June 1920 to June 1921), accepted some reforms in order to maintain the hegemony of the liberal political class. Neither man had the ability to create a new party of bourgeoisie capable of competing in a mass electoral system. Nitti's government was undermined by labor unrest, by his inability to deal with the coalition of rebellious students, veterans, and sundry adventurers who seized the disputed city of Fiume, and by the crushing defeat inflicted on the liberals in the elections of November 1919. Giolitti's failure was even more devastating. Long considered the most able of Italian politicians, he was hailed by all middle-class parties when he assumed the reins of government in the spring of 1920. But the prewar world in which Giolitti had operated with such mastery was irreparably damaged. The years had only deepened the suspicion between Giolitti and the reformists within the PSI, who feared that the prime minister wished to co-opt them without substantially changing the political structure. Giolitti's longstanding practice of neutrality in private labor disputes also cost him support among conservatives. After the strikes of autumn 1920, landowners and businessmen took their own measures to restore order.

Italian industrialization, which brought about an enlargement of state and private bureaucracies between the turn of the century and the end of World War I, had also created an ambitious and upwardly mobile bourgeoisie. Many young veterans, professionals, and students looked for a political party that would express their aspirations. The militantly proletarian and antiwar orientation of the PSI turned the middle class away. The failure of a mass veterans' movement in the election of 1919 added to the disillusionment. At first it seemed that the Fascist movement, formed in April 1919 by renegades from the Socialist and Syndicalist movements, could never assume the role of unifying various bourgeois interests. But fascism's program and social base, by 1921, made it an overtly rightist bourgeois party. These changes, coupled with the continuing crisis of the other middle-class political parties, brought success.

Like the maximalists, the fascists adopted a policy of "worse is better." Both wanted the postwar liberal governments to fail and the parliament to lose prestige. But the socialists only verbally attacked the state, whereas the fascists worked in conjunction with elements of the local gentry, police, and military to reassert the authority of a new model state that would be free from the threat of lower-class revolution. The fascists shared with the entire bourgeoisie a common sense of patriotic resentment, a desire for revenge, a disgust for revolutionary rhetoric, and a resolution to advance middle-class economic and social interests without consideration of worker and peasant demands. Landlords, harmed by strikes and loss of local prestige, joined businessmen and small shopkeepers, who were irritated by work stoppages and higher wages, and students and veterans, who sought a movement that would "make way for youth." As the reaction grew in force, it was fueled by the temporary successes of the socialist peasant leagues that had alienated small landowners, renters, and sharecroppers, and made an immediate counterattack more urgent.

CONCLUSION

By the end of 1920 the Italian revolution had failed. The division between maximalists and reformists grew deeper and prevented the PSI from developing coherent policies. The party itself had been overwhelmed by success. Its leadership could not agree on how to use the electoral strength that came on the national and local level in 1919 and 1920. Opportunities for cooperation with other reformist groups or with Nitti or Giolitti faded away. Instead, the PSI pursued a dream of a Bolshevik revolution totally inappropriate to Italian circumstances. The entire center and left of the PSI operated in an imaginary world where things would inevitably work out well. Occasionally leaders like Serrati realized that Italy was no closer to revolution, but these leaders lacked the will to redirect the PSI away from its myths. The reformists, fearing to operate on their own, pandered to the fantasies of the left. Now, in defeat, there was little reason to hold the party together, nor was there any guarantee that the PSI could rebuild its position in the face of a resurgent and vindictive bourgeoisie.

CHAPTER 4

The Creation of the Italian Communist Party, 1921–1926

From the time of the Congress of Bologna in October 1919, the extreme left of the PSI, headed by Amadeo Bordiga, favored splitting the party and creating an entirely new structure. Bordiga's influence grew throughout 1920 as Serrati seemed unable to steer a course between reformists and the Third International. The failure of the factory occupations and the obvious exhaustion of the working class after two years of continuous agitation by late 1920 made an alternative party organization very appealing. The Third International added to the momentum by leaving no doubt that it expected the full application of the twenty-one conditions for membership, including expulsion of the reformists and all those who refused the discipline of the International, an immediate party congress to ratify the decisions, the reservation of two-thirds of the seats on the new party executive for those who accepted unconditional membership in the International before the July Second Congress, and a change of name to Communist party.

Preliminary meetings were held by the party factions between October and December 1920 to discuss strategy and to prepare for the party congress, which was finally set for January 1921 in Livorno after Florence appeared too vulnerable to fascist disruption. The communist faction at the congress was divided into two important groups: those who believed in a disciplined and Leninist party based on the program outlined in Bordiga's *Il soviet*, and the Turinese *Ordine nuovo* group, headed by Gramsci, which was still strongly influenced by the worker-council movement. In addition, a number of maximalists wanted merely to satisfy the conditions for membership set by the Third International. Bordiga's absolute intransigence set the tone: full application of the twenty-one conditions, expulsion of the reformists, and the reorganization of the party into a disciplined cadre of professional revolutionaries.

At Livorno the only remaining question concerned the nature of the split. More specifically, how much of the center and center left would follow the communist faction? The most logical point of rupture would have taken the reformists out of the party. Then, Turati, backed by the CGL, might have cooperated with Giolitti or another moderate government on a program to stop the growth of fascism. Many observers, including Giolitti, gambled on such an outcome. But two things upset all calculations. The maximalist leadership refused to accept the twenty-one conditions *en bloc*, and the International proved totally unwilling to compromise. The reformists further blurred the lines by accepting Serrati's positions. When the voting occurred, it revealed that the leaders of the International had miscalculated. The split isolated the extreme left, leaving 14,000 reformists and the bulk of maximalists still together in the PSI. The new Communist party of Italy (PCI) took 58,000 or about one-third of the votes at Livorno, but only 42,000 later joined the new party. A large number of abstentions and political dropouts revealed the confusion that a good many maximalists felt about being forced into a split which seemed arbitrary and imposed from above. The only victor was Bordiga who had always wanted an ideologically pure party, even if it meant leaving the majority of maximalists behind. The major loser was the entire left because the combined membership of the new parties never equalled the 220,000 of the pre-Livorno PSI.

THE LEFT AFTER LIVORNO

The Congress at Livorno marked a new beginning for the proletarian movement. The old PSI had been a loose coalition of peasant leagues, cooperatives, provincial federations, the CGL, and the parliamentary party. Bordiga's new communist model promised to be completely different. The PCI was to be a tightly controlled and centralized organization, dedicated to advancing the cause of violent revolution. There would be continuous coordination between the party leadership, its members in parliament, and the cadres in the unions. In yet another break with the past, the Communist party would be closely bound, ideologically and organizationally, to the International.

The relationship between the PSI and the new PCI on the national and local level was understandably marked by bitterness and hostility. The two parties competed for the same electorate and for support from Moscow, because the PSI had not yet abandoned hope that it would finally be admitted to the Third International. Bordiga and the majority of communists firmly believed that the PSI was the single most serious impediment to the success of an Italian revolution. Given such attitudes, there was little chance that the two movements would cooperate to develop a strategy to deal with fascism.

ECONOMIC CRISIS AND THE
NEW BOURGEOIS OFFENSIVE OF 1921

In late 1920 or early 1921, Italy reached the low point of the postwar economic cycle. Layoffs were common as employers showed new determination to increase productivity and reduce labor costs. The onslaught caught labor unprepared. By 1921 many industrialists and landowners sensed that the situation had shifted in their favor, but the rapidity of change upset most political calculations. Giolitti had tolerated fascist violence in order to tame the revolutionary wing of the PSI. A break between the reformists and maximalists would have allowed the government to attract the unions and some moderate socialist parliamentarians into a new majority. (The General Confederation of Labor remained in control of the reformists after its congress in February 1921, but the communist faction took about one-third of the votes.) Simultaneously, Giolitti tried to strike a deal with the more political wing of the fascist movement by offering Mussolini and his followers a place on the national electoral list, which he drew up for new elections in the spring of 1921.

It turned out that fascist violence could not be tolerated on the local level without compromising the very authority of the government over the same local officials. Giolitti also lost his gamble on elections. After the April results, Mussolini, the reformist socialists, and the Catholics all abandoned the government, which resigned in May 1921. A succession of weak and ineffective governments under Ivanoe Bonomi and Luigi Facta followed, until Mussolini's March on Rome in October 1922.

THE PSI AFTER LIVORNO

The PSI, firmly under the control of the maximalists, had resolved none of its fundamental policy decisions by the defection of the communists. However, apparent success in weathering the Livorno crisis masked the seriousness of the problems besetting the PSI. Membership fell to 104,000 in 1921 and, under increasing pressure from the fascists, it declined further to 73,000 in 1922. In most working-class areas outside of Piedmont, the PSI remained dominant. The 1921 elections confirmed this favored position when the PSI elected 122 deputies to the PCI's 16.

Second thoughts on the part of the Communist International added to the confusion. Although in January 1921 the leaders of the International backed Bordiga, they soon realized that a Bordiga-dominated PCI would present new problems, and they sought an accommodation with the maximalists. As the stock of the maximalists rose, tension grew between the PCI and the International. Bordiga became more of an obstacle than a leader. Moreover, the Communist International's leadership became more realistic about the possibilities of revolution in Europe in 1921. In March the failure of an insurrection led by the Communists in Germany convinced Lenin of the wisdom of a more cautious policy. Revolution was now seen as a long struggle. In this perspective, the value of the PSI's broad worker support increased.

As early as its July congress, the International sought to undo some of the damage done at Livorno. At the Third Congress of the International, Lenin attacked the PCI's ultra-leftism and sought to circumvent the PCI leadership by direct agreement with the PSI. Had the negotiations been successful, they would have given control of the PCI to a coalition of Bordiga's opponents in the Communist party, and to the maximalists. The result would have been a larger but less cohesive PCI. Unfortunately, these new efforts ran aground on the same issue that blocked an earlier understanding. Serrati still refused to accept the mandatory expulsion of the reformists. The socialist delegation to the Congress of the International felt itself under attack on this issue and reacted by blaming the International for undermining the working-class movement. In October 1921, Lenin sent the German communist leader, Klara Zetkin, to Italy to try to work out with Serrati the expulsion of the reformists and acceptance of the other terms of the International. Zetkin also hoped to weaken Bordiga's hold over the PCI. The success of the second mission depended on winning over Serrati and the majority of maximalists. When that proved impossible at the October Congress of the PSI, Bordiga's leadership of the PCI was strengthened. The International temporarily suspended relations with the PSI.

The split between maximalists and communists was paralleled by the continuing division within the PSI between reformists and maximalists over how to deal with fascism. Throughout 1921 and 1922 the reformists sought to use the remaining power of the PSI in parliament to support a government committed to restoring legality in the country. The maximalists, caught up in negotiations with the Third International, were not about to make a serious overture to a bourgeois government.

The inability of the PSI as a whole to forge a coherent policy made another congress necessary. The party factions clashed once again at the Congress of Milan in October 1921. But neither side wanted to risk a second split within a year. In fact, the maximalists, with 47,000 delegate votes, firmly controlled the PSI. The reformists, with fewer than half that number, refused to admit that they could never seriously influence party policy. Like a bad marriage, the old round of mutual recrimination resumed. The unwillingness of either side to face the full consequences of the deep ideological conflict within the PSI crippled the party. The parliamentary delegation was unable to use its power constructively, and substantial sectors of the bourgeoisie moved to impose their own fascist solution to the crisis of the political system, which had been opened with World War I. The maximalists did not even win credit with Moscow for their firm stand against support for bourgeois governments. Using the refusal to expel the reformists as a pretext, the Third International broke off negotiations with the PSI after the October congress.

THE FIRST STEPS OF THE NEW PCI

As it tried to establish itself, the PCI faced the same issues that confronted the PSI: relations with the other proletarian parties, ties to the International, and a strategy against fascism. The circumstances of the formation of the PCI concealed a basic misunderstanding. The party was closely tied to the Third International, but Amadeo Bordiga, who commanded the support of a vast majority of militants, was extraordinarily independent and assertive. He was determined to follow the International only insofar as it agreed with his own revolutionary vision. Bordiga had staked his whole career on just the kind of split that had taken place at Livorno. He was determined to prevent any sort of reconciliation with the maximalists. He wanted an elitist revolutionary party, even at the cost of total political isolation. Bordiga was firmly convinced that the revolution would still be possible, but only if the PSI was eliminated. The road to revolution would reopen when the PCI formulated the correct ideological line for the workers. Alliances with other groups merely blurred the issues. Thus, for Bordiga and his followers the answers to all of the problems facing the PCI were quite simple. Italy was divided into two camps: the PCI was against all the rest, especially the PSI. As for fascism, it represented nothing new; it was merely a sign of desperation on the part of the bourgeoisie.

But the PCI faced its own crisis of credibility. It claimed to represent the true interests of the proletariat, but the split with the PSI had taken place solely on the leadership level. Those who followed the new Communist party had no clear ideological differences with the maximalists. The average communist militant was somewhat younger and perhaps more intransigent, but the differences were not all that substantial. Outside of Piedmont, where the PCI took 44.2 percent of the provincial votes at Livorno, and a few other centers (Venezia Giulia, Mantua, Bologna, Forlì, Naples, and parts of Sicily), the PCI had no assured mass following. The elections of May 1921 gave the communists only 16 seats to over 120 for the PSI. In Milan the disproportion of votes was 12 to 1 in favor of the socialists. The PCI had to prove that it was a true party, capable of competing on a national basis with the PSI.

THE LEFT, THE LIBERAL STATE,
AND THE DANGER OF FASCISM

The crisis of the parliamentary regime entered its final stage in 1922. The fall of Giolitti in June 1921 ended the last strong government that liberal Italy produced. His successor, the ex-socialist Ivanoe Bonomi, headed a weak and irresolute ministry that gave way to an even more shaky coalition headed by Luigi Facta in February 1922. These changes took place without a positive contribution from the left. The contrast with 1919, when the PSI was at the center of political life, was startling; now, just two years later, it had become an irrelevancy.

Discussions in both the PSI and PCI stemmed from the need to reverse this decline, but the options remained what they had always been. The reformists in parliament and in the CGL argued that the working-class parties had to support any antifascist coalition, even at the cost of abandoning its ban on interclass collaboration. The communists insisted on absolute intransigence, even at the cost of total isolation. The maximalists wavered and drifted. At times, they seemed willing to allow the reformists to try to reach some accommodation; mostly, they responded to the old militancy and pressure from the communists. Caught between strongly conflicting viewpoints, the maximalists fell back on tradition. Their strongest arguments were negative ones. They pointed out that none of the bourgeois parties really wanted the help of the socialists. The argument was all the more ironic because the policies followed by the maximalists had been responsible for the relegation of their party to the margin of political life.

The total isolation of the left was evident in July and early August 1922 when the unions called a protest strike against fascist violence on August 1. The fascists, strongly backed by middle-class opinion, crushed the strike and with it the spirit of resistance of the PSI and CGL. A simultaneous effort by Turati to break out of parliamentary isolation ended in failure as well. He tried to join the leaders of other parties for consulations with the king during a mid-summer crisis of the Facta government. For his pains Turati was denounced by the maximalists and forced to retreat. By autumn the PSI had been reduced to total immobility.

The communists fared little better. At the PCI Congress, held in Rome in early 1922, Bordiga continued to stress the struggle against social democracy as if it, not fascism, loomed as the greatest danger. No sooner did the PCI state its policies when it came under renewed pressure from the International to assume a more moderate position. If Bordiga seemed oblivious to the danger of fascism, Lenin, Karl Radek, and other leaders of the International certainly were not. But, so long as the PSI refused to expel the reformists, Bordiga was relatively secure from pressure.

Ironically, the Communist party bore the brunt of the fascist attacks. Its membership was 24,000 just before the March on Rome in October 1922, but the party was in decline in several major urban centers like Turin. Moreover, Bordiga's rigidity rendered communist policies more ineffective. True, with only sixteen deputies in parliament, the PCI could exert no real influence on the national scene, but it might have taken control of the CGL from the reformists, had the communists allied with the maximalists. Despite its militancy, the PCI was reduced to viewing the triumph of fascism from the sidelines. The chief asset of the party was its semi-clandestine organization. Of the major political movements, only the PCI had parallel legal and illegal apparatuses. Thus, despite the errors of its leaders, the PCI was better able to ride out the storm of repression.

THE FORMATION OF A REFORMIST PARTY

The fragile unity of the PSI was completely undermined by the failure of its attempts to stop fascism during the summer of 1922. An extraordinary party congress was called to resolve the conflict between factions. The reformists finally demanded an ideological break between socialism and bolshevism. Belatedly, they were willing to accept a party split on the issue, but the creation of a reformist party came too late to influence the events that would carry Mussolini to power. By October 1922 neither side disputed the necessity of the split, nor did they have illusions that their gesture would have much impact. The PSI was a kind of unwanted guest at the political table. Although the rupture between reformists and maximalists came over the refusal of the majority to accept a clear demarcation between the PSI and PCI, the root cause was their totally different approaches to socialism, which could be traced back to the turn of the century.

The reformists created the Unitary Socialist Party (PSU) in October 1922 with the charismatic Giacomo Matteotti as political secretary. The party won the support of a substantial part of the parliamentary group, including Turati and Treves, and the major leaders of the CGL. Had the split come earlier, it certainly would have had greater impact. The PSU program was gradualist and democratic. It put the emphasis of the restoration of democracy as a *sine qua non* for any social and economic progress.

The PSU's major defect was a latent conflict between the political wing of the party, which was strongly antifascist, and the labor leaders, whose corporativist and economic mentality led them into dangerous compromises with the fascists in order to protect the union structures from attack. After the fascist March on Rome of October 27–30, 1922 Mussolini sought to include labor representatives in his new government, but this move was blocked both by the fascists' conservative allies and by Matteotti. The PSU secretary sought instead to form a broad antifascist coalition in 1923 and 1924 that would extend from Catholics and bourgeois democrats to the maximalists. But the CGL leaders, who had been tempted by Mussolini earlier, could easily escape control by the PSU and would again be lured into discussions with the fascists.

THE FUSION ISSUE REVIVED

The October Congress of Rome marked a low point for the PSI. Serrati spoke as if the party assumed no responsibility for what happened in Italy between 1918 and 1922. Even after the reformists walked out to form the PSU, the maximalists, to their surprise, found that they were still unable to resolve the conflicts within the PSI. Two groups now battled for the remnants of the socialist legacy: a large and amorphous maximalist majority, still hoping to work out a favorable compromise with the Third International, and a pro-Moscow faction that called for fusion with the PCI. With the reformists out of the party, Serrati now opted for accelerated negotiations with Moscow. His erstwhile allies, Pietro Nenni (1891–1980) and Arturo Vella (1886–1943), found themselves defending the continued independence of the PSI as a political force.

When the fascists seized power on October 28 and 29, 1922, the attention of the left was focused on the Congress of the Third International in Moscow where, fusion between the PCI and PSI had become a major item on the agenda. In fact, Bordiga believed that the International's relentless pressure on the PCI to come to terms with the PSI was a much more serious danger than the fascist seizure of power.

At the meeting of the Third International in November and December 1922, the majority of the communist delegation fought any compromise with the PSI. The leaders of the International, however, pinned their hopes on a pro-fusionist faction within the PCI, led by Angelo Tasca, and on the eagerness of Serrati to arrive at a settlement. Under the watchful eye of the Comintern, a forced merger was arranged. The PCI reluctantly accepted the establishment of a common executive for the two parties to be followed by the convocation of a unity congress to ratify fusion. This process effectively took the decision out of the hands of the party organizations, which would meet only after the fusion process had been decided. Moreover, the communists were assured of a majority on all the committees. While seemingly favorable to the PCI, this accord concealed a threat to Bordiga's leadership because a natural alliance had formed between Tasca's group in the PCI and the fusionists in the PSI. Under the right circumstances these two groups might comprise a new majority within the PCI.

With agreement reached in Moscow by January 1923, the battle shifted back to Italy. The socialist opponents of fusion had been excluded from the negotiations, but they had been hard at work organizing their own Committee on Socialist Defense. Nenni had seized control of the *Avanti* from Serrati and used it to demand a renegotiation of the pact to preserve the autonomy of the PSI. Hopes for fusion received a serious setback when Serrati, who had been detained in Moscow until

February, was arrested on his return to Italy. With the party leader temporarily out of the picture, the majority of maximalists rejected the fusion pact, and remained immobilized in positions that Serrati had occupied from 1919 to 1922.

The struggle within the PSI came to a head at yet another special congress in April 1923. The issues were starkly posed: the International agreed to discuss minor points, but it held firm to the substance of the accord, which included expulsion of Nenni and Vella, the complete absorption of the PSI into the PCI, and acceptance of communist discipline and organization. Nenni and Vella, now in charge of the PSI, insisted on a simple alliance of the two parties with double membership in the Third International. In August 1923 the maximalist majority expelled the pro-fusionist Third International faction, headed by Serrati, Francesco Buffoni, Fabrizio Maffi, and Enzio Riboldi, from the PSI. With this gesture, the era of party splits that began at Livorno finally closed.

BORDIGA'S FALL

By mid-1923 the Comintern was increasingly unhappy with Bordiga. Tasca, who headed a rightist faction within the PCI, was much closer to the position of the International on the issue of a united front with the socialists. At the July meeting of the Executive Committee of the International, Bordiga was finally removed as secretary of the party, but he was replaced by the unworkable hybrid leadership of Palmiro Togliatti and Angelo Tasca. Togliatti, previously in the shadow of Bordiga and Gramsci, began as a brilliant student at the University of Turin. He came to the socialist movement later than Tasca, Terracini, or Gramsci, and in 1914 he almost ruined his career by opting for a Mussolinian stance on the issue of intervention. After the war, Togliatti gravitated to the PSI's far left, and from 1921 to 1923 he backed Bordiga in his intransigence within the PCI and the International. When it became clear in mid-1923 that the International would turn control of the party over to Tasca, Togliatti reluctantly shifted to a more flexible position.

Tasca's entry into the leadership of the PCI did not improve relations with the PSI, which deteriorated after the failure of the fusion project. The International now wanted a united front as a prelude to renewed negotiations for fusion. The possibility of new elections in early 1924 became a measure for how far the PCI had drifted from Bordiga's intransigence.

THE ELECTIONS OF 1924

The Fascist government called elections for the spring of 1924 in order to consolidate its majority in parliament. The Acerbo electoral law gave two-thirds of the seats in parliament to the list with a mere plurality of the votes. This reform, which grossly favored the fascists, was passed by a majority of liberals, fascists, and right-wing Catholics. Faced with this discriminatory electoral law, the left parties had to decide whether to boycott the elections or, if they decided to participate, whether to form an electoral alliance. After fruitless discussions in January and February 1924, it became clear that neither the PSU nor the PCI could reach an understanding and that the PSI would side with neither. In the end, the left went into the elections divided. The communists in alliance with the pro-Third International Socialists did poorly, winning only nineteen seats. Even more embarrassing for the new leadership of the PCI, Bordiga's followers fared better, and Togliatti and Tasca were beaten. Of the major figures, only Gramsci was elected. The PSU emerged with the largest number of votes and with twenty-four deputies; the PSI followed with twenty-two seats.

THE CONTINUING LEADERSHIP CRISIS IN THE PCI

Throughout 1924 and 1925 three factions continued to co-exist within the PCI: Bordiga's left wing; the so-called center, led by Gramsci and Togliatti; and the right wing of Tasca. But the triumph of the center group had been artificially imposed by the Comintern. Bordiga still held the loyalty of the party militants, and his prestige represented a threat to the party leadership. The rightist faction posed a quite different problem. Tasca questioned the entire political logic of the split that took place at Livorno and the choice of tactics thereafter. As an alternative, he proposed a larger and more open Communist party.

These divisions were apparent at the Como party conference of May 1924. The left won a large majority for its intransigent theses. With union support, the right finished second, while the official leadership continued to enjoy little support. That such divisions could not last had been apparent to Gramsci for some time. He understood that Bordiga had led the party into a direct confrontation with the International, and that the new leadership could not afford a similar mistake.

The decisions taken at the Fifth Congress of the International in July 1924 went a long way toward resolving the crisis within the PCI. As a result, Bordiga and his followers were totally excluded from the party leadership, and Gramsci took direct control of the secretariat. At the same time, the International Communist movement moved leftward and away from united-front strategies. While Bordiga and his followers continued to be a problem in Milan, Naples, and a few other centers, the leadership used all the disciplinary weapons at its disposal to eliminate these pockets of resistance and gain full control over the apparatus. The Congress of the International also mandated the integration of the profusion socialists (Serrati's group) into the PCI. This move effectively ended the period when fusion between the PSI and PCI was a real possibility. From this point until the Unity of Action pact in 1934, relations between the PCI and PSI were marked by varying degrees of hostility.

THE LEFT AND THE MATTEOTTI CRISIS

The murder of Giacomo Matteotti, the secretary of the PSU, by the fascists on June 10, 1924 led to a series of events that would plunge Italy into a dictatorship. Until Matteotti's death the government had operated within formal limits of legality. Although the elections of April were marked by extreme violence against the opposition, antifascists did manage to win about one-third of the seats in the new parliament. Within the Fascist party there was a debate between those who merely wanted conservative strong government and those who called for a single-party dictatorship. Mussolini himself acted ambiguously. After the elections he once again made overtures to the leadership of the CGL for a place in his government.

Matteotti, who was an implacable foe of any compromise with the fascists, made a sharply critical speech in parliament on May 30 that cited documented cases of electoral fraud and political corruption. Visibly angered, Mussolini, who muttered to his associates that they should take care of Matteotti, set off the series of events that ended in the murder of the socialist leader.

As word spread of Matteotti's disappearance, the opposition deputies called for the resignation of the government. To reinforce their protest they withdrew from parliament until the king removed Mussolini from office. This maneuver, referred to as the Aventine Secession, was led by liberal democrats like Giovanni Amendola who hoped that the monarch would act to restore constitutional government. Mussolini successfully countered their strategy by including a number of pro-monarchical conservatives in his government as a guarantee to the king, the Church, and the army.

The three left parties reacted very differently to the crisis. Initially, when it seemed that the government would topple, the communists broke with past policy and joined the other opposition parties on the condition that the Aventine would take direct action in the form of a general strike to bring down the government. The PCI lacked sufficient support within the unions to call such a strike by itself, and the Aventine opposition refused to move beyond the strict limits of legality in its attempt to remove Mussolini. In July the communists withdrew from the Aventine and returned to the Chamber of Deputies in order to carry out their protest more effectively. They were unable, however, to persuade the other parties to accept direct action or to mount an effective challenge to Mussolini on their own.

The PSU, as might be expected, leapt at the opportunity to forge a broad democratic front, but it gained little from the Aventine experience. The PSU had been crippled by the loss of the dynamic Matteotti and by disputes over policy between the union leaders and those who wanted to close the gap between the PSU and PSI. With the expulsion of the pro-Third International group from the PSI and the end of negotiations with Moscow, the way was theoretically open to reverse the results of the Congress of Rome of October 1922. Closer relations between the PSI and PSU seemed even more likely when Pietro Nenni led the socialists into the Aventine bloc. Nenni's belief that the restoration of democracy had to take precedence over all other objectives created an area of agreement between some maximalists and the reformists.

To its growing discomfort, the PSI soon found itself entrapped in a no-win commitment to the legalistic tactics of the Aventine bourgeois opposition. Nenni was attacked by the PCI, which sought to undermine the credibility of the PSI among the workers, and by the more rigid maximalists within his own party. Eventually, the policy of cooperation with the bourgeoisie became intolerable for a party that had been committed since 1912 to the principle of remaining outside all interclass alliances.

Pietro Nenni had staked his leadership on the success of the Aventine opposition, but the PSI drew little benefit from the alliance with middle-class antifascism. It was not a propitious moment for reformist tactics in any country. In 1924 the Labour-led MacDonald government collapsed in England, and the Cartel des Gauches alliance of radicals and socialists in France won the 1924 elections but broke down soon after. The inability of middle-class and socialist parties to work together was a persistent problem in the interwar period, but Italy, which never had a strong middle-class democratic tradition, provided less fertile ground than elsewhere. The PSI's rejection of bourgeois reformism in 1919 and 1920, when the middle class was badly shaken, constituted a missed opportunity; Nenni's acceptance of the Aventine alliance on terms dictated solely by the liberal parties symbolized only the weakness and isolation of the PSI. His strongest argument was that there was no practical alternative to participation, but this failed to convince the majority of his party. In September 1925 the directorate of the PSI voted to withdraw. Unable to reverse the decision, Nenni resigned as party leader and as editor of *Avanti!*.

Unlike Antonio Gramsci or Palmiro Togliatti, who worked on both a theoretical and practical level, Nenni responded primarily to tactical situations. He was now convinced that the PSI had to be reshaped on a less dogmatic basis. With this in mind, he joined Carlo Rosselli (1899–1937), another rebellious spirit of the socialist movement, to publish

Quarto stato. Rosselli, a student of the radical historian, Gaetano Salvemini, and later founder of the Giustizia e Libertà antifascist movement, wanted to blend socialism and bourgeois radicalism to forge a
new democratic mass party in Italy. Both Nenni and Rosselli sought to
escape from the prefabricated solutions that dominated maximalist
thinking for a decade. Although the ultimate aim was still socialism, the
PSI could no longer conceive of the struggle against fascism exclusively
in terms of a socialist program; nor could it afford a narrow alliance
with the PCI when the immediate objectives of the worker movement
coincided with those of all democrats. Thus, the old division between
reformists and maximalists was losing relevance, while the practical and
ideological split between socialists and communists became more pronounced.

Both Rosselli and Nenni demanded that the entire socialist tradition
be rethought in light of the political and ideological failures of the PSI
in 1919. Rosselli even questioned the turn-of-the-century victories that
the PSI had been unable to transform into permanent structural reforms. In short, the PSI had never made the psychological transition
from being a sect to becoming a national party. However, the common
point of renewal for both the reformist and maximalist traditions had
to be a struggle for a new democracy. In this struggle the PSI had to
be willing to shoulder its share of governmental responsibility. *Quarto
stato* set forth a modern political agenda based on a new awareness of
the nature of fascism, a new approach to postfascist institutions, and a
renewed effort for socialist unity.

In 1925 the PSI was far from accepting any such agenda. When Nenni's opponents succeeded in ousting him from the editorship of *Avanti!*,
they simply returned to the ineffectual policies of the past. It was a
fitting end to the long period of maximalist control of the PSI that, at
the moment of its suppression in November 1926, the party had little
more than 15,000 members and was already psychologically the second
party of the Italian left. When the maximalists took control of the PSI
at the congress of Reggio Emilia in 1912, they had no real alternative
to the reformist program. Their party administration amounted to little
more than a constant veto over any positive initiative. The result was
paralysis. Maximalism, unlike either communism or reformism, lacked
intellectual content. It remained a state of mind, a visceral rejection of
bourgeois society, and a rebellion against the centralized and disciplined
PCI. Maximalism might have reflected the attitudes of a large stratum
of Italian workers and peasants, but it was never a viable political option.
Its best argument came to be the lack of interest in true reform on the
part of the bourgeoisie, but maximalist intransigence was in large part
responsible for the failure of a democratic alternative in late 1918 and
in 1919. Serrati and Lazzari, however sincerely dedicated to the interests
of the working class, led the party down a blind alley. They followed

rather than led the masses by consistently underestimating the possibilities of reform and the dangers of fascism. The revolution was proclaimed, never achieved; lessons were administered, never learned; defeat was the more tragic and bitter because it need not have been so.

THE CREATION OF THE FASCIST DICTATORSHIP

On January 3, 1925 Mussolini, by now assured of the support of Church, industry, and army, challenged the opposition to unseat him. The government followed with a crackdown on the opposition press. The screw was tightened by gradual degrees until November 1925, when Tito Zaniboni, a member of the PSU, attempted to assassinate Mussolini. Zaniboni's arrest served as a pretext for the outlawing of the Unitary Socialist Party. Laws were also passed that abolished parliamentary government—making the prime minister responsible only to the king, and ending elected local government.

The dissolution of the PSU caught the party in a difficult moment. Differences between the political and syndical wings of the PSU had widened. The reformist leadership of the CGL moved ever closer to an apolitical strategy and expulsion of the communists from the labor organization. Turati and Treves were wedded to an Aventine opposition which had already been beaten. The dissolution of the party offered a chance for a new beginning. Many of the key leaders—Oddino Morgari, G.E. Modigliani (1872–1947), and Pallante Rugginenti (1892–1938)— were already in exile and would be joined by Turati and Treves. The reformists regrouped in Paris as the Socialist Party of Italian Workers (Partito Socialista dei Lavoratori Italiani—PSLI) in November 1926, which received almost immediate recognition from the Socialist International and from the French SFIO. When the CGL was suppressed also in November, Bruno Buozzi (1881–1944), a militant antifascist and long-time head of the FIOM, reconstituted the labor confederation in exile.

In a sense, the gap between the PSLI and the PSI had been reduced by defeat. Both parties now called for the restoration of parliamentary democracy as a precondition for future political action. Moreover, the reformists envisaged the restructuring of democracy in far more radical terms than a simple return to the old liberal constitution. Differences still remained between reformists and maximalists concerning the ultimate value to be placed on bourgeois democracy and over the pace of change. But, for the immediate future, the choice between democracy and socialism could be avoided, and a younger generation of reformists, like Giuseppe Saragat and Pallante Rugginenti, could set their sights on the reunification of the socialist movement.

The way to socialist reunification was not entirely smooth. The difficulties in applying any reformist program had also increased. Turati and Treves knew that the battle against fascism would be long. They believed that the proletariat alone could not carry on the struggle, but allies in the middle class were not easily found. The bourgeois and Catholic parties did not reorganize in exile. To compensate, the reformists looked to the United States, England, and France for help in the battle against Mussolini's dictatorship, but, until the mid-1930s, little interest could be stirred in the Italian antifascist cause in the western democracies. A whole sector of the socialist movement adopted a long-term strategy in the struggle against fascism that, however realistic, only encouraged the latent passivity within both reformism and maximalism.

GRAMSCI'S LEGACY TO THE PCI

In 1925 Gramsci acted decisively to destroy the remaining centers of Bordiga's influence in the PCI. The opposition faction, created by Bordiga, Bruno Fortichiari, and Luigi Repossi was dissolved, its leaders suspended, and several federations revamped. The onset of the fascist dictatorship, which brought an end to any normal political activity, accelerated this process by strengthening the party bureaucracy and lessening the influence of ordinary militants. Bordiga now found that the concept of an elite party worked against him.

The PCI also moved decisively to organize its underground resistance to fascism. This transformation was connected to the process of bolshevization, which meant restructuring the party on the basis of factory and geographical cells. Until this reorganization, the PCI had much the same territorial apparatus as did the PSI. Hereafter the Communist party would begin to differ significantly from the socialists on both the ideological and organizational levels. Within the labor movement in industrial centers like Turin and Milan, these cells became the only viable form of resistance and allowed the PCI to replace the PSI and PSU among politically conscious workers. However, the numbers involved were pitifully small—in the low thousands nationally, and only 600 in former revolutionary centers like Turin.

During these waning years of constitutional rule in Italy, the Communist party led the way in a more sophisticated analysis of fascism. Gramsci, Togliatti, and Tasca stood at the forefront of the effort to reshape communist understanding that the fascist regime was not simply another form of agrarian reaction, but rather a mass movement made up of many diverse groups. The communists tied fascism both to Italian capitalism's backwardness and to the transition to more modern forms of development that allowed for the mobilization of a large lower middle-class constituency against the workers.

The PCI was much less understanding of the role of social democracy. Only in January 1926 under Gramsci's prodding did the PCI's Congress in Lyons acknowledge that the battle against fascism would be long and difficult. It would probably have to be a two-stage process with a transition period between the fall of fascism and the victory of socialism. Although such a doctrinal advance allowed for the PCI to consider alliances with socialists or bourgeois democrats, there was little attempt to make such a shift until the united and popular front era of the mid-1930s.

The program drafted at the congress of Lyons was Antonio Gramsci's last contribution as a party leader. From February to November he led the PCI's parliamentary delegation in the face of increasing menaces from the fascist regime. Finally, in November when the opposition was outlawed, Gramsci was arrested and stripped of his parliamentary immunity. Togliatti, who had been sent in February as the representative of the PCI to the Comintern, moved into the leadership position.

Gramsci's legacy to the PCI and to the Italian left was enormously important, and came during the long years of his imprisonment. He offered independent and creative positions on important issues such as the importance of religion and the connections between political and cultural hegemony. Gramsci understood that if the working class were to seize power, it would have to triumph both in the political and in the cultural sphere by making itself the heir to the national tradition. He also realized that the struggle against fascism could only be won by creating the basis for a new state in an alliance with the peasantry and the lower middle class.

In a less positive way, Gramsci introduced some unhealthy practices into the life of the PCI. His leadership had been arbitrarily imposed upon a party that spiritually still belonged to Bordiga. Gramsci did not hestitate to use disciplinary weapons to break the potential opposition. However, he never carried these measures to the point of expulsion, or to the elimination of debate within the party.

Gramsci, who had been the representative of the PCI to the Comintern from 1922 to 1924, understood better than any other leader the need to harmonize the PCI's position with that of the International; but he also had the intellectual courage to criticize the tactics used against Trotsky within the Russian party and in the International. Togliatti also learned the importance of Soviet support. Both he and Gramsci were acutely aware that the survival of the leadership group depended on its internal unity and on its ability to shape policies so that they did not conflict with those of the Comintern. It fell to Togliatti to apply these lessons, for better or worse, during the most difficult days of Stalinism. But the long-term strength of the PCI was due in large part to the continuity of its leadership, which persisted despite purges and expulsions after 1928.

The end of its legal existence in 1926 closed an era in the history of the PCI. Under the leadership of Bordiga and the "center," the party was little more than a sect. Its doctrinal rigidity and revolutionary psychology were a holdover from maximalism; but communists showed a new and original determination to organize and act against fascism at whatever personal cost. They bore the brunt of police repression, and forged the most durable illegal apparatus. By 1926, with the elimination of all other competitors, the communists were poised to supplant all other parties on the Italian left. That they succeeded in doing so was a major development during the long years of exile and dictatorship.

CHAPTER 5

The Years of Exile, 1926–1943

THE REORGANIZATION OF THE SOCIALIST MOVEMENT

The period of forced emigration for Italian socialism can be divided into three periods. During the first, from 1926 to 1934, reunification provided the primary focus in the socialist camp. Both reformists and maximalists acted within the framework of the Antifascist Concentration, a democratic, interclass alliance of the PSLI, the PSI, republicans, the exiled CGL, and the Italian League for the Rights of Man (LIDU, which was formed in 1927). Only the PCI remained outside this bloc. The question of unity of action with the communists dominated the second period, which lasted from 1934 to 1939. During the final period—from the outbreak of the war in 1939 to the fall of Mussolini—the socialists turned their attention to the armed resistance to fascism. Through the entire exile experience, the socialists struggled vainly to redefine their ideology and modernize their movement. Central to this process was a definition of goals and methods that could be shared by all socialists. The failure to do this before 1926 had led to the formation of three different parties: maximalist, reformist, and communist. Each took a different position on the value of liberal democracy and on the future socialist society. The victory of fascism seemed to render many of these earlier divisions meaningless, and offered an opportunity to reformulate many of the policies that caused problems in the past.

After 1926 there was a new consensus over some of the issues that had separated reformists and maximalists. All socialists realized that lack of unity and doctrinal rigidity had contributed to their defeat. The starting point for reunification was a compromise on the question of democracy. Pietro Nenni now accepted the need for a restoration of bourgeois democratic liberties, while reformists agreed that democracy was a beginning, rather than an end in itself. Both rejected any return to the old prefascist liberal state.

Reconciliation was an ongoing process which took place within the framework of the Antifascist Concentration. The Concentration brought together the various parties and associations, hostile to the fascist regime, on a minimum program of democratic restoration. The decision to join the Concentration was an important step for the PSI, which had been reestablished in Paris in December 1926. Officially the new leadership in exile received its mandate from the now dissolved Italian maximalist directorate which had rejected Nenni's tactic of cooperation with the Aventine. Thus, the party position was somewhat ambiguous. Nenni, its dominant figure, was neither secretary nor editor of the *Avanti!*, but he was secretary general of the Concentration. The PSI still continued its international membership in the Bureau of Revolutionary Socialist Parties, which it had joined in 1925. By contrast, the PSLI belonged to the larger Socialist International which had been formed at Hamburg in 1923 and included the major British, French and German Socialist parties.

The intransigent wing of the PSI found its leader in Angelica Balabanoff, a Russian exile and one of the leaders of the maximalist faction that seized control of the PSI in 1912. Balabanoff returned to Russia after the revolution, but gradually became disillusioned with the bureaucratic authoritarianism of the bolsheviks. In true maximalist style she rejoined the defeated party in exile and became the embodiment of the tradition that led socialism to defeat from 1919 to 1922. She now insisted that the immediate aim of the PSI should be the creation of a socialist republic in Italy. This policy stood in obvious contradiction with the decision to join the Antifascist Concentration, and with the most recent positions of Pietro Nenni. Balabanoff could offer no alternative to membership in the Concentration short of total isolation. Instead, she and her allies in the PSI sought only to limit the damage of contamination with the reformists by a firm adherence to principle. But the orthodox maximalists were no closer to the communists than they were to the reformists.

In the PSLI, reunification with the PSI found broad support. The great names of Italian socialism, Filippo Turati and Claudio Treves, favored it, as did young leaders like Giuseppe Saragat (1898–1988). On one issue, however, the PSLI was firm: The maximalists had to choose definitively between the Socialist and Communist Internationals. No third way was possible. A reunified PSI had to belong to the Socialist International.

After an inconclusive congress in 1928, the PSI met in Grenoble in March 1930. The majority followed Nenni in accepting unity, while a minority, led by Balabanoff, broke off to form the small Maximalist Socialist party. Since the PSLI had already declared for unity at its congress in December 1929, the way was open for the reunification congress of July 1930 which created a single Socialist party for the first time since October 1922. The unification charter, presented by Treves and Nenni, represented a compromise between the two socialist traditions. It reaffirmed the marxist character of the PSI, and emphasized the validity of the class struggle and the long range goal of a socialist society. At the same time, the charter stressed the PSI's short term commitment to democracy and the understanding that reunification was based on an agenda that called for the restoration of democratic liberties during the transition from the fascist regime to the socialist revolution. Lack of political options for the new party facilitated agreement between reformists and maximalists. There was no question of an immediate alliance with bourgeois democratic parties because none existed in exile. The nature of the postfascist regime and the alliances necessary to achieve it could safely be put off for future debate. Moreover, the PSI did not face the renewed overtures for cooperation from the communist camp. The PCI viewed the move to the right by the maximalists as confirmation of the bourgeois nature of social democracy. The possibility of collaboration with the socialists was still phrased in terms that meant surrender to the demands of the Third International. Thus, with options blocked on both the right and left, reunification moved ahead. It enjoyed enormous popularity among socialist militants and membership doubled within a year. But the very ease by which reconciliation took place made it precarious. It remained to be seen if unity would survive more difficult tests.

THE PROCESS OF STALINIZATION
IN THE PCI

The PCI's transition from legality to life in exile was eased by the existence of a clandestine apparatus and by the support of the Third International; yet it was marred by the arrest of several major leaders, including Gramsci and Terracini, who were seized by the police in November 1926. Most of the others—Ruggiero Grieco, Angelo Tasca, Luigi Longo, Pietro Tresso, and Alfonso Leonetti—eventually found their way to Paris where Togliatti had established an exile center.

The communists had long believed that the struggle against fascism could only be waged by a combination of legal and illegal means. Therefore, unlike any other exile movement, the PCI was determined to maintain an active presence within Italy. The cost of this decision was incredibly high. Organizers sent into the country lasted about a month. The fascist police rounded up each underground network. The communists provided the regime with its most spectacular show trials, the most notable of which was the proceeding involving Gramsci, Terracini, and Mauro Scoccimarro in June 1928.

The Third International encouraged active resistance by providing direct aid to the PCI and indirect assistance for the families of leading party members through the "Red Help" organization. But this dependence on the International had its drawbacks. The communists in exile were almost completely cut off from other groups. The cost of expulsion from the party was extremely high and became an extra incentive to conform. Expulsion meant an immediate search for legal status, work papers, and moral and political support in the country of exile. After 1928 Stalin's domination of the International made these disadvantages more apparent.

From 1926 to 1928 the PCI tried to strike a balance between its former intransigence and the new policies outlined in 1926 by Gramsci. Within the exiled party Angelo Tasca became the leading exponent of a more flexible and open attitude. Internal debates revolved around the possibility of revolution in Europe and the seeming stabilization within the capitalist system. The victory of conservative forces throughout Europe after 1923 led to considerable soul searching within the Comintern and in the Soviet leadership. Nikolai Bukharin, who, along with Stalin, emerged as the most important figure in the post-Lenin leadership, theorized that the immediate revolutionary period had given way to a different stage in the development of monopoly capitalism. In this period, the state played a greater role in the stabilization of the system. New instruments of planning, and an increased role for the state as guarantor of the private sector, temporarily reinforced state capitalism and delayed the revolutionary crisis that was ready to engulf Europe after the war. In the PCI Tasca began to blend Bukharin's ideas with those parts of the Lyons Theses that allowed for a transition between the fall of fascism and the installation of a socialist state. The result was a new gradualism, which implied the need for allies in political battles during the antifascist struggle and until the onset of the anticapitalist revolution. Tasca's positions left open the possibility of a united front alliance with the PSI, but he could never convince the other leaders to go that far.

In fact, Tasca's moderation produced a counter movement within the PCI from a group of younger militants led by Luigi Longo (1900–1980) and Pietro Secchia (1903–1973). The party's left wing rejected any possibility of even a temporary stablization within capitalism, especially in Italy. Longo and Secchia argued that the country was in an immediate prerevolutionary stage that could be accelerated by pressure from below. They called for renewed aggressive action inside Italy to provoke the latent crisis.

In January 1928, at a party conference in Basle called to resolve the differing positions, Togliatti and Grieco seemed to side with Tasca against the left. The PCI reaffirmed the shift toward moderation at the sixth congress of the International in July 1928, when Tasca became the permanent representative of the party to the Comintern Executive Commission. But, almost immediately after the conclusion of the congress, it became apparent that Bukharin had lost the battle for control of Soviet policy to his former ally, Stalin, who differed sharply with Bukharin over the pace of industrialization and the balance between industry and agriculture. Stalin also held that world capitalism was much closer to a revolutionary breakdown. He argued that Communist parties everywhere had to organize for total war against all counterrevolutionary forces, including the social democrats.

As his battle with Bukharin drew to a conclusion, Stalin sought to impose his views on the various European parties in the Comintern. Inevitably, Tasca, the leading Bukharinist in the PCI, clashed repeatedly with Stalin until his recall to Paris in January 1929. Tasca's conflict with Stalin placed Togliatti, who shared the leadership with Tasca for over two years, in a delicate position. Unless he distanced himself from Tasca or forced the latter to recant, he too could fall victim to Stalin's wrath, and Longo and Secchia would assume control of the party.

In early 1929 Togliatti abruptly joined Longo and Secchia in arguing for an immediate transition to socialism. He also embraced Stalin's ideas on the equivalence of fascism to social democracy (social fascism), which made any consideration of alliances with the socialists impossible. The new policies resulted in a burst of activity inside Italy. Longo, who was put in charge of the internal apparatus, acted as though revolution was immediate. Old militants, like Camilla Ravera (1894–), Pietro Secchia, and Battista Santhià, were thrown into the battle only to be arrested shortly after they arrived in Italy. These almost suicidal attempts to establish a presence in Italy led to protests against the new policies by Alfonso Leonetti (1895–1984), an old friend and collaborator of Gramsci, by Paolo Ravazzoli (1894–1940), a key labor organizer, and by Pietro Tresso (1893–1943), who was close to Trotskyist positions. Leonetti, Tresso, and Ravazzoli, known as "the three", were soon joined by Secondino Tranquilli (Ignazio Silone, 1900–1982), who was one of the intellectual leaders of the PCI and a special favorite of Palmiro Togliatti. From prison, both Umberto Terracini and Antonio Gramsci also expressed serious reservations about the new course.

Togliatti was determined to save himself and incidentally, whatever remained of the old leadership nucleus, even if it meant acceptance of Stalinist methods, which would have been inconceivable in Gramsci's day. At the meeting of the Plenum of the Comintern in the summer of 1929, he publicly disavowed Tasca, who was expelled from the PCI. In June 1930 the "three" fell victim to the process of Stalinization and the series of major purges closed with Silone's expulsion in 1931. Gramsci's imprisonment probably saved him from a similar fate. Togliatti now abjectly accepted the crudest views of the crisis of capitalism. Bukharin's sophisticated ideas about organized state capitalism and planning were rejected out of hand. The identification of socialism with fascism cast the real differences between socialism and communism in grotesquely polemical terms. Worst of all, the party accepted the dogma that the current line of the party was automatically correct. Practice up to 1929 had been to allow a principled opponent, like Bordiga or Tasca, to remain within the party to preserve the potential for an alternative policy. This had allowed for the survival of most of the original founders of the PCI. Now the group was disbanded: Bordiga, Tasca, Leonetti, Ravazzoli, Silone expelled; Gramsci and Terracini in jail; Togliatti alone at the head of the party with the support of a new generation: Longo, Secchia, Giuseppe Dozza (1901–1974), Giuseppe Di Vittorio (1899–1957), Emilio Sereni (1907–1977), and Giorgio Amendola (1907–1980).

THE REUNIFIED PSI AND THE PROBLEM OF POLITICAL ALLIANCES

The death of socialism's two elder statesmen, Turati and Treves in 1932 and 1933, left Pietro Nenni as the dominant figure within the movement. The leadership of the reunited party was a hybrid of reformists and maximalists: Modgiliani, Saragat, Rugginenti from the PSLI; Nenni, Ugo Coccia, and Franco Clerici from the PSI. Nenni resumed his old post as editor of the *Nuovo Avanti!* with Rugginenti as his deputy.

The greatest problem for the PSI was to justify its continued existence to a younger generation of Italians. The party was blamed for leading the working class to defeat at the hands of the fascists. Its policies had been incoherent and its political tactics miserable. The legacy of the PSI in 1930 seemed to be only a series of lacerating ideological battles and bitter divisions. Reunification offered a chance to set all this aside. As the PSI sought to define its role, new issues emerged. The first concerned the party's status within the Antifascist Concentration. The Concentration was a fragile arrangement serving mainly as a bridge between the two Socialist parties.

The appearance of a new political movement clouded the future. After a daring escape from fascist imprisonment, Carlo Rosselli, Nenni's old ally on *Quarto stato*, reemerged in Paris in 1929 ready and eager to resume the battle against the regime. However, Nenni and Rosselli had taken quite different routes after their collaboration in 1925 and 1926. Nenni's interest had always been in the PSI, which he tried to renew from within. Rosselli had never been closely associated with the PSI and was more influenced by Gaetano Salvemini, another famous socialist dissident. Like Salvemini, Rosselli was drawn to socialism by its potential to renovate Italian society, but he was not a marxist. Rosselli believed that a new socialist movement would have to bridge the gap between the democratic and marxist traditions and could not afford to ossify politically or ideologically. Political clarification came from action. The socialists had to compete with the communists in a commitment to resistance inside Italy or they could never regain legitimacy.

In 1929 Rosselli, who was independently wealthy, formed a new political movement, Giustizia e Libertà (GL), that brought together radical democrats and socialists who could not accept the existing political options. However, GL initially defined itself as a broadly based movement of militants, fighting antifascism, consciously outside of the old political structures. To accentuate its innovative character, GL opened its doors to members from other political formations. Rosselli also tried to transform the Concentration into a kind of centralized superparty directed to waging a struggle within Italy. When the other parties rejected such activism, he kept GL out of the Concentration until a compromise was reached in 1931 that allowed GL to represent the Concentration for the struggle within Italy.

From the beginning Nenni sensed that GL was a serious rival. These suspicions were intensified in 1932 when Rosselli published an ideological charter that called for worker control of industry and the redistribution of land in favor of the peasants. Moreover, GL's commitment to activism seemed to undermine the moral position of the PSI and made many socialists uncomfortable knowing that their movement was not present in the internal struggle against fascism. All of these disputes came to a head in April 1934 when Nenni and Rosselli clashed over the latter's renewed effort to turn the Concentration into a superparty. The PSI withdrew from the Concentration, which promptly dissolved. The break with the Concentration, following soon after the deaths of Turati and Treves, cut the PSI from its reformist moorings. The party, once more without firm alliances, was now led by Nenni who was temperamentally disposed to a more militantly socialist course. The moment and the man converged in 1934 to push socialism in a new direction.

UNITY OF ACTION

From 1930 to 1934 the PCI, jointly directed by Togliatti and Longo, adhered fully to the Comintern position on social fascism. Longo gambled that the PCI's campaign in Italy would be a success, but by 1932 it was clear that this was a costly failure for which he paid by losing his leadership. Still, the activism probably made sense in the long term. Only by overestimating the potential for success could the Communist party have mustered the will to make the sacrifices necessary to keep sending underground labor organizers into the battle against fascism within Italy.

Togliatti survived Longo's failures, as he had the earlier Tasca crisis. In the process, he seemed to deepen his own analysis of fascism, which remained carefully hidden under the veil of Stalinist orthodoxy. In his *Lectures on Fascism*, written in Moscow around 1934, Togliatti grasped more clearly the techniques of rule, such as the leisure time and welfare organizations, which a mass-based authoritarian regime used to maintain consensus. Togliatti never completely abandoned the idea of a transition period between the fall of fascism and the triumph of the revolution or the need for tactical alliances with other political groupings. He had greater opportunities to apply these Gramscian ideas after 1934 when the theory of social fascism was abandoned by the Comintern. That year Togliatti departed for Moscow to become second in command in the Comintern hierarchy. Thus, from 1934 to 1939 he stood somewhat aloof from the day to day problems of the PCI. His decision to take a position in the Comintern was a change of heart from 1928 when he turned down a position in the Western European Bureau. By 1934 Togliatti wanted a larger stage than the PCI provided, and he understood the opportunities that were available through the change to united-front policies by the International.

After Togliatti's reassignment, the PCI was directed by Grieco, Dozza, Di Vittorio, and Longo, with the mixed results that collective leadership often gives. The new leadership had some difficulty applying the united- and popular-front policies. Nevertheless the shift in position by the PCI, coupled with the emergence of Nenni as the dominant personality in the PSI, opened the way for a new relationship between the two proletarian parties.

Extraordinarily complex problems faced the left in the mid-1930s. In no country had the proletarian-based parties achieved a majority. To gain power, the Socialist parties of England, Germany, and France had to make alliances with bourgeois Democratic parties whose lower middle-class constituencies saw little attraction in the typical socialist economic program. In fact, the fascists were winning the battle for the lower middle class as the political balance shifted to the right.

The challenge of winning over the key lower middle-class and peasant voter could be met by either a "national" or an "international" strategy. The national strategy, as outlined by the Belgian Henri De Man, or the French Neosocialist, Marcel Déat, demanded that the Socialist parties alter their rigid marxist orthodoxy in several important ways to attract middle-class support. State planning would be cast in the framework of a mixed economy, as would be the case with remedies for the depression. At the heart of the national strategy was the problem of political power. The neosocialists or neorevisionists argued that there was a race for power between the socialists and fascists that could be won by the left only by taking up some of the enemy's program. These theories found support among socialists who wanted practical solutions to the depression crisis; they believed the old debates over revolution and reformism were irrelevant.

Working against the national strategy was the middle class, who refused to accept any significant reform program. The record was as gloomy as could be: the failure of Mac Donald's Labour government between 1929 and 1931; the inherent instability of cabinets formed by the French Radical party and the SFIO from 1924 to 1926 and again from 1932 to 1934; the ouster of the German Socialist party from the government in 1930; and the inability of the Belgian Workers party to impose De Man's project on its coalition partners from 1935 to 1938.

The international strategy, as outlined by socialists from Nenni to Trotsky, was just as problematical. Power-sharing and relations with the lower middle class were, again, central. The major difference from the national strategy was the internationalists' belief that the proletariat, armed with an aggressively socialist program, could carry with it the bulk of the lower middle class, which had been directly harmed by the depression. Essential to success was the reestablishment of unity between the socialists and communists and an end to the isolation of the Soviet Union.

Adherents to both strategies agreed that immediate revolution was not possible; that a transition period between the defeat of fascism and the triumph of socialism was inevitable; and that interclass cooperation on some basis was necessary. But the national strategy was oriented toward short-term economic and political solutions that avoided a radical break with capitalism. The internationalists leaned toward a long-term perspective and were more confrontational in their economic and social policies.

The Communist parties were much more unified and opportunistic in their approach to the problem of political alliances. Almost overnight, they moved from extreme hostility towards the Socialist and bourgeois parties to a call for alliance. This put them at odds with the socialist adherents of the international strategy, and closer to the neorevisionists in the socialist movement who were, on most other issues, natural opponents of the communists.

The decision by the Communist parties to call for a united front with the Socialists came unexpectedly in the spring of 1934. The Third International abandoned social fascism under the impact of the terrible fate suffered by the German Communist party at the hands of Hitler. Then there were further shocks caused by the rightist antiparliamentary riots in Paris, and the rapid repression of the Austrian Socialist party, both of which took place in February 1934. The French Communist party reached an accord for unity of action with the SFIO in July 1934. Just before leaving for Moscow, Togliatti proposed a similar pact to the PSI and an accord was signed in mid-August. This Unity of Action pact was not a close alliance; rather, it was an agreement to consult and cooperate between the leadership of both parties. It marked a major change of position by the communists who had always avoided dealing with socialist leaders under any circumstance. The pact, signed in 1934, renewed in 1937, suspended between 1939 and 1942, and renewed thereafter, would be, as we shall see below, the cornerstone of socialist policy from 1934 to 1956.

THE IMPACT OF UNITY OF ACTION
ON THE PSI

Unity of action had a profound impact on the PSI, more so than on the Communist party, which viewed the pact not just as an alliance against fascism but also as another way to undermine the Socialist party and lead the proletariat to a correct revolutionary position. The most immediate consequence was to redirect the PSI back toward the left, and reopen the debilitating internal debate over alliances and tactics. This discussion was further complicated by the question of support for the USSR, which was an essential part of the pact but which raised the parallel issue of potential military support in a strongly pacifist movement. The Stalinist purges after 1934 revived the issue of the essential distinction between socialism and communism.

The majority, led by Nenni, made the alliance with the communists central to socialist politics. Nenni did not believe that conditions existed among Italian exiles for an alternative alliance. While he accepted the idea of a democratic phase and the need for alliances with the peasantry and the lower middle class on a transitional program between the fall of fascism and the onset of socialism, he really did not believe that Italian capitalism could survive the collapse of the Fascist regime. His revolutionary vision remained Jacobin, a kind of democratic seizure of the state which would then be used to carry out the revolution. But Nenni did not dwell on future projects. His commitment was to immediate action based on an unrelenting antifascism. The most direct way to fight fascism was on the international level where it seemed most vulnerable. Quite simply, the Soviet Union and the Communist parties were indispensible partners in any international antifascist front.

The minority in the PSI, led by the ex-communist Aneglo Tasca, G.E. Modigliani, and Giuseppe Faravelli (1896–1974), could offer no immediate alternative policies. The opposition to Nenni united in its belief that unity of action worked exclusively to the benefit of the PCI, by sapping the independent initiative of the Socialist party. Apart from an increasing anticommunism, the minority had little in common. Modigliani was a traditional pacifist and reformist, who had participated in the antiwar Zimmerwald conference in 1915. He now feared that support for the USSR would involve Italian workers in another war in the interests of the Soviet national state. Tasca, who belonged to both the French and Italian Socialist parties, attempted to apply theories of planning which were current in the French and Belgian movements to create a new non-marxist and anti-statist Italian socialism.

The minority was bothered by yet another aspect of the united-front pact. Unity of Action had always been justified as a step to the creation of a single party of the proletariat. Fusion was the goal of those like

Nenni, who relegated ideology to second place. But this possibility enraged Tasca who saw very real differences between socialism and Stalinist communism. Moreover, it was clear to the minority, if not to Nenni, that the PCI had done precious little ideological rethinking before it launched itself into the united front. The communists' rapid conversion smacked of the crudest form of expediency.

FROM THE UNITED TO THE POPULAR FRONT

In 1935, at the Seventh Congress of the Communist International, the new popular-front policy was announced. The communist movement now accepted a transition period and endorsed the view that the proletariat could not achieve a majority. Overnight communists became ardent champions of yesterday's despised bourgeois democracy. Middle-class liberals were suddenly transformed from latent fascists to allies in the struggle against Hitler and Mussolini. However, the popular front, which was dictated by the defensive needs of the USSR and by the rise of the far right in France and Spain, could only be applied with difficulty to Italian politics. Even Nenni was bewildered and troubled by the shift, which was based not on any change in the nature of capitalism, but on the interests of the Soviet Union.

Successful popular-front alliances between communists, socialists, and middle-class democrats were forged in France and Spain in 1936; but when the collective leadership of the PCI attempted a similar policy, the results were simply grotesque. Lacking a suitable democratic partner, the communists issued their appeal to sincere fascists, "brothers in blackshirts," who believed in the radical fascist program of 1919. This moral debacle compromised the positions of Mario Montagnana (1897–1960), Togliatti's brother-in-law, and Ruggiero Grieco (1893–1955). They went so far as to direct appeals to the fascists during the Ethiopian war and at the beginning of the Italian intervention in the Spanish Civil War, when even the Soviet Union opposed such initiatives. More successful was a recruiting drive among Italian immigrants in France. The PCI sponsored a frontist organization, the Unione Popolare Italiana, in 1936, which grew to 40,000 members within a year. Despite this success, it was not a brilliant period in party history. Togliatti, who had distanced himself from the operations of the PCI, finally decided, in 1938, to end the collective leadership by sending Giuseppe Berti to take charge. Berti, at that time a loyal Stalinist, moved with great ruthlessness to push aside Montagnana, Dozza, and Grieco.

THE PSI AND THE STRUGGLE WITHIN ITALY

One of the great weaknesses of the PSI throughout the fascist period was the lack of a solid apparatus within Italy. The socialists resented

GL, which had a small but heroic underground network, and they carried a permanent feeling of inferiority toward the communists, whose record of arrests and imprisonment by the regime far outstripped any other party. Defeat at the hands of the fascists had completely demoralized the majority of ex-socialists within Italy. The low point came when Emilio Caldara, the former socialist mayor of Milan, offered to support the Fascist regime in return for Mussolini's recognition of a loyal socialist opposition within the corporative state. This was only the most glaring example of a general collapse of will by many party and union leaders, and it gave the false impression that the Fascist regime enjoyed a measure of active worker support.

To remedy this situation, the PSI established a small but active Internal Center in 1934. Rodolfo Morandi (1902–1955), Bruno Maffi (1909–), and Lucio Luzzatto (1913–) became key organizers in Milan in 1934 and 1935. Morandi, who would be party secretary for many years after 1948, came to the PSI, along with Maffi and Luzzatto, from the GL underground. Earlier he had worked with Lelio Basso, another clandestine socialist operative, on the *Quarto stato*. Morandi rejected the eclectic activism of GL and the sectarianism of the PCI in favor of a PSI, which he felt could be renewed and turned into a viable political force. Morandi's study of Italian industrial development, published in 1931, convinced him that fusion between industrialists and fascism had gone too far to be reversed, and that the new postfascist order would have to be based on the proletariat. Under Morandi's direction, the Internal Center consistently took more radically socialist policies than did the party leadership in exile. A fundamental incompatibility developed between the mentality of the Internal Center and many of the older generation of party leaders in exile.

The Internal Center led a precarious existence. In April 1937, the fascist police arrested Morandi and Luzzatto; then another recruit from GL, Eugenio Colorni, took over but was arrested in 1938. Finally the leadership was passed to Eugenio Curiel (1912–1945), who emerged from the fascist student movement to play a role in both the socialist and communist undergrounds until he was killed during the Resistance.

THE SPANISH CIVIL WAR AND THE STALINIST PURGES

There was little that the left parties could do to counter fascist aggression until the outbreak of the Spanish Civil War in July 1936. Spain provided the first opportunity for the antifascists to pass beyond words. During the conflict the Italian exiles sent three thousand volunteers; well over half was from the PCI, the balance was from the PSI, GL, and the republican or anarchist movements. Luigi Longo became a leader of the International Brigades, while Nenni and Rosselli worked to mobilize support both in Spain and France on behalf of the Spanish Republic. Even Togliatti was involved as the official representative of the Comintern in 1937.

The Spanish Civil War both united and divided the parties of the Italian left. Disputes did not arise so much over the application of the united or popular front in Spain, as they did over communist persecution of all left dissidents, especially Trotskyists and anarchists. Evidence mounted that the communists were systematically eliminating their opponents as a counterpart to the purges taking place in the USSR. Togliatti's role both in Spain and the USSR during the purges still remains a mystery. He participated in the elimination of the Hungarian leader, Bela Kun, and of many German communists. Of those who served in Spain with the International, Togliatti was one of the few who survived Stalin's suspicions. He even launched his own purge of the PCI when he sent Giuseppe Berti to make the collective leadership pay for such errors as the "brothers in blackshirts" campaign in the application of the popular front to Italy. But the PCI, unlike the German, Polish, Yugoslav, and Hungarian parties, came through the experience relatively untouched. No top leader was executed or even expelled. Berti's methods, while harsh, did not fundamentally change the character of the leadership group as it existed since 1931.

THE PCI AND INTELLECTUAL DISSENT
UNDER FASCISM

Only the Christian Democratic party proved as successful as the PCI in recruiting young intellectuals who were disillusioned by the failure of the Fascist regime. The communists won the battle within the left on two very important levels. First, they transformed the experience of fascist prisons into a kind of training ground where many militants completed their ideological education. The communists formed prison collectives that carried on a relatively high level of political debate. By the end of the dictatorship there were perhaps 3000 communist activists in prison who rounded out their education in this way.

The PCI also gained ground during the fascist period by recruiting a large number of young intellectuals who had passed through the fascist youth movement. A few early adherents, like Giorgio and Antonio Amendola, Lucio Lombardo Radice, or Antonio Giolitti, came to the party from the great families of liberal Italy and had strong antifascist roots. Many more, however, came out of fascist student organizations and had collaborated on periodicals like Bottai's *Critica fascista* which had been at the center of intellectual ferment during the regime. Mario Alicata, Ruggiero Zangrandi, Pietro Ingrao, and Eugenio Curiel, among others, joined the party in this way. Communism responded to a belief that the fascists themselves had ingrained in the young: that the old liberal values were dead, and that new ideologies had to be collectivist and social, rather than liberal and individualist. Moreover, the PCI reaped the fruits of its constant activism. As disillusioned young intellectuals and workers sought a way of opposing the regime, they discovered that the only really active force against fascism on the left was the PCI.

THE HITLER-STALIN PACT AND THE RUPTURE OF UNITY OF ACTION

Anticommunism within the PSI exploded with the news of the pact of August 1939 between Germany and the USSR for Russian neutrality in the coming war at the expense of Poland . A minority, headed by Tasca, had long sought to end Unity of Action, but Nenni's position consistently predominated at party congresses until 1939. Even some prominent reformists supported the alliance with the PCI. Giuseppe Saragat, a marxist humanist and social democrat, was a strong advocate of the Soviet alliance and the united front in the face of the growing fascist danger and the manifest unwillingness of the western democracies to stand up to Hitler.

The split between Tasca and Nenni came to a head with the news of the Hitler-Stalin pact. Tasca, joined now by Saragat, ousted Nenni from the leadership and ended the Unity of Action pact with the PCI. But the victory was short-lived. The anticommunists did not have time to stamp their views on the party before France collapsed in June 1940. Moreover, Tasca, who led the anti-Nenni faction, opted for collaboration with the pro-German Vichy regime. Arrests and dispersion followed the Nazi victory. Nenni and Saragat found refuge in the south of France. The PSI directorate moved to Switzerland where it was controlled by such reformists as Ignazio Silone, Giuseppe Faravelli, and G.E. Modigliani.

If the news of the Hitler-Stalin pact stunned the socialists, it also left the communists somewhat nonplussed. Only Grieco and Sereni fully approved of the pact. Giuseppe Di Vittorio showed open embarrassment; Romano Cocchi (1915–1944), a member of the Central Committee, and the young militant Leo Valiani (1909–), left the party over the issue. Cocchi, vilified by his excomrades, died in a Nazi concentration camp, but Valiani went on to become one of the leaders of the postwar Action party.

Overall, however, the impact of the Hitler-Stalin accord on the PCI was less severe than it might have been. Although the party could not control individual reactions, dissent was unable to take organized form. Curiously, only in the PCI prison collectives could discipline be exercised on the issue. Umberto Terracini and Camilla Ravera, who dissented vigorously from the Hitler-Stalin pact, were expelled from their prison collective, which was led by the Stalinists Longo, Secchia, and Scocci-marro. Terracini's ouster meant that the last of Gramsci's close associates left the party, although he would be readmitted in 1944. The communists began to scatter when the French Communist party was outlawed in the fall of 1939. Giorgio Amendola was sent to Tunisia to work among the Italian community. Giuseppe Berti departed for New York where he resumed publication of *Lo stato operaio*, the party review. Togliatti, who had been in France in August 1939 to supervise the reorganization of the PCI leadership, was arrested by the French authorities in September, along with Longo, Di Vittorio, Montagnana, and most of the other leaders. Togliatti was held until March 1940, then released after negotiations between France and the USSR. Longo had less luck. He, too, was to be transferred to the Soviet Union; instead, he was handed over to the Italians in mid-1941, and remained in prison until the fall of Mussolini in 1943. Di Vittorio, Sereni, Dozza, Celeste Negarville, and Giorgio Amendola attempted to create a new party directorate in the west, while Togliatti resurfaced in Moscow and began to broadcast messages to Italy.

By 1941 the PCI became more active within Italy. Older cadres returned from abroad to set up networks in Turin and Milan. They made contacts with the young intellectuals who had been attracted to the PCI from fascist youth organizations and with young militant workers. With few exceptions, almost the entire leadership of the Communist party was reassembled in southern France or in Italy during the first years of the war. The only potential problem for the PCI was the confusion that resulted from the separation between Togliatti in Moscow, and the cadres in the West, who operated without real direction. An attempt by Togliatti to send his own man, Umberto Massola, ended in failure when Massola was unable to get along with the other leaders.

ON THE EVE OF LIBERATION

The Nazi invasion of the USSR in June 1941 allowed the left to return to the united-front policies, which had been followed from 1934 to 1939. In the south of France Nenni made contact with Amendola, Dozza, and Sereni. Amendola enthusiastically accepted the formation of a broad antifascist front with the PSI and GL. But the years of exile had not been happy ones for the Italian left. On the positive side, the PSI regained its unity and the united front was one step toward overcoming the rupture of Livorno. The price was high, however. Reunification between reformists and maximalists was possible only because defeat and exile made the old disputes irrelevant. Party unity began to come apart by 1938, as conflicts re-emerged over relations with the communists. In theory, the alliance between the PCI and PSI should have symbolized a new cooperative era on the left. In fact, the united front simply sapped the strength of the PSI. The communists made the pact a one-way street. It bound the socialists, while the PCI kept almost total freedom of action. There was no consultation on the "brothers in blackshirt" campaign, nor were the socialists allowed to discuss the Stalin show trials or the Nazi-Soviet pact.

The differing reactions of the PSI and PCI to events of the 1920s and 1930s reveal why the communists emerged as the dominant party on the left after the war. The socialists remained passive and divided, without a unifying ideology. When Nenni renewed the process of unity of action in 1942 on the same basis as before the war, he risked crippling the entire party. As for the communists, they came through the troubled years of exile and Stalinism in remarkably good shape. The leadership group survived the purges, although most of Gramsci's old collaborators were out of the party. Togliatti, now the supreme leader, showed himself to be intelligent, ruthless, and resourceful. The communists also profited from the sacrifices they made within Italy. It was a party psychologically and politically prepared for the postfascist battles.

PART TWO

The Left and the Republic

CHAPTER 6

The Fall of Fascism and the Establishment of the Republic

The end of Mussolini's government came suddenly and dramatically on July 25, 1943. In an all-night session on July 25, the Fascist Grand Council voted to return power to the king. Out-voted and shaken, the Duce meekly submitted to arrest after he informed the monarch of the decision of the Grand Council. During the years of exile, the leaders of the left parties dreamed of a violent overthrow of the Fascist dictatorship. When it came, Mussolini's downfall was the work of conservative monarchists, dissident fascists, and the military, who aimed to make the transition to another regime as painless as possible. Marshal Pietro Badoglio, the new prime minister, had served the Fascist regime throughout its existence. King Vittorio Emanuele had signed the decrees in 1925 and 1926 that established the authoritarian state. Together, they represented the fusion of prefascist elites with the Fascist regime.

In its effort to make the transition to the new postfascist world, the Badoglio government moved rapidly to restore the constitution as it existed before 1922. The flight of the king and Badoglio from Rome to Bari on September 8 cast doubt on the conservative restoration. The royal government left without warning or preparation as the Germans seized control of the capital. The left justly claimed that the monarchy had abandoned its claim to power, but, trapped between the Nazi occupiers of most of Italy and the Allied-supported government in Bari, there was little that the left parties could do. The antifascist parties were not entirely passive, however. On September 9 they created the Committee of National Liberation (CLN) as a potential alternative government. The more radical parties on the CLN—the Socialists and Action Party—attempted to pass a declaration that the monarchy had fallen, but neither the moderate liberals nor the Catholics would accept it.

The antifascist exiles, who had been sustained during the hard years of exile by the ideal of a revolutionary Italy, were now faced with a totally unforeseen situation. Nothing prepared them for the way fascism fell. The assumption on the left had always been that the old order would be washed away. Projects for economic and social reconstruction had been formed on the premise that Italy would be totally free to choose its own destiny. The socialists took an especially abstract view of the postwar; the communists, bound by a special tie to the USSR, were more sensitive to the context of great-power relations. Palmiro Togliatti understood the limitations with which Italy found itself. The obstacles to revolution were formidable. Most important, a revolution would not be tolerated by the Allies. The British stressed continuity with the monarchical state. The Americans were initially more flexible on reconstruction in 1943 and 1944, but, eventually, they too accepted the notion of continuity. The second limitation to the left's efforts to impose a revolutionary solution arose from the ability of the conservatives to manage the transition. As Italy passed from fascism, the distribution of industrial and financial power, and the complicated interconnection between the state and private sectors of the economy, remained as they had been under fascism. Nor were other institutions seriously threatened. The Church emerged from the fascist experience as the country's most complete political and social infrastructure. The bureaucracy and judiciary defied efforts to purge them of their fascist past.

The way Italy was liberated helped the old order to survive. Although the lines shifted constantly, three zones emerged: an expanding area, initially in the South, which was administered by the Badoglio government; a zone closer to the front, which was directly controlled by the Allies; and Nazi-occupied Italy, which was administered by the Germans directly, or by Mussolini's Italian Social Republic. Liberation came rapidly to the South, well before the conditions for revolutionary change could be created. Nearer the front, military considerations prevailed. Only in the North, where the left organized a partisan army, did the possibility of seizing political control exist, but this chance diminished with the advance of the Allies.

Ideological obstacles also faced the left. During the Interwar Period neither the socialists nor the communists had developed a comprehensive theory to counter orthodox economics. Every socialist government from 1920 to 1939 had foundered on the resistance of national and international finance to accept unconventional policies. The most notable experiment, Léon Blum's Popular Front government of 1936, and its reformist capitalism, met with such hostility from financial circles that they helped bring down the Blum cabinet after less than a year in office. The Belgian De Man plan was discredited by the inability of the Belgian Workers' party to impose it on its coalition partners. The left had a vision of a socialist economy, but it had no transition plan other than a revolutionary seizure of power. Since that was impossible, left-wing governments were forced to work within the framework of capitalist thinking on economic matters. The road map simply offered no route to the destination.

The left's inability to contest the overall strategy of capitalist reconstruction after 1943 placed it in the position of accepting a neoliberal system which in Italy was not even softened, as in France or England, by a measure of systematic planning. Four trends marked Italian economic reconstruction and undermined the left's ability to shape events: an adherence to the liberal market system; rapid reassertion of discipline in the workplace; continuation of the management of state enterprises in the interests of the private sector; and the integration of Italian reconstruction into the American dominated international economy.

THE COMMUNIST STRATEGY AFTER 1943

The Socialist, Communist, and Action parties, which represented the left between 1943 and 1946, could not agree on a basic political model to propose to the Italian people. The communists set an extremely modest agenda. Among the masses, the myth of Stalin and of the USSR was so powerful that it reduced the question of revolution to the arrival of Soviet troops. "The 'big moustache' (Stalin) is coming" was the cry of countless peasants and workers. At the other end of the spectrum was Togliatti, who had little interest in sponsoring a violent seizure of power or even of opening a full-scale debate on the nature of the socialist society. He came very early to the idea that "progressive democracy" should be the aim of the party. This meant the establishment of representative institutions and the insertion of the PCI into the broadest possible antifascist front until its position in the country could be assured. Discussion of revolution, an unlikely possibility anyway, would only frighten Catholic and liberal allies. More radical communist leaders, based in the partisan armies of the North, called for a direct proletarian and peasant democracy, but Togliatti almost completely ignored these calls in favor of a defensive strategy: the propagation of the myth of revolution among the masses, while assuring the conservative and Catholic elites that the PCI would do nothing to realize it.

THE SOCIALISTS: EVER DIVIDED

Within the PSI old divisions reappeared. The majority of socialists drew far more revolutionary conclusions from the war and resistance than did the communists. They understood that the simplistic idea of revolution that enflamed the maximalists in 1919 was no longer possible; but they held the unshakable conviction that the bourgeois state could not survive the fall of fascism and certainly could not overcome the problems of postwar reconstruction. Unlike the communists who played down their social and economic program, the socialists pressed ahead with calls for sweeping changes: a Socialist republic, based on the classic alliance of industrial and peasant labor; major nationalizations; and a vast purge of those guilty of collaboration with fascism.

The socialists even had seeming advantages in the postwar struggles. Unlike the new Christian Democratic party, which was tied to the Vatican, or the communists, who were constrained by loyalty to the USSR, the socialists could offer a uniquely Italian alternative. But lack of external support proved disastrous on the practical level. Two factors weakened the socialist position from the outset. The first was the failure of the party to organize within Italy during the fascist period. The socialists had few ties with the young who found themselves drawn by its role in the Resistance to the more dynamic PCI. The leadership counted on the PSI's historical appeal to the Italian working class. Such residual loyalties existed, but they were not followed up by concrete steps to build a mass base. As a result, the socialists faced a precipitous decline after their initial electoral successes.

The second limitation faced by the Socialist party was the old nemesis of internal division. The reconstructed PSI was a fusion of four constituencies: the majority of the exile party that followed Nenni in calling for the creation of a social republic to be achieved in alliance with the communists; the Swiss exiles under Silone, who supported an interclass democratic republic, open to Europe; old-line socialists, who had emerged during the crisis of fascism and had reorganized the PSI in Rome in September 1942; and the young militants of the underground Internal Center, who formed a new Movement of Proletarian Unity (MUP) headed by Lelio Basso. Basso, who had collaborated on the *Quarto stato* of Nenni and Rosselli, and was strongly influenced by Lenin and Trotsky, envisaged a movement that would be pro-Soviet while it competed with the communists for the loyalties of the radicalized workers of the North.

The MUP was formed in January 1943, a few months after the PSI was reconstituted in Rome. Instead of challenging both the socialists and communists by extending the MUP from its base in Milan to a national organization, the young revolutionaries of the Internal Center agreed to merge with the old-line socialists on August 22, 1943. The new party, created as an uneasy truce between hostile tendencies, became the Italian Socialist Party of Proletarian Unity (Partito Socialista Italiano d'Unità Proletaria—PSIUP). It was plagued by a lack of strong political cadres and by an inferiority complex toward the communists. The PSIUP took a position on the far left of the National Liberation Committee. But the party undermined its own militant position by signing a Unity of Action pact with the much more moderate communists on August 25, 1943. Because the aim of the pact was fusion between the two movements, one of the first political actions of the PSIUP was to declare that its independent existence had only limited value.

THE FAILURE OF AN INTERCLASS
ALTERNATIVE: THE ACTION PARTY

In terms of day-to-day politics, the natural ally of the PSIUP was not the PCI, but a new political formation that developed out of the Giustizia e Libertà and a parallel but independent liberal-socialist movement founded by Guido Calogero and Aldo Capitini at the Scuola Normale of Pisa around 1940. Calogero and Capitini, like Rosselli, attempted to blend liberal values with a socialist economic system, which they felt was the only way to organize a mass society. They hoped to create an individualist socialism that would lay the basis of a democratic Italy for the first time in its history.

In July 1942 the nucleus of the Action party (PdA) came together: Lodovico Ragghianti, Enzo Enriques Agnoletti, Tristano Codignola, Carlo Francovitch, Franco Venturi, Alessandro Galante Garrone, Riccardo Bauer, Norberto Bobbio, and Altiero Spinelli. Collectively, they represented the finest of Italy's democratic and socialist intellectuals. The PdA hoped to escape from the rigid categories of the old political world by offering a radical, interclass alternative to both the communist left and to the conservative order.

Although the PdA was second only to the communists in its participation in the armed resistance, the party had yet to be tested electorally. Nor had the liberal and socialist wings of the Action party agreed upon a common program. This internal conflict became apparent in January 1943 when the PdA attempted to set its future course. A deep division, becoming more debilitating over time, appeared between radical democrats, like Ugo La Malfa (1903–1979), Ferrucio Parri (1890–1981), and Riccardo Bauer, and socialists like Emilio Lussu (1890–1975). The Action party, whose natural constituency was in the lower middle class, could never define its objectives clearly enough to unite bourgeois and working-class voters on an interclass basis. The party merely assumed that disillusionment with fascism would create a natural electorate for its program. In the end, the PdA remained a party of brilliant leaders with little following.

The PdA received a severe blow when in June 1944 it was excluded by the communists from participation in the new General Confederation of Labor on the grounds that it was not a true proletarian mass movement. Togliatti instinctively understood the weakness of the PdA and treated it with contempt. The Communists, Socialists, and Christian Democrats (none of whom had faced an electorate for twenty years) divided the leadership of the labor movement on the assumption that they had mass support among the workers. Instead of backing the Action party, which did have some support from white collar workers, the PSIUP myopically followed the communists in their argument that the actionists had no right to participation in a proletarian organization. As a result, the PSIUP weakened a potential ally and increased its dependence on the PCI, while the Action party, unable to build a following among workers in the South, accentuated its bourgeois character and deepened divisions within the party. Despite these problems, the Action party represented, with the PSIUP in 1943 and 1944, the most intransigent wing of the Committee of National Liberation, and it was the closest ally of the PSIUP in pressing for the immediate proclamation of a republic.

THE COMMITTEE OF NATIONAL LIBERATION

The Committee of National Liberation emerged on September 9, 1943, out of the wartime accords between the parties of the left—PCI, PSIUP, and PdA. The left alliance was made possible after the reversal of communist policy following the Nazi attack on the USSR in June 1941. The communists then called for a new united front. In October 1941, Nenni and Saragat for the PSI, Silvio Trentin and Fausto Nitti for GL, and Emilio Sereni and Giuseppe Dozza for the PCI signed a pact of cooperation. This alliance was broadened in 1942 to include the Catholics; during the following year it included the liberals and a small southern based party, Democracy of Labor, which was the personal vehicle of the ex-prime minister, Ivanoe Bonomi.

From the outset, the nascent Committee on National Liberation accepted the rule of parity and unanimity. The consent of all parties was necessary to make a decision. This turned out to be a trap, which ensnared the left in an endless series of compromises. The conservatives had only to fall back on the least common denominator of the status quo to block calls for fundamental change. Moreover, political life centered on the South, where the left parties had never been strong, and where local notables who did not want a radical break with the past were at their best. The right wing wanted to maintain the CLN as a temporary alliance of parties, not as an alternative government resting on the revolutionary will of the people. Initially, the parties of the CLN were bound by common antifascism, but they were split on the question of the monarchy. The left was republican, but only the PSIUP and the PdA really pressed the issue. The Democracy of Labor and the Liberal party had strong sympathies for preserving the monarchy without Vittorio Emanuele. The Christian Democratic party (the successor of the pre-Fascist Popular party) was officially neutral, but tended to favor the monarchist cause by delaying a decision.

With the fall of Mussolini's government, a potential split developed between the CLN and Badoglio's government. The PdA and the PSIUP pressed for a declaration that the royal power had lapsed when the king fled Rome without leaving a transitional governmental authority. The left wing of the CLN wanted that body to declare itself the de facto government of Italy. The first decrees of the Badoglio government went in the opposite direction. On August 2, 1943, Badoglio dissolved the fascist lower house and called for elections to a newly revived Chamber of Deputies immediately following the end of the war. Significantly, no mention was made of the royal senate in the decree. The government implied that the continuity of the prefascist liberal state and of the various institutions which had been contaminated by fascism would not be an issue.

Faced with Badoglio's actions, the CLN revealed its fundamental internal conflicts. The liberals and Bonomi wanted to delay a decision on the monarchy until after the war. The socialists and actionists wished to make a stand on the issue of the republic, but could not win the support of the PCI, which preferred to place the antifascist fight above all else. In October 1943, the CLN bowed to the conservative principle of state continuity by agreeing to defer the institutional question until after the war. To balance the concession to the conservatives, the CLN pressed for the elimination of the Badoglio government and its replacement by a government of national unity based on the CLN.

From October 1943 onward, the CLN was officially opposed to the royal government, which had been recognized by the British and Americans. At the Congress of the antifascist parties, held in Bari on January 28 and 29, 1944, the socialists and actionists again failed to win a declaration in favor of a republic. They were unable to play the key card of mass pressure because the North was still under Nazi control. Moreover, the position of the PCI was extremely ambiguous. Neither the communists, nor the Catholics wished to provoke an open confrontation with the right and with the Allies. The Congress did form a permanent executive committee as an alternative government-in-waiting.

THE "SVOLTA DI SALERNO":
THE PCI SUPPORTS BADOGLIO

The conflict between the CLN and the Badoglio ministry continued unresolved into the early spring. Badoglio had almost no support from the major political parties, but they could not force him out without the consent of the British and Americans. The impasse was broken when the Italian Communist party abruptly changed policy in favor of the Badoglio government, the so-called *svolta* di Salerno. This shift is often unfairly seen as merely dictated by the interests of the Soviet Union, but Togliatti's motivations were much more complex. He had been convinced that the transition to socialism would be much longer than most of the PCI leaders imagined. Alliance politics would be necessary in the struggle for the new society. These political battles would involve a struggle for hegemony over mass institutions within the capitalist order. With this as his starting point, Togliatti devoted much of his energy, not to revolution, but to the establishment of the PCI within the political and cultural infrastructure of the state. He believed that over the long term, there would be a basic contradiction between democratic political forms and capitalist economic structures, but the resolution of this conflict would be neither simple nor rapid.

Ironically, Togliatti followed a strategy that gave primacy to politics over economics. Little stress was put on the struggle for economic control of reconstruction. The Communist party sought to expand its base as far as possible within a system that it admitted in advance would be capitalist. To build up mass organizations and establish itself as the preeminent proletarian party, the PCI had to remain well within the legal order. Through the Unity of Action pact with the socialists, Togliatti ensured that the PSIUP would not act independently to become a rival on the left by challenging communist control of the labor movement. The PCI could then claim to represent the bulk of the Italian working class in seeking an understanding with the Catholic Church, which controlled the other mass movement in the country. Togliatti was willing to forego the PCI's revolutionary program in order to forge this coalition with the Catholics.

Togliatti's policies were the product of his own evolution during the fascist era, but they also coincided with the European strategy of the USSR. In 1943 Stalin dissolved the Comintern as a gesture of good will toward his capitalist allies, and stressed the importance of national unity as essential to winning the war against fascism. Stalin also accepted the rough division of Europe into spheres of influence. Togliatti, who well understood Stalin's policies, knew that a revolutionary outcome was possible only with Soviet support, and that the USSR had had no role in the liberation of Italy. His definition of the "partito nuovo" or new party, as a mass movement working within the context of a "progressive democracy," fit both his reading of the Italian political situation and of Soviet foreign policy.

Throughout 1943 and 1944 the PCI systematically sought broad interclass alliances. Giorgio Amendola was the architect of this early frontist policy. As the son of Giovanni Amendola, a Neapolitan and leader of the liberal opposition to Mussolini, Giorgio understood the complexity of the political situation in the South and the need for cooperation with other political parties. Even before the fall of Mussolini, he worked out an accord in Milan between the parties of the left and the Catholics and liberals. When Mussolini's government fell, Amendola shifted the base of operations from Milan to Rome where he represented the PCI on the Committee of Opposition Parties.

The PCI moved simultaneously in the summer of 1943 to consolidate its position on the left. On September 28 it renewed the Unity of Action pact with the socialists. The new pact aimed at the harmonization of policies between the proletarian parties in the short run, and at complete fusion in the long term. While the communists sought to use the pact to keep the PSIUP from taking an independent line, the socialists tried to use it to push the communists further to the left. Both the PSIUP and the PdA took more radical positions on the proclamation of the republic and hostility to Bodoglio's government. In late 1943 the PCI seemed to shift toward the intransigence of the socialists, as old-line revolutionaries, like Luigi Longo, Pietro Secchia, and Mauro Scoccimarro, who had few contacts with the old political establishment, returned to take the place of Amendola at the leadership of the PCI. By the early months of 1944, the Communist party wavered between joining the PSI and PdA in open conflict with the royal government or following the frontist line of Amendola.

As long as Togliatti remained in exile in Moscow, the issue was unresolved. Then, on March 14 the USSR officially recognized the Badoglio government, and on March 27, Togliatti finally arrived in Naples. Without hesitation he allied the PCI with the bourgeois parties by offering his support to Badoglio. Togliatti declared that the primary aim was victory over fascism, and that institutional and economic questions could wait until peace had been achieved. In siding with the Christian Democrats and liberals, Togliatti cut the ground from under those who wished to use the partisan movement in the North as the basis for a revolutionary democracy. Longo, Secchia, and the others on the left of the PCI, who counted on the "wind from the North" to radicalize political life, were forced to align themselves with Togliatti's conservative strategy. The isolated socialists and actionists soon followed suit.

POLITICAL CONSEQUENCES OF THE SVOLTA

The "svolta di Salerno", or turnabout of April 1944, was the logical conclusion of the policies already outlined by Amendola and by Togliatti. By ending the deadlock between the CLN and the Badoglio government, Togliatti rendered an enormous service to the conservatives and gave the PCI a national profile making it the privileged partner of the center-right parties. A series of compromises rapidly followed Togliatti's *svolta*. On April 6, the CLN executive approved the constitution of a war cabinet. As part of the arrangement, Vittorio Emanuele stepped aside on April 12 in favor of his son, Umberto, who became Lieutenant General of the Kingdom. With the institutional question temporarily settled, the liberals, Catholics and communists moved to create a government of national unity under Badoglio on April 24.

Togliatti used these negotiations to establish a direct link with the Vatican. He was more than willing to recognize the Christian Democratic party as an equal partner with the PSIUP and PCI, if it would improve the Communist party's standing with the church. What began as a series of concessions by Togliatti to the Catholics, led ultimately to Communist acceptance of the entire Lateran Treaty as part of the republican constitution in 1947. As compensation, the Communists received little but recognition as a party that seemed to accept the status quo.

Togliatti balanced incompatible positions throughout the immediate postwar period. At the same time, the PCI embodied the myth of direct action as it was defined by the Resistance bands, as well as the pragmatic, conservative adherence to national unity at all costs. By monopolizing the myth of the Resistance, the PCI did two things. First, it drained the Resistance ideal of any revolutionary potential and ensured that the northern partisan movement would never pose a threat to the political order. Then, ironically, the conservatives used the PCI's alleged monopoly of the Resistance to justify abandoning the ideals of militant antifascism as corrupted and politicized by the communists.

THE PCI AND CULTURAL ANTIFASCISM

Despite the inherent contradictions in the politics of the PCI, the party under Togliatti developed an extraordinarily close relationship with the young intellectuals who were emerging from the fascist university system. In June 1944, as one of his first major acts, Togliatti began to publish *Rinascita*, a cultural-political periodical which gave a voice to the intellectuals who rallied to the PCI. While the older leaders were dispersed to various positions outside of Rome, Togliatti surrounded himself with younger men. He seemed to feel more at home with the generation that came politically of age in the late 1930s than he did with his comrades in exile from the 1920s. These young intellectuals, like Mario Alicata, Antonello Trombadori, Aldo Natoli, Pietro Ingrao, Fabrizio Onofri, Luigi Pintor, Paolo Bufalini, Alfredo Reichlin, and Massimo Caprara, were born in the decade from 1915 to 1925, and shared a common experience of university life under fascism. In one way or another, they all supported Togliatti's vision of progressive democracy as a long-term struggle for control of democratic institutions. They provided the leadership of the PCI throughout the 1960s and 1970s.

More than any other left-wing party, Togliatti's PCI broke with the maximalist and Bordigan politics, which had failed so miserably between 1918 and 1922. The PCI emerged as a mass party seeking to become an indispensible partner of the center and right. As early as 1944 the communists accepted the classic social democratic stand, that true representative democracy was incompatible with capitalism and would gradually undermine the latter as it became stronger. The cost of accepting an essentially antirevolutionary position was high. The PCI undermined aggressive action by the other parties of the left. It subordinated both the PSIUP and the PdA to its own conservative ends and thwarted the emergence of an alternative strategy. As a result, the economic and social agenda of postwar Italy was set by the conservative American-backed parties.

TOWARD A GOVERNMENT OF THE CLN

In April, Togliatti brought the PCI into Badoglio's government. Nenni, who was initially critical, followed suit a week later, and on April 22, a new Badoglio cabinet was formed with socialist and communist participation. The *svolta* revealed the power of the PCI to influence the policies of the other parties of the left. The PSIUP backed off when it had to choose between its leftist program and the Unity of Action pact. The PdA, faced with isolation, accommodated itself to the communist positions.

Badoglio's government was short-lived. On June 10, the PSIUP and the Action party forced Badoglio's withdrawal in favor of the former socialist and prefascist prime minister, Ivanoe Bonomi, now president of the CLN. The new ministry represented a victory for the entire National Liberation Committee, because it was the first to be officially designated by the CLN. But this limited success did not shift the political balance in favor of the left. The Bonomi cabinet rested on an uneasy compromise between the conservatives and the left. The government promised to allow a constituent assembly to decide the institutional question. The oath of office was modified to make it neutral with regard to the monarchy, and the government kept its power to issue legislative decrees until the end of the war. All of these decisions, embodied in a decree of June 25, 1944, ostensibly favored the left. The creation of the office of Lieutenant General of the Realm, to be occupied by Vittorio Emanuele's son, Umberto, was a major gain for the monarchy. The semi-retirement of the old king, who had been totally compromised by fascism, made the monarchy, as an institution, much more acceptable to moderate opinion.

THE RECONSTRUCTION OF
THE LABOR MOVEMENT

The most dramatic change in the balance of power on the left could be seen in the labor movement. The old pre-Fascist General Confederation of Labor had been under the control of the reformist wing of the PSI. After 1943, the new labor confederation became a source of power for the PCI. The communists realized immediately that the union confederation represented a vital link with the masses and would serve as a trump card in negotiations with the conservatives and Catholics.

In August 1943 Bruno Buozzi, Italy's best-known labor leader and long-time head of the Metal Workers Federation, was asked by the new Badoglio government to take control of the fascist union structure. Buozzi, a reformist socialist, consulted with his party colleagues and then demanded that the communists be included as well. The socialists scrupulously followed the terms of the Unity of Action pact, but they also recognized the great strength that the PCI had already built among industrial workers. The communist-led strikes of March 1943 in Turin signaled the crumbling hold of Mussolini's government over the country. The PCI designated Giuseppe Di Vittorio to head the agricultural section, while Buozzi assumed overall supervision of the union bureaucracy. The agreement was far from satisfactory, however. The mandate, which came from the Badoglio government, made it only a temporary expedient until a new syndical movement could be created.

The creation of the General Confederation of Italian Workers (CGIL) was delayed by the Nazi occupation of Rome and problems of resuming political activity in the South. When negotiations resumed, the communists surprised the PSIUP by pressing for the inclusion of the Christian Democrats to parallel the unity of the three mass parties within the CLN. Buozzi agreed, but the Catholics' participation in what had been a marxist-oriented syndical movement posed new problems. Two fundamentally different ideas entered into conflict. The traditional left had organized workers, on the basis of class, in close alliance with the socialist political movement. The Catholics insisted on a politically neutral union, decentralized structures, and muting the idea of class conflict. The PSI accepted much of the Catholic position in the final Pact of Rome on June 3, 1944, which set up the CGIL.

Just before the stipulation of the pact, the socialists were dealt a severe blow when Bruno Buozzi was arrested and executed by the Nazis. Leadership of the CGIL passed to the communist Di Vittorio, and to the long-time Catholic labor organizer, Achille Grandi. The Vatican, which had always resisted the idea of uniting with marxist unions, surprisingly accepted the Pact of Rome, but, as an insurance policy, moved to set up a parallel structure, the Christian Association of Italian Workers (ACLI) in August 1944. In October the Church also created a powerful small landowners association, the Coltivatori Diretti, which became a major source of Christian Democratic electoral power.

The Pact of Rome put off many of the most difficult issues. The balanced leadership of the CGIL, nominally independent from any one party or ideology, was somewhat artificial. The exclusion of the Action party from the leadership was even more arbitrary. But the weakness of the CGIL lay elsewhere. The failure of the left to control economic policy during the reconstruction deprived the CGIL of a favorable context within which it could press its demands. As a result, labor's gains were fragmented, piecemeal concessions that did not fundamentally alter the balance of power in the factories.

THE LEFT AND THE PURGE
OF FASCIST COLLABORATORS

The purge remained a major weapon at the disposition of the left in the struggle to remake Italy after fascism. Several pieces of legislation dealt with the process of defascistization. One of the first was issued on December 28, 1943. It set an objective of eliminating fascists from local government and state agencies, but the law lacked a mechanism for enforcement. A second decree law of April 12, 1944 abolished fascist legislation on political crimes, imposed the death penalty on major fascist officials who figured prominently in either the March on Rome or the construction of the dictatorship, and established a judicial procedure for weeding out fascists. On July 28, 1944, the government appointed Count Carlo Sforza, an ex-foreign minister and strong antifascist, as High Commissioner for Sanctions against Fascism and established a special court to try cases. Finally, a decree of October 1944 gave the High Commissioner power over promotions at the highest level of the civil service and allowed wider latitude to retire or dismiss civil servants.

Despite good intentions on the part of the government and the close identification of PSIUP and the PdA with the purge, it bogged down almost immediately. Judges were reluctant to apply retroactive legislation and demanded clear causality between each individual and a specific crime. The mere holding of high office was deemed insufficient. Wide latitude was given to those who could argue that they did their duty for the state and king, not for the regime. The results were predictable. Of thirty-six death sentences, only two were carried out. In all, 890 sentences were issued by the purge tribunal: in 1945, 158 acquittals and 183 guilty verdicts; in 1946, 158 acquittals, 128 guilty verdicts, and 65 amnestied; in 1947, the last year of the purge, 24 acquittals, 67 guilty verdicts, and 30 amnestied. Even in cases arising from the pro-Nazi Italian Social Republic, the only punishable crime was collaboration with the Nazis. Participation in the regime was not in itself a crime.

Those who favored the purge faced the problem of setting limits and accountability in a country where, after twenty years of fascism, too many people had been involved with the regime. Neat distinctions became impossible. Even high officials could claim that they served the king, and not Mussolini. Badoglio and Vittorio Emanuele shared more guilt than many of those on trial. Moreover, in the North the purge became too closely identified with the communist-led partisan movement. Middle-class Italians came to see the process as an attack on their property and civil rights. By late 1944, Togliatti, who was extremely sensitive to these considerations, designated Mauro Scoccimarro, the PCI's official representative on the purge commission, to reassure Italians that only the corrupt and violent would be targeted. Despite these reassurances, hostility to the whole idea of the purge spread in the middle class and made it more sympathetic to calls for an end to active defascistization.

THE LEFT AND BONOMI

In August 1944 the Unity of Action pact was renewed by the PCI and PSIUP. Although the new accord called for coordination of policies on the political and syndical level, it did nothing to eliminate the dramatically different orientations of the PSIUP and PCI. The split on the left was the more unfortunate in light of the possibility that the CLN of North Italy (CLNAI), which was controlled by more radical elements, might shift the balance in favor of the left. As the Germans retreated, the CLNAI began to seize real power in the newly freed areas, often before the Allies could arrive.

The possibility that the CLNAI might finally break the continuity of the state faded when the Catholics and liberals, backed by the CLN in Rome, rejected any such option. The communists also dismissed any use of their power in the unions and partisan movement to seize direct power. Togliatti, who continued to believe that the essentially Catholic and conservative balance in the country could not be reversed without Soviet support, did not even wish to raise the specter of republicanism and resented the socialists' insistence on the issue.

In November 1944 the Bonomi government resigned. During his ministry the agenda of the left had stalled. Little progress was made on the purge. The government also began to back off from electing a constitutional assembly with broad powers to decide on the future of the monarchy. When the cabinet crisis began in November, it was widely viewed as an effort by Bonomi to free his government from the constraints imposed by the left wing of the CLN. The form that the resignation took was in itself an affront to the left. Although Bonomi formally held power under the Lieutenant General, he was the officially designated candidate of the CLN. When the prime minister by-passed the CLN by submitting his resignation directly to Umberto, he seemed deliberately to strengthen the monarchy's claim to legitimacy.

As a successor to Bonomi, the PSIUP and the PdA nominated Carlo Sforza, only to find his name vetoed by the British as too republican and independent. Once again, the communists broke ranks by opting to join a new version of the Bonomi government without the participation of either the actionists or socialists. The new Bonomi ministry gave four cabinet posts to the Communists: Togliatti at Justice, Scoccimarro at Occupied Italy, Fausto Gullo at Agriculture and Antonio Pesenti at Finance. But the powers of the PCI were merely symbolic. The communists lacked the will to impose an economic program, and

Togliatti had no wish to offend conservative and Catholic Italy by insisting on the purge or on an immediate decision on the republic.

Despite this public rupture between socialists and communists over Bonomi, the PSIUP renewed the Unity of Action pact with the PCI on December 10. Nenni simply refused to consider any possible concentration of left-wing forces that would act independently of the PCI. By his own unwillingness to pressure the communists, Nenni had no way of making credible his own fight for broad powers for the new constitutional assembly.

THE PERILS OF SUCCESS:
THE PARRI GOVERNMENT OF 1945

Without the participation of the socialists and actionists, the second Bonomi government lasted only a few months. The socialists again put forward a candidate, Pietro Nenni. To the chagrin of the socialist leader, he was arrested briefly by the Allies in May 1945 for making an unauthorized speech, and subsequently withdrew his candidacy. The Catholics, cautiously but prematurely, advanced their leader, Alcide De Gasperi. On June 12, when Bonomi finally resigned, Ferruccio Parri, a leader of the PdA, emerged as the consensus candidate of the left to form the next government. He did so on June 19 with an ambitious program of economic recovery and consolidation of the gains of the Resistance in the form of workers' councils, the purge, and the convocation of a constitutional assembly.

Division and confusion plagued the Parri government from the start. The split within the PdA between a democratic reformist wing, headed by Ugo La Malfa, and a militant socialist faction, headed by Emilio Lussu, had grown deeper as it became clear that the Action party had very little room to maneuver between the traditional forces of the left. Within the cabinet, difficulties in forging a consensus also grew as the Christian Democratic party moved away from its earlier commitment to the Republic.

THE REOPENING OF THE DEBATE
WITHIN THE PSIUP

Even more serious for the future of the Parri ministry were new signs of a rift within the PSIUP. The National Council of the party met from July 20 to August 1, 1945 to debate the old questions of relations with the PCI and of the place of democracy within socialism. The fundamental split between right and left reappeared. Those who opposed an exclusive Unity of Action pact with the PCI also had doubts about the idea of a single party of the working class on the communist model.

The social democrats, led by Saragat, argued that the role of the PSIUP was to find a third way between the Soviet and the Western models.

Morandi, Basso, and the other fusionists within the PSI, who advocated both an aggressively leftist policy and merger with the PCI, failed to show how these two positions could be reconciled while the communists were following a strategy that placed them well to the right of the PSIUP. Still, Nenni received the backing of 76 percent of the party delegates at the National Council for policies that had no possibility of becoming effective. Although Nenni was not personally enthusiastic about fusion, his leadership suffered from other defects. He failed until much later to see the impact the Soviet-American split would have on European political life. He hoped to forge a neutralist international bloc in alliance with British Labour, which had just scored a stunning upset of the conservatives and formed a new government. But Nenni grossly overestimated the ability of England to proceed independently of the Americans and misjudged the balance of power within the Labour party.

The official position of the majority, expressed in a motion of Sandro Pertini (1896–), revealed the PSIUP at its worst. The party's call for a single party of the working class resembled the 1919 decision by the PSI to join the Third International. Both gestures were made with the same blissful ignorance of the consequences. Of course, the delegates who voted in 1945, with the exception of Lelio Basso and his friends, did not intend to merge the PSIUP with the PCI in the foreseeable future. The vote was implemented for the same reason the PSIUP made many of its gestures: it sounded noble and was emotionally satisfying. However, by October 1945 the center-right and center-left of the PSIUP agreed to delay the question of immediate fusion with the PCI. The socialists were becoming increasingly aware that the communists were far better organized, and that fusion would spell the end of the socialist tradition.

The reformists within the PSIUP began to organize to combat the leftward course of the party. By late 1945, the philosopher U.G. Mondolfo, and Giuseppe Faravelli, had revived Turati's old *Critica sociale* with a call for an end to the Unity of Action pact and a return to an autonomous policy. But the reformists in the PSIUP faced the old problem of finding support with an essentially interclass appeal to workers and the lower middle class. In 1945, and for many years thereafter, there was no political space in that direction.

THE FALL OF PARRI AND THE BEGINNING
OF CHRISTIAN DEMOCRATIC RULE

Paralysis within the PSIUP had become most acute just when the Parri government needed solid support to survive. In November 1945, the liberals provoked a political crisis by withdrawing their backing from

Parri's government over the question of the powers of the constitutional assembly and the new demand of the right for a referendum on the question of the monarchy. The Christian Democrats and the communists accepted the crisis without really doing anything to save Parri. The humiliation was especially bitter for the socialists. Nenni was not even seriously considered among the successors. Instead, V.E. Orlando and Francesco Nitti, two relics of the prefascist past, ventured forth—before Alcide De Gasperi put together enough support from the liberals and communists to form a new government in December 1945. Never had the logic of the CLN worked so dramatically against the left, nor had the left been so divided in its response.

The formation of the De Gasperi government marked only one dimension of the left's defeat. Hopes for a constituent assembly which could freely decide the question of a republic also disappeared. Instead, the De Gasperi government deferred the institutional question to a popular referendum. This option favored the right, which could bring to bear the mass of disillusioned southern voters. But the retreat of the left did not stop here. Under terms of a decree of March 16, 1946, the constituent assembly was not granted ordinary legislative power but would be limited to drafting a constitution, setting electoral legislation, and ratifying treaties.

The De Gasperi government also brought about the end of the purge. On January 1, 1946 it announced that career prefects and police officers would replace CLN appointees throughout the North and that the High Commission for Sanctions against Fascism would conclude its work by March 31. The end of the purge and the acceptance of the administrative continuity of the state were inexorably linked. All that remained was for Togliatti, the justice minister, to propose a major amnesty decree on June 8, 1946, which the courts then used as a pretext to free practically everyone. Togliatti, who seemed strangely unconcerned, never used his control of the justice ministry to attack the legal underpinnings of the fascist legal system. The law codes, designed by the fascist minister Alfredo Rocco, remained in effect and were applied and interpreted by the same bureaucrats who had worked under fascism. This seeming inattention to details carried over into other ministries under PCI control. The party designated Mauro Scoccimarro (1895–1972), a staunch militant who understood little of economic questions, as treasury minister. In general, the PCI subordinated immediate reforms to its long-term strategy of turning the party into an accepted national force, even at the price of a conservative and capitalist reconstruction.

THE DEEPENING CRISIS WITHIN THE PSIUP

Whatever the errors of the communists, they at least followed a coherent strategy. The PSIUP merely stumbled from one miserable expedient to another. The party was increasingly consumed by internal disputes centering on the unresolved relationship with the PCI. But this issue only masked the debate over two radically different conceptions of socialism. The battles that had been fought decades ago, between Turati and the revolutionary left, were about to be replayed between Nenni and Saragat. Nenni, pushed by the neomaximalists, Basso and Morandi, succumbed to the illusion of an Italian revolution.

The fall of the Parri government accelerated the process of internal dissolution of the PSIUP. The party split in four directions. On the extreme left, Lelio Basso launched a new version of *Quarto stato* with a demand for a break with the reformists and the creation of a single party of the proletariat. The center left, dominated by Nenni and Morandi, paid lip-service to revolutionary positions but was unwilling to break up the party. On the center right were two veterans, Sandro Pertini and Ignazio Silone. Silone, in particular, sought to stamp his Europeanist and humanitarian socialist ideals on the party, but both men still opted for unity with the left wing. On the far right were the *Critica sociale* group and Saragat, whose strong anticommunism led them to accept a split with the left.

The neomaximalists and ultrareformists also disagreed over party organization. The Leninist Basso called for democratic centralism on the model of the PCI with much less emphasis on electoral competition. He wanted a strong secretariat and a renewed effort on the part of the PSIUP in the factories by the formation of factory cells (*nuclei aziendali socialisti*—NAS). The socialists realized that the PSIUP had lost ground to the communists among the most politically conscious workers. Basso and Morandi feared that the party might lose contact with the labor movement unless it made a serious organizational effort. The influence of the communist model on the PSIUP's left could also be seen in Morandi's decision to launch the Istituto di Studi Socialisti as a counterpart to the PCI's Gramsci Institute. The party's right wing disagreed on almost all counts. Knowing that it was in almost permanent minority status, the reformists refused to strengthen the power of the secretariat to enforce discipline in the name of democratic centralism. They also rejected the factory cell organization of the party as an effort to circumvent the traditional territorial party apparatus.

To succeed in conciliating opposed conceptions of socialism, the PSIUP needed leadership far beyond the capacities of Pietro Nenni. The socialist leader found himself forced to abandon position after position: support for the Parri government, independence within the Unity of Action pact, the role of intermediary between Catholic and communist cultures or between rival camps in the Cold War. The PSIUP under Nenni fell into a one-sided alliance with the PCI and into uncritical support for the USSR. Later, when the Socialist party shifted rightward in 1956, Nenni mustered the same uncritical support for the Christian Democrats and for the Americans.

CONCLUSION

The political struggles of the postwar period revealed the dramatic shift in the balance of power on the left. Before the onset of full dictatorship in 1926, the PCI had been the third party of the Italian proletariat. Throughout the 1920s and early 1930s the communists remained sectarian and isolated. Only with the first Unity of Action pact in 1934 did the PCI break out of its self-imposed limitations. It proved far more adept than the PSI in exploiting the opportunities offered by the united front. In fact, the communists seemed constantly to confound the socialists with their flexible and aggressive tactics.

While the communists moved ahead, the socialists consumed their energies by reopening the old debates which paralyzed and divided the party between 1919 and 1922. Unity of Action once again became the central issue in the internal socialist battles. For a time, the struggle against the Nazis and the fascists seemed to overshadow all other issues, but, quite rapidly, the tendencies of the Interwar period reemerged with new force. The communists were rewarded for their efforts at clandestine organization in Italy. They moved to the forefront of the union and cooperative movement and established a privileged relationship with avant-garde culture. Under Togliatti's leadership, the PCI staked out a solid claim to a share in the national political tradition and became a privileged partner of the right-wing parties. If anything, Togliatti seemed excessively cautious in his political options. He was willing to pay any price for his goal of incorporating the PCI into the new democratic political system.

The socialists were uncertain of the value of their own party. The party operated under no clear strategies or principles. Even when the socialists were correct in opposing concessions to the right, they undercut their own intransigence by refusing to operate independently of the PCI. Nenni and Morandi did little to encourage the Action Party, which might have been a useful ally in creating a third force between rival political blocs. By the end of 1945, it was clear that the PSIUP was heading toward a new split that would almost destroy it as a political force.

CHAPTER 7

The Cold War and the Creation of a Bipolar Political System

TOGLIATTI'S "NEW PARTY" IN 1946

By the end of 1945 the PCI had 1,770,891 members, a fourfold increase over 400,000 at the beginning of the year, and a quantum leap from the mere 10,000 members of 1943. Party rolls continued to grow in 1946 to reach 2,252,170 members in 1947. But the party's substantial organizational effort went well beyond numbers of militants. By the end of 1945 the PCI was flanked by a series of allied associations that dealt with various constituencies and interest groups. Of great importance was the Unione delle Donne Italiane, a feminist organization formed in October 1944. Two-thirds of the active partisan units were communist inspired, which translated into control of the National Association of Partisans of Italy. Other frontist groups were the Association for the Defense of the National School, the Association of Renters and Homeless, the Italy-USSR Association, the Italian Association of Democratic Journalists, the Movement for the Rebirth of the South, and the Italian Union for Popular Sport. The PCI won its most important battle when it gained control of the Lega delle Cooperative, which had been one of the bastions of reformist strength before 1922. The cooperative movement became an important force in the rural economy of much of central and northern Italy. Control of the Lega delle Cooperative, in turn, reinforced communist control of local government in the Red Belt, which stretched over the southern half of the Po Valley, including important centers like Bologna, Parma, Modena, and Reggio Emilia. The PCI used efficient delivery of municipal services and honest government to further enhance its national image.

The various organizations under PCI control allowed the communists direct access to the mass base of the PSIUP. In their enthusiasm for the united front, the socialists had merged their own organizations into those controlled by the communists. As it lost control over its own following, the PSIUP became further dependent on the Communist party. Only the Catholics had a comparable system of mass organization: the extremely powerful Coltivatori Diretti under Paolo Bonomi for small landowners and renters; the Associazione Cristiana dei Lavoratori Italiani (ACLI) to rival the CGIL, the Federation of Catholic University Students, Catholic Action, the Catholic Scout movement, various women's groups, and the Comitati Civici to mobilize the electorate. Both the Catholics and communists had begun to lay the groundwork for these organizations under fascism; their rival networks made Italy a bipolar system by 1946.

THE CGIL AND THE POLITICAL PARTIES

One of the major points of contact between the Catholic, Communist, and Socialist mass parties was the CGIL. The two major challenges faced by the Confederation in the postwar period were to redress the balance between labor and management (which, under fascism, had shifted dramatically in favor of the employers), and to deal with the immediate issues of shortages, unemployment, and inflation. A strong syndical movement, capable of reintroducing the unions into the factory and of gaining some control over work conditions, had to be recreated from the ground up.

The CGIL was founded as the result of a compromise between communists and Catholics in June 1944. After Buozzi's death the socialists were relegated to a minor role, and the Action party was completely excluded from the leadership. The communist Giuseppe Di Vittorio, and the Catholic Achille Grandi (1883–1946), led the CGIL in an uneasy partnership. The formally equal leadership was made more difficult when it became apparent that the communists alone controlled forty percent of the delegates at the First Congress of the Confederation in January 1945. The PCI strategy, however, was to do nothing which would threaten the unity of the labor movement. Therefore its basic compromise with the Catholics held.

The CGIL was discouraged from putting forward too aggressive an agenda. Worker councils were gradually dismantled and the purge of fascist collaborators in industry ended in 1946. As a result, the Confederation never really succeeded in enlarging the role of the factory commissions, which had been the only means of direct access into the single plants and had been reconstituted by the Buozzi-Mazzini accord of 1943. Contracts were still negotiated on the national level with little autonomy for the local unions. These national accords established salary scales by region, sector, sex, and age, but efforts on the part of unions to control piece work or the deadening factory conditions failed by 1947. The left also lost all control over economic policy to the liberal Luigi Einaudi, who pursued strongly deflationary policies. Unemployment rose, forcing the unions further on the defensive as they struggled in vain to protect the existing level of jobs. The CGIL alone could do little to reverse the deterioration of its position. It was subject to the strategies of the political parties that controlled it. The Communists remained reluctant until after 1947 to antagonize the Christian Democrats.

THE CULTURAL STRATEGIES OF THE PCI

The PCI's ties to the main traditions of Italian intellectual and political life were reinforced by the adherence of some of the most influential families of liberal Italy: Giorgio and Antonio Amendola, the sons of the liberal leader who was murdered by the fascists; Concetto Marchesi, a distinguished academic from one of Sicily's oldest families; Antonio Giolitti, the grandson of the Piedmontese statesman, and Lucio Lombardo Radice, the son of the liberal philosopher and pedagogist.

But the PCI again went beyond collecting famous names in order to organize its own sphere of culture on the left. Essential to success was the party's relationship with the Einaudi publishing house and its list of authors. It was Giulio Einaudi who initiated one of the most important cultural events of the entire postwar: the publishing of Gramsci's collected works. The monopoly of the Gramscian legacy was one of the PCI's cultural trump cards until the 1970s.

The PCI appeared open to the newest trends in politics, sociology, literature and the arts. In the summer of 1945 it sponsored *Società*, a review under the direction of Ranuccio Bianchi Bandinelli, Cesare Luporini, and Romano Bilenchi. Luporini was one of Italy's noted existential philosophers. Even more open to new ideas was *Politecnico*, edited by the novelist Elio Vittorini with the express intention of bridging the gap between avant-garde culture and the PCI.

Togliatti, a man of extremely traditional taste in culture, manner, and dress, initially seemed to enjoy the idea that his party was the center of so much intellectual ferment. He even made a conscious effort to welcome a number of leftist Catholic intellectuals into the party, as if to say that this small fringe was a first installment on the incorporation of the entire Italian tradition. Franco Rodano, a Catholic who, much to the dismay of the Vatican, converted to the PCI, prominently figured as one of Togliatti's closest political advisers.

The onset of the Cold War and the renewed Stalinization of culture eventually soured this relationship between the PCI and artists and intellectuals. In 1946 and 1947, when Soviet standards of socialist realism were imposed on the international communist movement, the PCI conformed at the cost of a series of clamorous ruptures with Vittorini's *Politecnico* and with the neorealist movement in film.

THE LEFT AND THE DE GASPERI
GOVERNMENT

The two chief aims of the left in early 1946 were the abolition of the monarchy, and control of the constituent assembly. The referendum on the monarchy was scheduled for June. The parties of the left united in their support for a republic, but a mood of cynicism in the country made predictions difficult. The liberals, monarchists, and a new, rightist Everyman's party (Uomo Qualunque) showed great strength in areas south of Rome. The PCI carefully avoided any repetition of the 1919–1920 experience when the left provoked a bourgeois reaction by its revolutionary rhetoric. Togliatti also sought to keep the Catholic party from shifting more dramatically to the right, especially as it was becoming clear that the Christian Democrats had been adopted by the middle class as its main defense against the left. The PCI's aims continued to be the establishment of democratic institutions and the legitimization of the party as a recognized force within this framework.

A test of the PCI's willingness to cooperate came with the skirmish over economic policy during De Gasperi's first government (December 1945–June 1946). Scoccimarro, the Communist minister of finance, had developed a public works program to stimulate employment, financed by greater taxes on wealth. But, when Scoccimarro clashed with Epicarmo Corbino, the liberal treasury minister, who received the support of De Gasperi, the communists backed down and abandoned their program. Allocation of the costs of reconstruction and strategies of state intervention in the economy were settled in favor of the private sector.

TOWARD THE BREAK-UP OF THE PSIUP

Despite internal wrangling and confused policies, the PSIUP was not a political corpse. In the winter of 1946, at the time of its annual congress, the party had about 850,000 members with strong concentrations in the historic bastions of Lombardy, Emilia, and Tuscany. Moreover, the party had a surprising success in the administrative elections that were held in early 1946 as a preliminary to the referendum. It finished with 24 percent of the votes—only one percentage point behind the PCI. More than anything else, this achievement bore witness to the historic loyalties of the Italian working class.

The Congress of Florence in February 1946 came at a delicate moment for the PSIUP. At its own congress in January, the PCI intervened directly in the internal socialist debates by relaunching the idea of fusion between the two parties with federation as a first step. The offer was designed to provide backing for the Socialist party's left wing, and to keep the PSIUP from straying too far from the overall objectives of the PCI.

During the socialist congress, what promised to be a major debate over ideology ended by clarifying nothing. The victorious alliance of Nenni, Basso, and Morandi gathered about 380,000 delegate votes to an equal number that went to the various motions of the center and right. But disputes over unity of action, future political strategy, and party organization were papered over until after the referendum on the Republic. The split over the alliance with the communists continued to be central. Unlike almost every other socialist party in western Europe, the PSIUP revealed that it was unwilling to assume organizational and ideological independence. In France, where the socialists faced a large Communist party, there was no doubt that the SFIO would continue as a distinct movement with its own values. One of PCI's achievements was that it permanently shook the socialists' resolve about the value of their own party. But the causes of self-doubt stemmed from the lacerating debates between 1921 and 1922, when the PSI split again and again in its effort to define a relationship to the communist movement. Class conflict, the product of extreme social and economic inequality, made the issue of proletarian unity sharper than elsewhere in developed Europe. The memory of how division paralyzed the movement before the March on Rome worked in favor of the movement for a single party of the proletariat and against the development of an English- or German-style social democratic movement. This historical legacy weighed especially heavy on Nenni, who was convinced that the left was defeated only when divided. But it is still surprising that, in an era of Stalinist tyranny over the communist left, the PSIUP could not unify around certain core values, allowing the party to survive as a major force.

THE REFERENDUM ON THE REPUBLIC

The victory for the republic in the June referendum, by a 54–46 percent vote, was a triumph as well for the left parties that had actively campaigned for it, but the results were mixed at best. Every province south of Rome voted for the monarchy, while all the northern provinces voted republican. The number of spoiled ballots cast doubt on whether the republicans won an absolute majority of all votes cast.

The electoral results also altered the relationship between the main political parties. The Christian Democrats with over eight million votes—35.1 percent of the electorate—became the largest party in the country. To the surprise of most observers, the PSIUP finished second with 4,700,000, or 20.7 percent of the votes, to the PCI's 4,300,000, or 18.9 percent. The minor parties finished badly. The Action Party dissolved when its nonsocialist wing, headed by Parri and La Malfa, broke off and joined the Republican party. A socialist remnant under Lussu eventually merged with the Socialist party. A similar process took place within the Liberal party, whose left wing, headed by Manlio Brosio, left the party after the referendum.

The alteration in the role of the Christian Democratic party within the political system had been underway for some time. The Catholic party had won considerable support from small landowners and from the urban middle class. Faced with a choice between offending his basic constituency and conciliating the left, De Gasperi did not hesitate. The communists were extremely attentive to this shift in the political winds. Togliatti moved to bolster the PCI's position within the government. Under no circumstances could the party be ousted until it had consolidated its position as the premier party of the Italian left. The third place finish for the PCI in the constituent assembly elections showed that there was still work to be done on that score.

Although the PCI remained a partner in the new coalition formed by De Gasperi after the elections, Togliatti did not stay on as justice minister. Nenni, as vice president, was the most prominent leader of the left in the cabinet, but the new government represented a breakdown of cooperation between the socialists and communists. The PSIUP remained determined to press for economic reforms, but found itself excluded from any important economic ministry. Despite rising unemployment and an inflation rate of 30 percent, the communists pulled back and offered no support within the government to their socialist allies. Yet pressure from below forced the PCI to adopt a two-track policy: official moderation in Rome, and increased agitation in the streets and factories. With good reason, De Gasperi complained of communist duplicity, although the PCI from its perspective had little alternative.

THE RENEWAL OF UNITY OF ACTION

On October 27, 1946 the Socialist and Communist parties negotiated yet another renewal of the Unity of Action pact. More than ever, the communists used the pact to block the PSIUP from becoming a rival on the left. While the agreement seemed to call for less coordination on the policy level, it pushed local and provincial cooperation to an unprecedented degree, and further weakened the dynamism of the Socialist party. The PSIUP, which took the pact seriously, gave up a large measure of grass-roots autonomy, while failing to advance the goal of fusion between the two movements. The PSIUP and the PCI formed "Peoples Blocs" for a second round of local elections. This time the socialists finished well behind the better-organized communists. Moreover, the Christian Democrats received a warning from their conservative electorate that fraternization with the left in the government would be punished. The Catholics lost to rightist parties in the major cities.

The socialists, especially, were bitter, confused, and more divided than ever about the causes for their party's electoral decline. The glue that held the PSIUP together began to dissolve rapidly. The decision was made to advance the date of the party congress to January 1947. Basso felt that the time was right to press for the expulsion of the rightists; Saragat raised a cry of alarm over the harm which the Unity of Action pact was doing to the Socialist party. It promised to be a grim and unpleasant meeting, and it more than lived up to its advance billing.

THE CONGRESS OF ROME AND THE BREAK-UP OF THE PSIUP

The Congress of Rome, which split the PSIUP into two separate movements, was a victory for Lelio Basso but a defeat for practically every other socialist leader. When the party met in January 1947, there was little hope that unity could be salvaged, but that did not make the break any less painful. Led by Giuseppe Saragat, the majority of reformists walked out to form the Socialist party of Italian Workers (Partito Socialista dei Lavoratori Italiani—PSLI). The very name revealed the power of memory and tradition. It recalled the party formed after 1926 by the exiled reformists in Paris; at that time, however the party had the leadership of Turati and Treves and the legacy of Matteotti behind it. In 1947 little remained of the glorious reformist tradition. The reformists left the PSIUP with high hopes and great individual prestige, but with little preparation. In fact, the party was ironically referred to as the Partito Senza Lavoratori Italiani (PSLI) or Party Without Italian Workers. The PSLI had been formed by two groups bound together by a common hostility to Stalinism and to the abject subservience of the PSIUP to the PCI. However strong the basic motivations, it was not enough to forge a coherent party. The Critica Sociale group, inspired by Turati's vision of parliamentary socialism, was reformist in a classical sense; but the Iniziativa Socialista group was an odd mixture of anticommunism, economic radicalism, internationalism, and neutralism.

The split pushed the PSIUP further to the left without creating a viable social democratic alternative. This failure to strengthen either the right or the left was fatal. The PSIUP was no more capable of defining a viable position after the split in 1947 than it had been between 1943 and 1946. Those who pressed for a single party of the proletariat had always pointed to the persistence of anticommunism and reformism in the PSIUP as the two major obstacles to success. However, it was painfully clear that the communists did not want fusion on the basis of an entirely new party; they merely wanted to absorb the remaining viable organization of the PSIUP. Any other policy would have destroyed Togliatti's postwar "new party."

The greatest responsibility for the socialist debacle fell on Pietro Nenni, who had been so important to the survival of the party in the 1920s but who now seemed unable to sustain the PSIUP as an autonomous party. Unity of action with the PCI was the immediate cause of the break, not because the idea was bad in itself, but because the PSIUP could not defend its own positions within the terms of the pact. The PSI had had the same difficulty during the years between 1934 and the outbreak of World War II, but then the struggle against fascism offered some justification for Nenni's policies. Now, applied without alteration to the postwar era, an uncritical united front was a formula for disaster. Neither Nenni nor Morandi were capable of presenting a united front policy that would maintain the PSIUP as a force between the communists and Catholics or as a reasonable intermediary in the dialogue between the proletariat and the middle class. Because, in practice, they accepted many of the same policies as the PCI, they had no way of countering Basso's call for complete ideological and political fusion with the communists. Finally, the socialist leadership refused to admit that fusion was totally impractical on any reasonable terms. The PCI would have undermined its work of twenty years by accepting a new party. Nor would the impact of a merger have had a positive impact on the political system. Rather, it would have accentuated the existing polarization.

The split within the PSIUP weakened the entire left. The formation of two socialist parties diminished the importance of both. De Gasperi now had the possibility of ousting the communists and socialists from the government, while coopting the PSLI as a cover on his left. A weakened PSIUP also could not contest the supremacy of the PCI on the left. Nenni hoped that the PSIUP would have been drawn closer to the proletariat once it was purged of its reformists, but this did not happen. In January 1947 the party had slightly over 900,000 members. Two years later, the membership was cut in half, just when the PCI solidified around veteran leadership and ever more firmly established its position within the working class. Most of those who dropped out of the newly renamed PSI did not pass over to the reformists. Instead they simply opted out of active politics.

The reformists had even fewer options. The PSLI hoped to become the nucleus of a third force that would alter the political balance of power. But, when De Gasperi ended the three-party government by excluding the left, the PSLI found no support for the third-force idea among the workers, and no room to grow in the polarized political system. Although 52 of the 115 socialist deputies and 7 of the 15 members of the party directorate went over to the PSLI, this victory was achieved solely on the leadership level. Most socialist militants did not understand or, when they did, they rejected the logic behind the split.

When the reformists left the old PSI in 1922, they had a so'id power base in the CGL and in the cooperatives. After 1945 these advantages were lost. The PSLI had no significant standing within the CGIL or in the Lega delle Cooperative or, for that matter, in the country. By leaving the PSIUP the reformists severed themselves from the working class and lost all chance to alter the policies of Italian socialism.

Almost immediately after the Congress of Rome, the socialists changed the name of their party back to the PSI and reaffirmed loyalty to the Unity of Action pact. The new secretary of the PSI, Lelio Basso, emerged as the real victor at the congress. Basso was determined to stamp a new ideological rigor on the PSI. He believed that the political system had already passed the point of class warfare where no middle ground between the proletariat and the bourgeoisie existed. Other party leaders did not necessarily share these drastic conclusions, but they did little to challenge them. Nenni continued to believe that there was still life in the three-party coalition idea. Morandi seemed uncertain that the break with the bourgeoisie had been reached. Centrists, like Pertini and Silone, were clearly dismayed at the outcome, although they remained within the PSI. In Silone's case this desision to stay with the Socialist party would be temporary.

THE DEBATES OVER THE CONSTITUTION
AND THE CRISIS OF THREE-PARTY
GOVERNMENT

The split within the PSIUP allowed De Gasperi to reorganize his three-party government for the third and last time. In the new coalition the left lost control of any ministry that set basic economic policy. The socialists received only Industry and Commerce and Public Works. The PCI, which feared to be associated with economic policies over which it had no control, willingly acquiesced to a diminished power. Togliatti merely hoped to maintain the PCI in the government for as long as possible in order to prolong a formal relationship with the Christian Democratic party. But De Gasperi was under pressure to break with the communists and socialists from his anticommunist and conservative electorate, from the Vatican, which had accentuated its anticommunism, and from the United States, whose aid was vital for any reconstruction.

An immediate split was impossible, however. In February the peace treaty with the Allies was about to be signed (February 10) and the constitution still had not been passed. The status of the 1929 Lateran Treaty—an issue of overriding importance to the Church—remained at the top of the agenda. The Socialist and Action parties, along with much of the lay left and center, opposed inclusion of the treaty, which gave a privileged position to the Church, in the new constitution. The key vote on Article 7 would be cast on March 25 by the communists.

In a move that helped shape the political system for the next two decades, Togliatti instructed his party to vote for the inclusion of the Lateran Treaty in the Constitution of the Republic. This choice, which codified Italian law on such matters as divorce, was again guided by Togliatti's long-term strategy, rather than by short-term considerations. He understood that the days of the coalition were numbered, but he wanted to maintain a privileged relationship with the Catholic Church and the Christian Democrats. There was no question in his mind that the PCI and the Christian Democrats, the two national and mass parties, would have to reach a compromise. A vote against the treaty would have become a permanent source of friction with the Catholics. By accepting the Vatican's position he hoped to remove the religious issue from working class politics. Whatever considerations were behind the PCI's stand, its position was a blow to the other parties on the left who hoped to establish a religiously neutral republic. The article passed by a vote of 350 to 149, with the 103 socialists comprising the bulk of the opposition vote and the 95 communists providing the margin for victory.

Although the left had a relatively strong position in the Constituent Assembly, Togliatti took the position that the constitution would never be a socialist document. At best, it was a transition to socialism. The new constitution did nothing to break up the large concentrations of private power. No real reform of local government was attempted. In 1948 the Corte di Cassazione further restricted the progressive character of the Constitution by deciding that its provisions were of two kinds: those that had immediate force of law, and those that were mere social and economic objectives to be realized in concrete legislation. Nevertheless, from the communist perspective, the Constitution was not totally bad. The PCI liked the strong parliamentary form of government in which some account of the opposition views had to be taken to make the system function.

THE BREAK-UP OF THE WARTIME
COALITION GOVERNMENT

Despite cooperation between the Christian Democrats and the communists on key provisions of the Constitution, De Gasperi ousted the left from his government in May 1947. He acted in response to pressure from industry, from the Catholic party's lower middle-class constituency, and from the United States. Not only was American economic support vital, but, in the struggle with Yugoslavia over Trieste, it did not hurt to ensure the solid support of the western anticommunist governments.

The formation of the PSLI with its substantial parliamentary delegation cushioned the impact of the ouster of the PSI and PCI. By reaching out to the Social Democrats, De Gasperi avoided shifting more drastically to the right. However, the PSLI did not join De Gasperi's new government immediately after the break-up of the three-party coalition. Saragat set his sights on control over economic policy, which was in the hands of the liberal Luigi Einaudi. But pressure from within the party for a share of the political pie led the reformists to join the government in December, 1947. Having abandoned their political virginity, they found that they enjoyed power and patronage so much that they remained a part of most governments thereafter. The formal justification was that the social democratic presence guaranteed secular and democratic politics in what might have been a clerical-dominated government. However correct this stand, it had little to do with socialism.

THE COLD WAR AND POLITICAL LIFE

The expulsion of the communists and the socialists from the government triggered a series of changes that brought the Cold War directly into Italian politics and isolated the left within the parliamentary system. For the PSI the margin for maneuver was drastically narrowed. Nenni mistakenly expected the reconstituted De Gasperi government to fail. The socialists futilely proposed a motion of no confidence in September 1947 with the hope that the other lay parties would join against the Catholics; but the PSLI and the center-right Liberal party refused to vote with the left. Attempts to find support for the third-force idea on the international level were equally unrewarding. Nenni and Basso looked in vain to the British Labour party as an ally in the struggle to keep the international socialist movement from splitting along Cold War divisions. The PSI was not admitted to the Socialist International's Congress held in Zurich in June. Later that summer the PSI's efforts received another blow. In August, Nenni and Basso visited Poland to lend support to the Polish socialists, but the gesture was cut short in September with the proclamation of the Cominform and the subsequent destruction of any pretense of an independent Polish Socialist party.

The organizational meeting for a new Communist International was held in Poland in September 1947. The French and Italian Communist parties, the only nonruling parties to receive invitations, were bitterly criticized for their passivity. The PCI reacted by aligning itself totally with Moscow. The decision to back Soviet positions limited Togliatti's aspirations to play a national role. The PCI remained in almost permanent opposition until the early 1970s. Henceforth it concentrated on building its organizational and electoral machinery, its hold on local governments, and its propaganda campaigns. Politically, the 1948–1960 period saw the party engaged in defensive maneuvers (such as a series of politically motivated strikes and factory occupations which usually ended in defeat and exhaustion for the workers), in order to preserve positions won during the Resistance years. But one important caveat must be added to understand fully the PCI position. Even during the worst days of the Cold War, the Communist party routinely voted for seventy to eighty percent of ordinary legislation and was quite active on the level of parliamentary committees in fashioning compromises. Communist opposition was most visible symbolically when it fought against NATO, the Marshall Plan, and the early steps toward European integration.

In its state of relative isolation, the Unity of Action pact with the socialists took on new importance for the PCI. But, for the socialists, this same Unity of Action pact remained an insurmountable obstacle to an independent role. It forced the Socialist party into the same isolation as the PCI suffered. The PSI rubber-stamped the alliance with the communists and supported the creation of the Cominform, despite the elimination within the communist bloc of the Rumanian Socialist party in January 1948, the Hungarian and Czech parties in June, and the Polish and Bulgarian socialist movements in December. Instead, Nenni blamed the Americans for the polarization that was taking place in Europe. He opposed the Truman Doctrine and became increasingly hostile to the Marshall Plan, just as he would later oppose the creation of NATO. The automatic support the PSLI gave to the American initiatives widened the gap between it and the PSI.

The defeat of the left in 1947 altered the Italian political system. Given the party's basic commitment to the Soviet model, the PCI sided wholeheartedly with the USSR in the confrontation between East and West. The socialists, however, closed the door by themselves. Their continued loyalty to Unity of Action made it impossible for the PSI to act as a bridge between left and center. Little or nothing remained of a third-force alternative. When the National Council of the Action party formally voted to merge with the PSI on October 20, 1947, most of the independents or ex-Actionists had already opted for one or the other side of the Cold War division. Riccardo Lombardi and Vittorio Foa joined the PSI where they played an important role; Tristano Codignola, Leo Valiani, and Aldo Garosci joined the PSLI.

TOWARD THE RUPTURE OF THE CGIL

Difficulties for the labor movement increased as the Cold War political climate became more uncertain. Not only did conditions within the labor market become less favorable, but management used the isolation of the left to attack the gains of the communist and socialist labor unions. The unions fought a losing battle to protect what they had won in the immediate postwar years. The workers councils, set up in the 1944–45 period, were abolished after 1947 and conditions on the assembly line deteriorated. As the Italian economy was integrated into the new international structure, wages for workers were held as low as possible.

High unemployment made it difficult to fight back. Following the wave of political strikes between 1948 and 1950 against the Marshall Plan and NATO, there was a gradual loss of labor militancy.

In 1946, Achille Grandi, leader of the Catholic contingent in the CGIL, began to protest against political strikes by the confederation. When Grandi died in September 1946, his successor, Giulio Pastore, was politically closer to De Gasperi. The expulsion of the communists and socialists from the government made the issue of CGIL politics even more urgent. At the congress of the CGIL in June 1947 the communist faction had 55 percent of the delegates and the socialists 22.6 percent. The Catholics had only 13.4 percent of the membership and their Social Democratic and Republican allies only 2.1 percent and 2 percent respectively. To prevent the CGIL from making life difficult for the government, a compromise was reached in 1947 that demanded a three-fourths majority for political strikes. The battle over Marshall Plan aid tested this understanding. In December 1947 the CGIL refused to take a stand on the issue, but the confederation was badly divided with the Communists and Socialists opposed, and the Catholics, Social Democrats, and Republicans in favor of the American initiative.

UNITY OF ACTION AND THE ELECTIONS OF 1948

By late 1947 the Italian electorate was almost completely polarized. The socialists cast the elections (called by De Gasperi in early 1948) in the context of past struggles against fascism as they appealed for the unity of all left forces against the danger from the right. On December 28, 1947 the PSI and PCI created the Popular Democratic Front to fight the rightist bloc in the 1948 elections.

In courting a direct left–right confrontation, the new Popular Democratic Front contradicted the policy that had been followed by Togliatti since 1944. Between 1944 and 1946 the PCI conceded in order to preserve its position in the government; but now it was forced to fight in opposition under totally unfavorable circumstances. The socialists, who feared that they would lose badly alone, pressed the PCI on the need for the bloc. At the PSI's congress in January 1948 the party voted to form a common list with the PCI. Riccardo Lombardi, Sandro Pertini, and a few others opposed a move that led to defections of the remaining reformists to the PSLI and undermined the image of the party in the minds of the voters. Lombardi argued cogently that, if the electoral bloc did not conquer a majority, the PSI would be crippled as a force able to bridge the gap between the PCI and the DC. Nonetheless, the party's left wing rejected all counsels for caution. In a dazzling display of optimism, Morandi insisted that Italy could elect a Communist-Socialist government and still receive Marshall Plan aid. Nenni argued that the

PSI, weak and uncertain as it was, could act as guarantor of democracy within an alliance with the PCI.

The PCI was in much better shape. In January 1948, at the time of its Sixth Congress, the PCI had 2.3 million members—almost 60 percent in the North, 23 percent in central Italy, and 17 percent in the South and on the islands. It had become the preeminent party of the proletariat. The bulk of its membership was from the industrial working class and from agricultural day laborers. Little support came from the middle classes, but the party had established itself as a national force to be reckoned with and had displaced both the reformist and maximalist traditions in the hearts of the workers with its curious blend of revolutionary idealism and practical reformism.

Despite the seeming prosperity of the PCI, there were serious difficulties. Togliatti, who had always sought to avoid the danger of political isolation, found it forced upon the party. The Italian government was increasingly conservative. The Catholic Church, industry, and powerful agricultural interests had been mobilized against the communists. The party leadership was well aware that the slightest misstep on the national or local level would result in a crackdown on the party. Other pressures came from the Soviet Union where the process of Stalinization of the arts was proceeding rapidly. The PCI had amassed an eclectic coalition of intellectuals and artists. A typical example of this support was Elio Vittorini's relationship with the PCI. Vittorini, the author of several critically acclaimed novels, founded the review, *Il politecnico*, in September of 1945. He wanted to bring the best of the new culture to an Italian audience, but he was also quite close to the PCI. Vittorini's defense of the avant-garde, and his rejection of Soviet criteria for the arts, won a rebuke from Togliatti in December 1946 that was followed by formal rejection in early 1947. Loss of party support forced Vittorini to fold *Il politecnico* by the end of the year.

Despite the shadow cast by the *Politecnico* affair, the highpoint in the relationship between left-wing intellectuals and artists and the PCI came during the elections of 1948. Many intellectuals backed the Popular Front as a way of rejecting the Cold War polarization and confessional politics being imposed upon Italy. For its part, the PCI muted the crackdown on the arts in order to maintain a broad base of support as it took its case to the country. The joint lists of the communists and socialists attracted the support of such cultural luminaries as writers and critics Luigi Russo, Massimo Bontempelli, Salvatore Quasimodo, Cesare Brandi, Sibilla Alerano, Carlo Bo, and Giorgio Bassani; artists Carlo Carrà, and Renato Guttuso; and academics Arturo Carlo Jemolo, Nino Valeri, and Guido Calogero.

The elections of April 1948 became a referendum on the events of the past year. On the one side were the Christian Democrats, the Social Democrats, the republicans, and the liberals. Communists, socialists, and a handful of left independents made up the opposing bloc. The entire context for the election worked against the left. Anti-Americanism, the glue for the coalition, proved ineffective. Using a stick and a carrot, the Americans announced that all Marshall Plan aid would be cut off if the left won the elections. Then the United States persuaded France and Britain to return their zones of occupied Trieste to Italy. Simultaneously, the communist seizure of power in Czechoslovakia in February 1948 led to negative publicity for the PCI during the weeks before the voting. However, the crucial factor working against the left was the swing of the lower middle-class vote in favor of the center right.

The left lost badly in April 1948. The Popular Front took only 31 percent of the votes and 183 seats. Alone, the Catholic party won 48.5 percent of the electorate and 305 seats—an absolute majority in parliament. The consequences of the staggering defeat for the communists and socialists, and subsequently for the entire working class, were enormous. Defeat for the socialists was particularly galling. They had foolishly calculated that the alliance with the PCI would not damage the party; instead, the electorate saw the party as a mere replica of the PCI with no program or principles. A massive defection of support left the PSI with only 40 parliamentary seats—in contrast to the 115 that the PSIUP had before the split, and the 63 that remained in the PSI on the eve of the elections. Communist voters, concentrating their preferences on certain candidates, managed to elect far more candidates than did the socialists on the joint lists. At a hastily called party congress in June, the PSI tried to recover its balance. Basso's strategy of a frontal attack on capitalism, organic unity with the PCI, and the rejection of any parliamentary strategy, had left the PSI in shambles. A centrist faction, headed by Alberto Jacometti and Riccardo Lombardi, took over the leadership of the party with a mission of restoring a base for independent socialist politics. But the party had been permanently damaged. Many of those who had advocated independence were out of the party. Other more radical activists defected to the PCI as the most effective means to achieve change. Membership dropped from 780,000 to 531,000.

There was no easy solution to the ills besetting the PSI. The socialist-communist alliance had left the socialists dependent on the communists within the unions and in many local governments. The Christian Democrats and its allies, with their absolute majority, did not need the mediation of the socialists. For want of a better policy, the new leaders of the PSI reaffirmed the Unity of Action pact in July, but requested the dissolution of the Popular Front.

The inability of Lombardi and Jacometti to find political space between the two blocs became painfully evident when the PSI was ousted from the union of western Socialist parties (COMISCO) on March 4, 1949. The party's left wing was able to reclaim the leadership in a congress at Florence in May 1949. A majority headed by Nenni and Morandi, and strongly backed by the PCI, took 51 percent of the delegates against 41 percent for Lombardi's independent faction and 8 percent for a rightist group headed by Romita (who soon left the PSI for the PSLI). The communists intervened by financing memberships in the PSI, by using the jointly controlled mass organizations to favor the socialist left, and by funneling funds through left socialist federations to allow Nenni to create the review *Mondo operaio* in December 1948.

The centrist Riccardo Lombardi argued in vain that the PSI ought not cut itself off from the other Western European Socialist parties, or commit all its prestige in a hopeless campaign against the Marshall Plan. As an alternative, he suggested that the party work to protect the interest of the proletariat within the western bloc. But these warnings went unheeded as the PSI returned, in 1949, to a policy of almost complete acceptance of communist hegemony: full support for Stalin's trials in the eastern bloc, total hostility to the United States, rejection of Tito's third way. Nenni, who temporarily lost all hope for a third force, accepted the new party line. The party leader cast his lot completely with the left—even to the point of closing the door on possible reconciliation with dissidents of the PSLI (Faravelli, Mondolfo, Mario Zagari) who opposed Saragat's abject pro-Americanism. For his troubles, Nenni took away little more than the Stalin Peace Prize in 1951, which he returned after the Soviet invasion of Hungary in 1956.

Morandi, a dedicated advocate of working class unity, believed the elections confirmed the repressive nature of the capitalist system and of the objective continuity between the Fascist and the Christian Democratic governments that defended capitalism. Under such circumstances the only strategy was to emphasize the unity of the proletariat which, more than a simple pact with the PCI, now seemed vital for the survival of the working class. The independence of the PSI paled in importance to the survival of the proletariat. But Morandi went even further. Rejecting the libertarian instincts that shaped his socialism during the 1930s, he now called for his own version of Basso's centralized Leninist party (although, belatedly, Basso began to have second thoughts). The PSI, however, lacked the sense of historical purpose and the ideological coherence that gave life to the PCI's organizational efforts. More than ever, the PSI under Morandi seemed indistinguishable from the PCI. But even Morandi could never completely transform the Socialist party. Despite the application of Stalinist purges and committees of ideological vigilance during the years when he was party secretary, the PSI never totally broke with its democratic traditions.

CONCLUSION

The period from 1947 to 1949 was one of almost unrelieved bad news for the left. The PCI fell into an isolation never desired by Togliatti. While the party maintained a solid apparatus, it no longer had the same freedom of maneuver that marked its actions from 1943 to 1946. The only firm ally of the PCI was the Socialist party; but the PSI had become a shadow of its former self by a combination of its own errors and by communist deliberate strategy. Two lessons had to be assimilated by the left from the experience of the Popular Front. First, the PSI and PCI did not do as well by merging their forces as they did by operating independently. More important, the PCI had to understand that its policy of using the Unity of Action pact to weaken the PSI undermined the entire left. Only a viable Socialist party could provide the left with a majority; alone, the Communists could not do it. But the leaders of the PSI themselves almost destroyed the party through their rigid and uncreative adherence to the principles of the Unity of Action pact. The experience of the Popular Front left the maximalist tradition clinging to life in a dying party.

CHAPTER 8

The Left in the Years of Centrism, 1948–1960

THE PCI AFTER THE 1948 ELECTION

The years between the elections of 1948 and 1953 were marked by extreme polarization. Conformity was imposed on both sides of the Cold War division, as Italy retreated from the gains made by the left in the new republican constitution. The establishment of a constitutional court, a generalized system of regional government, and the revision of Fascist legal codes were put off. Instead, the government pressed for legislation to control dissent. The Christian Democrats and their allies, with an absolute majority in the parliament, rarely had to negotiate with the opposition. The Socialist and Communist parties were as politically marginal as they would ever be during the years of the Republic.

The economic situation until the boom years after 1958 also worked against the left. Permanent employment in manufacturing rose only 8 percent during the early years of the decade, and unemployment remained high, especially in traditional labor-intensive industries such as wood working, food processing, and textiles. Factory conditions were harsh and primitive. Within the plant, traditional patterns of hierarchy and deference were once again imposed after the upheaval of the Resistance years. A 48-hour, six-day work week was common. After particularly bitter strikes between 1949 and 1951, labor militancy subsided and union membership declined. Employers used lockouts and selective dismissals of political activists to break the unions. Of 164 workers at the Fiat plant who were fired for political reasons between 1949 and 1953, 30 were on the factory internal commissions. The divided trade-union movement became more dependent on political parties and less effective in labor management struggles.

The new period began badly for the PCI. On July 14, 1948 Antonio Pallante, a young rightist, attempted to assassinate Togliatti. When they heard the news, communist militants in the North threatened open insurrection. The CGIL called a nation-wide strike in protest. The vacationing Giuseppe Di Vittorio rushed back to Rome to regain control of the CGIL. Longo and Secchia, in charge of the PCI apparatus, knew that any violence might offer a pretext for greater repression and that no help could be expected from the Soviet Union. Only in a few cities of the North, like Genoa, Turin, and Bologna, did the communists have any chance at even temporary victory.

The news that Togliatti would live eased the tension, but the crisis spilled over into the internal politics of the CGIL. The alliance of communists, socialists, Catholics, and some minority Republican and Social Democratic factions never broke down as a result of the split within the PSIUP because the majority of socialist union leaders stayed with the PSI. The Cold War, Marshall Plan aid, and the elections of April 1948, had a much greater impact. On each of these issues the communists and socialists opposed the Christian Democratic government.

The government, pressed by the Vatican and the Americans, began to work for the creation of non-communist unions. On August 5, 1948 the Catholic factions, led by Giulio Pastore, broke off from the CGIL. Vatican pressure and American money were behind the establishment of a new Catholic-dominated union confederation, which initially took the name of the Free General Confederation of Italian Labor (Libera Confederazione Generale Italiana del Lavoro—LCGIL) in October 1948. Then, in May 1949 the Republicans and Social Democrats also left the CGIL and formed the Italian Federation of Labor (Federazione Italiana del Lavoro—FIL). The Americans failed to engineer a merger between the Catholic and Social Democratic splinter groups. Instead, the Social Democrats and Republicans created the Unione Italiana del Lavoro (UIL) in March 1950. The LCGIL and some members of the FIL merged to form the Italian Confederation of Worker Unions (Confederazione Italiana Sindacati Lavoratori—CISL) which became the major Catholic union organization. By 1950 there were three politically dominated labor organizations (CGIL, UIL, CISL) unable to work together on a common strategy and often acting at cross purposes. Autonomous and company unions appeared to divide and weaken the worker movement further. The CGIL, which had been 55 percent communist, was now 70 percent PCI controlled. The socialist factions found, once again, that they had less leverage within the Confederation. Management, sensing the weakened position of labor, hardened its stand in contract negotiations. The result was a series of bitter strikes that took place in all major industries throughout the years of 1949 and 1950.

The Cold War cut through nearly every aspect of Italian political life. In July 1949 Pius XII excommunicated believing Marxists (i.e. all members of the PCI, its allies and voters, and the readers of the communist press). Denunciations of the red menace rang from every pulpit in Italy, as the Church and the government sought to isolate the Communist Party.

Within the PCI the situation was equally disquieting. Intellectual allies were proving more restive with the controls that were being imposed on the world Communist movement by the Soviet Union. The music critic Massimo Mila attacked the Stalinists for rejecting Prokofiev, Shostakovich, and Khachaturian. Prominent scientists were expelled from the PCI for protesting the Cominform's imposition of the biological theories of Soviet geneticist Lysenko, while the PCI dutifully defended the Soviet scientist. Even Pablo Picasso came under attack; although within the PCI, Renato Guttuso, a prominent artist, defended the Spanish painter against Soviet criticism. There was also a growing coolness between the PCI and prominent neorealist film directors. Lucchino Visconti, Roberto Rossellini, and Vittorio De Sica had been initially greeted with enthusiasm by the PCI as they made the first ground-breaking films in the immediate postwar period.

Until 1949 the alliance between the PCI and intellectuals seemed to hold. Then things began to change. A new sensibility appeared in novels and films as the younger generation of writers and artists abandoned their neorealist beliefs. The PCI seemed culturally less attractive, now that it was under pressure from the USSR to conform. Communist intellectuals, like Emilio Sereni, became Stalinist cultural policemen as they mobilized writers and artists behind the USSR. It was a slow process, but, beginning in the 1950s, writers and artists began to abandon the PCI. Still, the party continued to attract significant support, and in 1951 Togliatti eased tensions by replacing Emilio Sereni with the more tolerant Carlo Salinari as head of the party's Cultural Affairs Commission.

The communist world began to close in on itself. Unable to affect national policy directly, the PCI turned its energies to a series of campaigns against the Marshall Plan, NATO, and the European unification. The party leadership believed that only by a shift in international competition in favor of the USSR could its domestic position be improved. But the PCI's loyalty to the USSR could also be seen as a mirror image of the ardent pro-Americanism of the De Gasperi governments.

The hard line leaders, Longo and Secchia, were in charge of the PCI apparatus during these years. They devoted their energies toward building up the PCI, especially in the South. In 1954 the PCI reached a membership of 2.1 million, overwhelmingly drawn from the workers and peasants. The party had little middle-class support. Under Secchia the organization of the party was rigidly centralized and hierarchical; a combination of Stalinism and reaction to rightist repression. Dissent was strictly limited. When in 1951 Valdo Magnani and Aldo Cucchi, communist parliamentarians from Emilia, attacked the lack of party democracy and overdependence on the USSR, both were expelled from the PCI as Titoist traitors; although Magnani later rejoined when the party took positions similar to his own.

Even Togliatti was not entirely secure during these years. He had recovered from the assassination attempt in 1948, but in August 1950 he had a serious auto accident. The recovery period turned out to be more difficult than anticipated, and in December, Togliatti went to the Soviet Union to recuperate. While in the USSR, Stalin pressured him to accept the leadership of the Cominform and to abandon control of the PCI to Longo and Secchia. It is unclear to what extent Secchia encouraged the Soviets. Like many of the old guard, he had never been in favor of the "new party" which Togliatti had created after 1943. He rallied a majority of the Central Committee of the PCI to support Stalin's request. But Togliatti, who had lived through the Stalinist purges of the 1930s, refused to abandon his base in the Italian party for life in Moscow. After recovering his health, he returned to the leadership of the PCI and began systematically to undermine Secchia's position in the party.

In this effort, Togliatti was aided by a number of external changes. The most important of these was the death of Stalin in March 1953. Inspired by the emergence of a new collective leadership in the USSR, Secchia attempted to turn the anti-Stalin "cult of the personality" argument against Togliatti. The effort backfired. Togliatti had not so much created a cult around himself, as he had gradually withdrawn from the old guard and surrounded himself with younger leaders. Togliatti now proceeded to use these leaders against Secchia in his own version of collective leadership. Then Secchia received a mortal blow when Giulio Seniga, his top aid and head of the party's Vigilance Committee, defected with party funds and important documents on July 25, 1954. Seniga sought to rally the Stalinist true believers against Togliatti's PCI, but even Secchia was forced to denounce him as an American agent. After the Seniga incident, Secchia's days in the party leadership were numbered. In 1955 he was replaced by the more liberal Giorgio Amendola as head of the Commission on Organization.

THE ELECTIONS OF 1953 AND THE "SWINDLE LAW"

The elections of June 1953 were held under quite different conditions from those five years earlier. In 1952 the government proposed a law that gave to the parliamentary list (which won a majority) an extra premium to bring it up to 65 percent of the seats. This legislation, known as the "swindle law," recalled an earlier fascist electoral reform and was designed to perpetuate government by the center right. In November 1952 the Christian Democrats, Republicans, Liberals, and Social Democrats agreed to support the legislation. The law passed the Chamber on January 21, 1953, but the government parties faced serious defections within their own ranks. The electoral law accelerated the emergence of an independent left movement in the area between the Christian Democratic party and the PCI–PSI bloc. Radical democrats and nonparty socialists such as Gaetano Salvemini, Norberto Bobbio, Arturo Carlo Jemolo, Leo Valiani, Ernesto Rossi, Ignazio Silone, and Mario Pannunzio formed a loose group of lay democrats, who delivered their message in such reviews as *Belfagor, Il ponte, Il mondo, Nuovi argomenti,* and *Lo spettatore italiano.* Some within the group were close to the socialists; others, like Silone and Nicola Chiaromonte participated in the pro-American Congress for Cultural Freedom, but they shared a common dislike for the narrow clerical government that had been imposed upon Italy after 1948. During the battle over the swindle law, this group coalesced into an active third force. The jurist Piero Calamandrei and Tristano Codignola defected from the Social Democratic party. Ferruccio Parri broke ranks from the republicans. With other dissidents they formed *Unità popolare* in February 1953.

Nenni, who was an able tactician and sincere democrat despite his many contradictory policies, now actively encouraged the formation of the independent left. Instead of running a common ticket as in 1948, the socialists and communists separately appealed to all those who opposed the new electoral law and the climate of repression that had governed Italy between 1948 and 1953. The strategy paid off handsomely as the Christian Democrats lost 8 percent or two million votes, and all the minor governmental parties emerged weaker. On the right, the monarchists and neofascists gained, but the real change was the recovery of the left. The PCI received 22.6 percent of the vote and the socialists slightly over 12 percent. Combined with the extreme right and the left independents, the socialists and communists prevented the Christian Democrats and their allies from gaining a majority.

THE PSI UNDER MORANDI

From 1949 to 1953 there seemed little to distinguish the PSI from its larger communist ally. Morandi believed that the Social Democrats had absorbed the old PSI tradition and that a new socialist identity would have to be found in alliance with the communists. In a speech in Milan in March 1952, Morandi even argued that Stalin was part of the ideological heritage of the PSI, a view shared neither by Nenni, nor by Lelio Basso. After his failure to lead the party to victory in alliance with the PCI, Basso began to rethink his own version of Leninism and to contrast it with the rigid Stalinism that prevailed in the PCI after 1948.

The problem for the doubters was that the PSI's constitution, adopted in 1949, gave strong disciplinary powers to the secretariat, now in the hands of Morandi. But Morandi's control of the party was not absolute. Nenni, as the historic leader, commanded enormous respect. Moreover, Morandi's concentration on improving party organization met limited success. On paper, membership jumped from 400,000 to 700,000, but these figures were exaggerated and came mainly from the South, rather than from socialism's traditional base in the industrialized North. Morandi wanted to create schools to train party cadres and potential candidates from the ranks of the working class, but what he created was a lifeless bureaucratic structure. Despite the efforts of the party secretary, the PSI remained a traditional party marked by low membership relative to votes, a weak presence in the factories (especially after the factory cell experiment ended in 1954), and a party whose concentration of power fell within a few large federations, the parliamentary delegation and the directorate. One-third of the party members still came from Emilia and Lombardy.

One of the great difficulties for the PSI remained the party's absolute dependence on the PCI. Within the unions Morandi accepted joint lists with the communists. Electorally, in certain areas such as Sicily, the PSI was on the verge of disappearing into communist-dominated Blocchi del Popolo. By 1953, 70 percent of the Socialist-party cadres worked in frontist organizations that were largely PCI controlled. Culturally, the PSI featured Gramsci in its theoretical reviews as often as the communists did. In 1950, while the PCI was promoting its Gramsci Institutes in various cities, the PSI closed down its Istituti di Studi Socialisti.

The influence of the left wing within the PSI reached its peak at the Congress of Bologna in January 1951 when Basso was excluded from the leadership, and Nenni barely avoided a call to merge the party with the PCI. After the congress, Nenni began to define a more independent role for the PSI. Changes within the Social Democratic camp encouraged him to open new political ground between the Catholics and Communists. Saragat's pro-American leadership of the PSLI after 1947 was not popular among all members of his party. Social Democrats, such as Faravelli and Mondolfo, hoped for reconciliation between the PSLI and the independents still within the PSI. In 1949, when Morandi and the left regained control of the PSI, the remaining reformists, headed by Romita, broke off and eventually formed the Partito Socialista Unitario (PSU) with the dissidents from the left wing of the PSLI. The PSU was designed to compete with the PSI, while working to nudge the Social Democratic party over to the left. But Romita used it to strike a deal with Saragat in January 1952 that led to a merger of the PSLI and PSU into the Partito Socialista Democratico Italiano (PSDI). The new PSDI split almost immediately over its support for the "swindle law," when its left wing joined with other independent leftists to form the *Unità popolare* movement. This was the opportunity that Nenni hoped to exploit in 1953.

At the thirtieth party congress in January 1953, the PSI took a small step toward recovering its independent position as an alternative working-class party that would bridge the gap between proletarian and bourgeois Italy. Lombardi argued that there was little purpose in developing a party organization, as Morandi sought to do, if the PSI sought only to mirror ideologically the PCI. Lombardi's reentry into the party directorate, and the reactivation of an autonomous socialist current in the CGIL, symbolized the new drive for autonomy.

After the 1953 elections, Nenni took another step toward reasserting an independent socialist position. In July 1953, speaking to the Chamber of Deputies, he hinted at what would become a totally new strategy for the PSI when he defined the socialist alternative as the insertion of the working class masses into the government majority. In so doing, he indicated that his party would be the privileged intermediary with the Christian Democrats—a role the PCI had always claimed for itself.

The period of detente following the death of Stalin in March 1953 opened new perspectives for the third force idea, but Nenni realized that greater independence from East Bloc positions was necessary if the strategy were to succeed. Foreign policy was a major area over which the PSI had surrendered autonomy in the Unity of Action pact. The united front was based on the willingness of the PSI to accept the USSR as embodying fundamental socialist values. This deference had gone on for so long that it was difficult to reverse. In 1954, and again at the Thirty-first PSI Congress in Turin in 1955, Nenni called for a dialogue with the Catholics; but, for the Christian Democrats, acceptance of a western orientation in foreign policy was the neccessary starting point for any such dialogue.

By 1955 a real impasse had been reached in Italian politics. The left had been excluded from most of the major decisions in domestic and foreign policy. Italy had accepted Marshall-Plan aid and embarked upon an American-oriented economic reconstuction. As a result, the country had opted for the military and political alliance with the United States in NATO, and for the Atlantic and Western European models of economic integration. By 1955 all of these fundamental choices had been successfully made against the votes of the left. Only when the PCI and PSI broadened their appeal, as in the elections of 1953, did they achieve a measure of success. These elections reawakened in the PSI a desire to resume its independence and to redefine its role within the political system.

THE KHRUSHCHEV SPEECH:
DE-STALINIZATION IN THE USSR

The years from 1953 to 1956 severely tested the leadership of the PCI. Despite the victory of the left in preventing the passage of the "swindle law," the elections of 1953 disappointed the PCI. It made few gains in the North; success came in the South, where Giorgio Amendola had charge of the party machinery, and used broad interclass appeals to draw votes to the PCI. Togliatti, ever-sensitive to the shifting public mood, understood that the thaw following Stalin's death might allow the PCI to return to policies that had been successful between 1944 and 1947. At the December 1953 meeting of the party's central committee, he backed Amendola's flexible southern tactic. The jolt felt by the PCI in the factory elections at Fiat in 1955, when it lost control of the internal commission to the Catholic union, added a special urgency to the effort to escape from isolation. In 1955 Amendola's assumption of control over the party's internal apparatus marked a major step away from a rigid Stalinist direction in the party.

The difficulties facing the PCI were not only internal, however. The death of Stalin and the effort of the new Soviet leadership to separate itself from his legacy led to the rehabilitation of Marshal Tito of Yugoslavia, and threw into crisis the leadership cadres that had developed after 1948 in eastern Europe. Few Soviet bloc leaders could adjust easily to the new reality, and changes soon followed in Hungary and Poland. When Khrushchev made his famous report on Stalin's crimes to the Twentieth Congress of the Soviet party in February 1956, the pace of change became irresistible.

The French and Italian delegations to the Soviet party congress were shown copies of the Khrushchev report at the time of the congress; Pietro Nenni was informed of it by the Soviet leader himself. This did not lessen the shock for the socialists who had always supported Stalin as a man of peace. The first reaction of both Nenni and Togliatti was similar. Both tried to minimize the impact of the report. Nenni, in March 1956, placed the excesses of Stalin in the context of the rapid industrialization of the USSR. But Lelio Basso saw the speech as throwing into doubt the monopoly that the USSR heretofore enjoyed as the leading socialist state. Prompted by Basso, Nenni began to make more sweeping criticisms. The socialist leader, as if suddenly recalling his own statements from the 1920s and 1930s about the historic differences between the socialist and communist traditions, argued that the single-party system in the USSR was at the root of the problem. The Twentieth party Congress gave the socialists a sense of purpose and mission that allowed them to set their party off from the PCI, especially in foreign policy and support for the USSR, which represented the foundation for the Unity of Action pact.

Although Togliatti reported on the Khrushchev speech to the PCI's central committee in March and April, debate within the party did not occur until the *New York Times* published the entire report on June 4. In the face of increasing pressure, Togliatti attributed the problems of the Stalin era to too much personal power and to bureaucratic degeneration. It was a typically cautious answer that tried to balance criticism with loyalty to the USSR, but it avoided fundamental issues. Rather than attack the crimes of Stalin, in which he had some role during the purges of the 1930s, Togliatti took the occasion to reassert the autonomy of the Italian model. He used the term "polycentrist system" to describe a new structure for the communist bloc that would be based on the different traditions of various Communist parties.

Individual communists went beyond the position of the leadership. Umberto Terracini argued in the communist daily, *L'unità*, that the Khrushchev report raised questions about fundamental legality within the Soviet Union and urged abandoning the outdated theory of the dictatorship of the proletariat. Fabrizio Onofri of Bologna, one of the young intellectuals who was the pride of Togliatti's new party, resigned from the PCI. He was soon followed by the able economist-politician Antonio Giolitti, who crossed over to the PSI after 1957.

HUNGARY AND POLAND

No sooner had the Khrushchev report been digested than two more crises rocked the communist world. In June the first reports of rioting in Poznan began to emerge from Poland. Changes in Hungary had been underway for over a year, but the internal situation in both countries exploded in September and October 1956. In Poland, the formation of the Golmulka government in September averted outright rebellion, but in Hungary, Imre Nagy, the new prime minister, faced a rapidly deteriorating situation in which the Communist party had lost all credibility. When Soviet troops moved in at the end of October to oust the Nagy government and crush the Hungarian resistance, most of the leadership of the PCI lined up behind the USSR. Only Giuseppe Di Vittorio, the head of the CGIL, expressed the widespead skepticism within the party over the official Soviet version of events. He publicly denied that the Hungarian movement was the work of American agitators. On October 29, 1956, 96 communist intellectuals appealed to Di Vittorio to go to Budapest. A massive exodus from the party took place. Politicians, journalists, artists, academics, and rank-and-file militants left the PCI. In all, Hungary cost the PCI 250,000 members. Some, such as Eugenio Reale and the historian S. F. Romano, joined the PSDI; Giolitti, Furio Diaz and Sergio Bertelli entered the PSI; and many, like Onofri, remained as independents on the left.

After 1956 a whole area of left-wing dissidence was created outside the PCI and would eventually become a constituent part of the new left in the 1960s and 1970s. Journals like *Opinione* of Franco Fortini, Roberto Guiducci, and Gianni Scalia; Giolitti's *Passato e presente*; and Onofri's *Tempi nuovi*, expressed real frustration with the caution of the PCI and served as a bridge for a younger generation of militants whose critique of the PCI and of the entire political system would be more sweeping. Raniero Panzieri, a dissident socialist who became the intellectual guide of the New Left movement for worker autonomy, published *Quaderni rossi*; Piergiorgio Bellocchio edited the *Qaderni piacentini*; Lucio Coletti

La sinistra; and Mario Tronti *Classe operaia*. This dissidence reflected a belief that the official left was too slow to respond to the changes taking place both within Italy and internationally. The Khrushchev Report and Hungary set off the first wave of a phenomenon that threatened to escape control by the PCI.

In December 1956 the PCI met to assess the damage. At the party congress the leadership did all it could to limit debate on the events of the year. As he did after the crisis over the Khrushchev speech, Togliatti used the Hungarian revolt to define more accurately the PCI's own position on its independent route to socialism. While rejecting Terracini's call to modernize ideology by dropping outmoded concepts such as the dictatorship of the proletariat, Togliatti outlined policies that were based on an Italian route to socialism. Without abandoning the party's nominal adherence to revolutionary ideology or its residual loyalty to the USSR, Togliatti simply widened the gap between theory and practice by returning openly to his strategy of building up the PCI within the existing system. The refusal to criticize Soviet actions and de facto establishment policies served to enrage the dissidents on the left and right of the PCI.

THE RUPTURE OF UNITY OF ACTION

In August 1956, Nenni suggested to Pierre Commin, the secretary of the French SFIO, that Commin set up a meeting between himself and Giuseppe Saragat. It was Nenni's most dramatic gesture yet—to create an alternative to the alliance with the Communist party—and he did not even attempt to win the backing of the followers of Morandi within his own party. The meeting between the two socialist leaders took place at the resort of Prolognan, against the background of a rapidly deteriorating situation in eastern Europe. Saragat set a high price for any agreement on future socialist reunification. He wanted precise guarantees for the western orientation in foreign policy, acceptance of NATO, and a formal schism between the PSI and PCI. Although Nenni tacitly admitted that Saragat had been correct about the relationship of socialism and democracy, he was not yet prepared to face another split within his own party on these issues, nor did he wish to deal with specific ideological questions. He preferred to set a concrete agenda for cooperation between the PSI and the PSDI in ending centrist government. To achieve this goal, Nenni was ready to offer two major concessions. The PSI would never form a government solely with the PCI in the event that the left won a majority. Nenni stated this indirectly when he told Saragat that the United Front was no longer valid as a policy, and that the country would not accept a PSI-PCI government. Second, he declared that the PSI was prepared to respect Italy's alliances. Although he had broken with the united front strategy, Nenni understood that he could not alter the policies of the PSI overnight. Thus, he sought to exploit new opportunities for his party without raising too many issues.

The Hungarian crisis in October forced Nenni to go further then he might have in August in breaking with the united front. After Hungary, Nenni returned his Stalin Peace Prize and began to speak of socialism and communism as operating in two different ideological worlds. Years of subservience to the PCI fell away in Nenni's speech to the parliament on November 12, 1956, which attacked the USSR for its actions in eastern Europe. But the socialists could only go so far. A sizable portion of the PSI rejected the break with the communists. Moreover, the PSI had prepared no alternative within many of the frontist organizations. Finally, the failure at Prolognan demonstrated how difficult it was for the leaders of the PSI to develop a basis for cooperation with the PSDI.

The PCI responded cautiously to these efforts to reorient socialist policy. Togliatti tried to slow down, but could not stop the momentum for change in the PSI. In October 1956 he offered to replace the Unity of Action pact with a simple consultative agreement. When this was signed in November, an era of socialist-communist relations, dominated by futile efforts to overcome the split that had taken place at Livorno more than thirty years earlier, finally ended. The communists still counted on the left wing of the PSI to curb Nenni's autonomist faction, which now sought to reintegrate the PSDI and to begin a new relationship with the Christian Democrats. The PSI's left wing (Raniero Panzieri, Tullio Vecchietti, Lelio Basso, and Vittorio Foà) gambled that the process of de-Stalinization within the PCI would proceed rapidly enough to offer an alternative to Nenni's move to the right. But within the socialist left, there was little agreement. Vecchietti headed those socialists dubbed "carristi" (after the term for tanks to recall their support for the Soviet invasion of Hungary), who favored the old relationship with the PCI and with the USSR. Unfortunately the arrest and execution of Imre Nagy, and the new Soviet attacks on Tito, promised little for the future. Basso, after years on the fusionist left, now moved closer to Riccardo Lombardi, who advocated true independence for the PSI. Others, such as Panzieri, rapidly evolved toward more revolutionary schemes for direct worker control, which would eventually take them out of the PSI and into various "new left" movements.

The persistent inability of the PSI to define clearly a new political strategy was evident at the party congress in Venice in February 1957. Nenni's autonomists managed to end unity of action with the PCI, but the left countered by limiting the extent of the policy changes which might have been drawn from the break with the communists. Though no majority existed for any policy, Nenni continued to redefine the role of the PSI within the political system. He would be aided by a rapidly changing economic and social context, as the Italian economic miracle began to take hold.

THE IMPACT OF THE ECONOMIC MIRACLE

After World War II, Italy continued to have a large state sector that had been inherited from the bank and industrial takeovers by the Fascist government during the depression. At the beginning of the 1950s, state holding companies such as the Istituto per la Ricostruzione Industriale (IRI) controlled 62 percent of iron production, 60 percent of cast iron, 42 percent of steel, 25 percent of electrical energy, 80 percent of ship building, and 60 percent of arms manufacturing. This large state sector that had been organized in a network of state and parastate firms—the IRI which controlled much of heavy industry, the ENI which was the oil trust, the IMI in banking, and the RAI-TV which controlled radio and television—was a major source of political as well as economic power. It became a powerful weapon in the hands of the Christian Democratic party which ran it after 1956 through the Ministry of State Participations.

The economic system that survived fascism and was carried over into the Republic was cumbersome and relatively inefficient. Beginning in the mid 1950s, however, Italy experienced the most profound economic changes in its history. The GNP rose at an average of 6 percent per year. Individual income, which increased three times between 1860 and 1960, saw half the gain come between 1950 and 1960. The boom was fueled by a 10 percent average annual rate of gross investment. Export industries led the way, spurred by the development of a European free-trade economy, and by relatively low wages and high industrial unemployment, which allowed investment and profits to far outstrip labor costs.

The alterations in Italian society were just as profound as those in the economy. There was a flight from agriculture and a massive restructuring of the rural economy. Rapid growth widened the gap between North and South and created the slums that mushroomed around the great northern cities. It also led to a speculative boom in urban land values and a tremendous shortage of housing. The new demands on urban centers put greater pressure on the system of public health, schools and sanitation.

THE CRISIS OF CENTRIST GOVERNMENT

These changes were not long in finding their way into the political system. A new generation of Catholic leaders, such as Amintore Fanfani and Aldo Moro, entered politics less bound by rigid Cold-War dichotomies. Fanfani emerged on the political scene in the mid 1950s, promising a more activist and dynamic approach to government than had been achieved under the center-right coalitions, even if this meant enlargement of the governmental majority toward the left. Such overtures found a ready acceptance in the PSI. As early as 1953, Pietro Nenni revealed a willingness to work with the Catholic party and had sided with the Fanfani group within the Christian Democratic party by backing the election of the leftist-Christian Democrat, Giovanni Gronchi, as president of the Republic in 1955. After the failure of the Unity of Action pact, both the Social Democrats and the Christian Democratic left sought to lure the socialists into the orbit of the government parties. But the PSI faced some fundamental choices. How far did it want to move toward the center? Did the party wish to continue to compete with the PCI for working-class votes, or did it wish to compete for new untapped sources of electoral strength among the new middle class? Finally, what kind of an accord did the PSI hope to reach with the Christian Democrats?

The elections of 1958 provided a partial answer for both the Catholic and Socialist parties. The Christian Democrats, in 1958, gained votes mainly from the smaller parties on their right. The Democrazia Cristiana went from 40.1 percent to 42.4 percent of the electorate, while the PSI jumped from 12.7 to 14.2 percent. The PCI, which expected to do badly, held to its 1953 levels. The minor governmental parties suffered setbacks that increased their discontent with the coalition governments of the 1950s. In fact, within the PSDI, criticism of Saragat's centrist politics led to the defection of several notable Social Democrats, such as Giuseppe Faravelli and Mario Zagari, leaders of the 1947 split, and Matteo Matteotti. After the elections, Fanfani, the secretary of the Catholic party, launched the idea of dropping the right-wing Liberal party, and of creating a Christian Democratic-Republican-Social Democratic coalition as a bridge to a formal government with the PSI. He was, however, blocked by right-wing opposition within his own party and in March 1959 ceded the secretariat to the diplomatic Aldo Moro. But Moro, even more than Fanfani, was committed to the idea of an opening to the left. As one of the most prominent leaders of the *dorotei*, the largest faction within the Christian Democratic party, he was in an ideal position to push his party toward the left. Even if movement toward an understanding between the socialists and catholics temporarily became stalled, a return to the old center-right coalitions of the late 1940s and early 1950s was out of the question. The result, in 1959 and 1960, was a series of brief temporary parliamentary expedients that culminated in the disastrous Tambroni government of April 1960, which survived in parliament with neofascist support until it was ousted in July on a wave of popular protests and strikes.

Although the socialists seemed to be rewarded in 1958 for their move to independence, the new course was far from universally accepted within the party. At the congress of Naples in January 1959, a three-way division appeared in the PSI. On the right, Nenni and his allies favored a dialogue with Fanfani. On the left, Vecchietti called for a resumption of united front. The centrist Lombardi urged tough negotiations with the Catholics on concrete programs and reforms. In practice, however, Lombardi agreed with the right wing of the party that the future lay in a dialogue with the Catholics. He implicitly accepted Nenni's position that a government with the PCI was impossible and that no alternative to the rule of the Christian Democrats was possible in the immediate future. Nenni and Lombardi disagreed fundamentally on the terms under which the understanding with the Catholics would be reached, but not over the need for some accord. At the congress of Naples, the left mustered all its resources to stall an understanding with the Christian Democrats. Nenni, who was unable to command a majority for an opening to the Catholics, temporarily lost his majority to the combined factions of the left (Vecchietti and Basso). The disarray within the Socialist party and the unsettled conditions within the Catholic camp contributed to the crisis which surrounded the Tambroni government in 1960. Once Tambroni's failure proved that there was no way to return to the past, the long awaited "opening to the left" was at hand.

CHAPTER 9

The Opening to the Left: New Beginning or False Start

Domestic and international developments that took place after 1955 made possible the alliance between the Christian Democratic and Socialist parties. The death of Morandi in that year, followed the next year by the Khrushchev speech, Hungary, and the rupture of the united-front pact, combined to push the PSI toward the center. Similar changes took place within the Christian Democratic party, beginning with the election of leftist Giovanni Gronchi to the presidency in 1955, the emergence of Fanfani and Moro, and concluding with the Tambroni crisis of 1960. No practical center-right majority existed, as it had in the early 1950s, unless neofascist and monarchist votes were included. Even within the Social Democratic party Saragat was being pressed for an understanding with the PSI.

The changing attitude of the United States was another decisive factor. By 1960 some American diplomats saw the opening to the socialists as inevitable and were able to influence the new Kennedy administration which seemed sympathetic to moderate reformism. The death of Pius XII, who epitomized the spirit of the Cold War, removed another obstacle. The papacy of John XXIII opened a period of liberalization within the Catholic Church. Finally, the attitude of the business community slowly changed as a result of the "economic miracle" and entry into the European Economic Community in 1957. Industrial giants, like Fiat, which controlled the influential Turinese daily *La Stampa*, favored an opening to the PSI, as did Enrico Mattei, the powerful head of the state oil trust, ENI, who lined up the newspaper, *Il Giorno* of Milan, behind the venture.

When Tambroni fell in July, Aldo Moro began to work for the formation of a centrist government led by Fanfani and made up of the Christian Democratic, Republican, Social Democratic, and Liberal parties. Unlike the classic center right coalitions of the 1950s, Fanfani's government would also have the parliamentary support of the PSI. But the process turned out to be slow and difficult. Within the Catholic party, the right, backed by Catholic Action and Cardinal Siri of Genoa, mobilized against any understanding with the PSI.

Progress came first on the local level. By January, 1961, Catholics and socialists had formed municipal alliances in Milan, Genoa and Florence. Then, in September 1961, a pact was reached for the Sicilian regional government. Although eventually forty such regional and local coalitions were worked out, there was a limit to local government cooperation. The Catholics wanted the socialists to abandon all local alliances with the PCI— a move that would have radically altered the balance of power in much of North and Central Italy. The socialists flatly refused.

Both the Catholic and Socialist parties recognized the need to embark on a program of reforms. The boom created too many social and economic problems, but, for the first time, it opened the possibility of resolving long-standing inequalities that plagued Italian society. The socialist Congress in March 1961 gave Nenni a mandate to negotiate with the Catholics for a program of concrete reforms. Then, at the congress of the Christian Democratic party in January 1962, Moro reaffirmed his faith in the center-left solution. In a gesture to appease American fears, Nenni contributed an article to the journal, *Foreign Affairs* in January 1962, indicating PSI acceptance of Italy's membership in NATO.

Finally, on February 2, 1962, Fanfani resigned as prime minister in order to form a new government that would have formal socialist support (although not yet full PSI participation). The program for this first step towards a center-left coalition called for regional government, reform of laws dealing with public order, a unified school system to age 14, reform of the sharecropping contracts, and the nationalization of the electrical power industry. This latter point was a test of the center-left's determination not only to break up a concentration of private power or to allow for cheaper energy rates, but to put in the hands of the state a powerful instrument for controlling investment decisions.

When the new Fanfani government presented itself to parliament, the PSI still abstained. Suspicion persisted on both sides. During the spring elections for a new president of the Republic, the PSI joined the rest of the left in backing the Social Democratic leader Giuseppe Saragat, while the Christian Democrats successfully advanced the conservative Antonio Segni. In June, however, the law on the nationalization of the electrical industry began its parliamentary itinerary and finally passed in the fall. The Fanfani government also secured legislation to create an autonomous region for Friuli-Venezia Giulia and to establish an anti-Mafia commission. In May 1962, Ugo La Malfa of the Republican Party presented to parliament his "Additional Note" to the annual economic report of the Bank of Italy. La Malfa, who often expressed the views of the more progressive sectors of industry, backed the new agenda of the center left by calling for state planning to deal with the distortions caused by the boom.

With the passage of energy nationalization the PSI had reached a crossroads. Two groups composed the majority in favor of the center-left: Nenni's autonomist faction and the center, headed by Antonio Giolitti and Riccardo Lombardi. After breaking with the PCI in 1957, Giolitti began to formulate a socialism to deal with the economic prosperity and consumerism that were just beginning to spread into Italy. Absorbing the economic theories of Keynes into his own socialism, Giolitti outlined a regulated market economy to a PSI that had heretofore lacked an adequate economic theory. Instead of making yet another ritual bow before Marxist orthodoxy, he suggested that the socialists attempt to regulate and shape the neocapitalist system through control of investment and the wise use of economic and fiscal policy.

Lombardi reached similar conclusions about the need to plan for structural reform as a step to a left-wing government. Structural changes would highlight the contradictions between the positions of the Christian Democratic party and its essentially conservative capitalist base. The reforms themselves would create a certain momentum from which it would be difficult to draw back. Lombardi argued that the PSI had to be willing to withdraw at any moment from the center-left alliance and shift back to the left if that were necessary to put pressure on the Christian Democrats. He was far more reluctant than was Nenni to abandon the PSI's former identity by entering the center-left coalition. From 1943 to 1960, the PSI had remained true to the socialist principles that had inspired it. The party continued to be emotionally maximalist. Right or wrong, its political options, as set by Basso or by Morandi, had been dictated by a sense of idealism. In breaking with this past, Lombardi wanted to ensure that the PSI would balance benefits and risks in the new alliance. Optimistically, if an aggressive center-left strategy were to fulfill its promise, it might split the Catholic party and allow the PSI to expand its political base.

If Lombardi's idea of the center left was aggressive, Nenni's was much more defensive and cautious. Those in the PSI who followed the old party leader responded more to political than economic considerations. The stress on programs and planning, so dear to Giolitti and Lombardi, was not shared by most socialists, who worried about immediate political problems. Nenni, although interested in planning, feared a shift by the Catholic party back to the right, which would bring to power an even more repressive government than that faced by the working class between 1948 and 1953. Thus, Nenni wished to protect the institutions rather than force them in new directions. Lombardi hoped to initiate a crisis between progressives and conservatives in the Christian Democratic Party; Nenni felt that Catholic unity was vital to the success of the center left and was willing to concede much to achieve it.

A third option emerged out of the crisis of 1956 that was critical of the Soviet Union, the PCI, and the path traced by Giolitti or Lombardi. These socialists went back to the most libertarian ideas of Morandi in the 1930s, who sought to create a socialism that would arise out of autonomous worker organizations. Morandi was unable to achieve much during the early 1950s as secretary of the PSI, but in 1957 Panzieri and Libertini published their "Sette tesi sul controllo operaio," which called on the PSI to accept a radical leftist course. Their new strategy was based on three points: a stress on marxism as a doctrine of worker autonomy; violent hostility to the Italian system of neocapitalism and to the bourgeois values of consumerism that were behind it; and a desire to base the new organization of the socialist movement on factory level worker organizations. Panzieri offered no technocratic solution, as did Giolitti and Lombardi, but rather sought a break with parliamentary and bureaucratic solutions of all sorts. A substantial part of the PSI had always been attracted by this idea. Basso and Morandi in the immediate postwar, Morandi during his secretaryship of the PSI in the 1949–1955 period, and now Panzieri in the late 1950s, urged the PSI to find political space in the areas that were ignored by the PCI when the communists accepted the national and parliamentary strategy outlined by Togliatti in 1944. Panzieri felt that the boom had created a new situation with which no party, including the PSI, seemed willing to deal. When Panzieri found himself unable to persuade the majority of the party, he broke with the PSI and moved toward the extreme left where he found an audience in the student movement and among the restless young workers, who rebelled against both the capitalist system and against the solutions offered by the communist-controlled CGIL.

However, within the PSI the more cautious strategy of Nenni won the day. Nenni had no grand design for politics, but acted by intuition and short-term tactics. Now, in the center-left, the PSI found itself drawn into a policy of cooperation that diminished the party's own sense of purpose. The center left failed to realize many of the possibilities which had been inherent in the strategy. The Catholics, backed by the American progressives in the Kennedy administration, wanted to use the alliance with the PSI to block permanently the progress of the Communist party, but, instead, the PCI gained votes. Equally disappointed were many socialists, who wanted the center left to undermine the Catholic party and open the way for a left alternative that would involve the PCI. None of these expectations was achieved. The center-left coalition governments seemed to weaken both the Catholics and the socialists and to strengthen the communists, but these electoral shifts were not so pronounced as to force a real change in either direction.

The socialists hoped that reforms would generate new economic growth and investment. In turn, new revenues would pay for schools, housing, and other social services that were called for in the program. Reforms would create their own momentum and lead to an organic alteration of the capitalist system. The socialists also gambled that the working class would accept improvements in noneconomic areas and would not absorb the potential investment surplus in new wage demands. As it turned out, neither of these premises worked. The workers greeted the arrival of the PSI in the government with aggressive wage demands. The pent up frustration at not fully sharing in the gains of the economic boom exploded by 1962. To make matters worse, it soon became clear that one reform did not automatically lead to another, so that nothing could generate the necessary momentum.

Paradoxically, most of the concrete gains for the center left came during the Fanfani government of 1962 when the PSI remained outside the government. Limited regional government, the introduction of a unified school to age 14, and the nationalization of the electrical industry, came with relative ease, but by early 1963 a limit had been reached. Stalled in parliament were laws for general regional government, for the reform of sharecropping contracts, and for planning of urban land use. Moreover, just as the first true center-left government was about to be formed at the end of 1963, the economic boom came to an abrupt end. The growing economic crisis diminished the margin for accommodating worker demands and led to confrontation with organized labor.

LABOR AND THE ECONOMIC BOOM

The 1950s had been difficult times for the Italian labor movement. The bitter fruits of the splits in the CGIL during the 1948–1949 period were harvested in the mid-1950s, when the CGIL lost its majority on the internal commission at Fiat to the Catholic CISL, which, in its turn, was beaten by a company union. Negotiations for national contracts often ignored local grievances, a fact taken advantage of by management to encourage dissident union activity. Employers dismissed union activists and handed out anti-strike bonuses. The unions were also drawn more completely into the political orbit. The UIL and CISL were tied to parties that were almost constantly in the government and caught up in Cold-War politics. On the other side, the CGIL was completely dominated by the PCI. By the end of the decade, the three major confederations faced serious organizational obstacles. Local and provincial unions were underfinanced and understaffed. No dues check-off system existed to ensure steady income, and the unions received less than half the dues owed them. A decrease in union membership made financial problems even worse.

At the beginning of the 1960s, the unions had much to prove and could not afford to be complacent about demanding a fair share of the economic boom. Moreover, several changes had taken place in the work force that altered the balance in favor of the unions. A new young generation of workers, uninterested in the old splits of the 1940s, arrived in the factories. They seemed less fearful of losing jobs in a period of economic expansion. The new worker attitudes inevitably affected the unions themselves. Quite different methods of negotiation emerged. In 1959 the three metal-worker unions held a joint strike, and in December 1960 they won from Intersind, the association of state-controlled industries, the right to company-level bargaining. These local negotiations allowed fresh leadership to rise within the unions. The new decade also saw a decline in religious polarization and a weakening of the ties that bound the UIL and CISL to the government parties. All three confederations competed to represent the new workers who moved from the rural areas and the South to the industrial cities of the North.

By 1962, just as Fanfani formed his first government with outside support of the PSI, worker demands led to a major wave of strikes in both the public and private sectors for increased wages and better working conditions. Wage demands cut into profits and investments. In 1962 and 1963 labor costs went up by 35 percent and the growth in demand translated into serious problems. Although the Gross National Product jumped a healthy 5 percent and industrial output increased in 1963 by 8 percent, consumer demand also rose by 8 percent, leading to a surge in imports and resulting in a balance of payments deficit. Government expenditures also led to a parallel growth in the budget deficit. The Bank of Italy called for severe reductions in public expenditures, for a balanced budget, limitations on salary increases, and restrictions on credit—all of which were at odds with the PSI's program for structural reform. In 1963 Ugo La Malfa, the influential budget minister, now argued that planning and structural reform demanded a simultaneous incomes policy to hold down wages. The newly militant unions rejected this and began a new wave of strikes in 1963 and 1964. Salary increases now began to outstrip productivity. The bitter industrial conflicts that pitted workers against police put further pressure on the PSI to produce immediate gains before they opted formally to join a government.

THE OPENING TO THE LEFT

The national elections of April 1963 served as a warning that the center-left idea would be no panacea for the ills besetting the political system. During this campaign the Vatican took an uncharacteristically aloof position. Pope John XXIII granted an audience to Khrushchev's daughter and son-in-law and published the reformist encyclical *Pacem in Terris*. The electoral results revealed a strong advance for the communists; by moving from 22 percent to 25.3 percent in 1963 they clearly recovered from the crisis of 1956. But neither the socialists nor the Catholics did as well. The PSI dropped from 14.2 percent in 1958 to 13.8 percent. Conservative voters punished the Christian Democrats by moving to the right-wing Liberal party, which had opposed the center-left. The Catholic party lost four percent, dropping from 42.4 percent to 38.3 percent, which the Liberals picked up as they moved to 7 percent. Only the Social Democrats, who increased from 4.5 percent to 6.1 percent, gained from favoring the rapprochement between socialists and Catholics.

The elections of 1963 marked an involution of the political situation. The two major parties of the center-left coalition had reason to be far more cautious and defensive. Lombardi urged the PSI to hold back and wait for better terms. Nenni, who feared the potential for a shift to the right, resolved to press ahead with the center-left experiment. To force a change of direction, Lombardi would have had to ally with the extreme left of the party, but it offered only subordination to the PCI, which Lombardi had always opposed.

In May 1963 Aldo Moro, the secretary of the DC, attempted to form a new government with the formal participation of the PSI. Moro was determined to succeed where Fanfani failed by forging the first center left coalition. Perhaps the most complex and ambitious of the postwar Catholic prime ministers, Moro genuinely believed that the political system had to be open to the left. The inclusion of the socialists was part of a larger strategy that he hoped would contain the growth of the PCI. Only later, when the center-left formula bogged down, did Moro shift to the more daring alternative of bringing the communists within the sphere of governmental parties. The second stage involved great risks and eventually cost Moro his life.

Nenni clearly favored entry but could not persuade a majority of the central committee. Unable to win socialist support, Moro withdrew in favor of a conservative Catholic, Giovanni Leone, who formed an interim government without socialist participation. The Leone government was merely "a vacation ministry" to get through the summer months. By autumn, the opening to the PSI was again on the agenda. This time, the PSI decided to join the government at its party congress in October, 1963, but Nenni's autonomist majority was fatally weakened by the opposition of Lombardi, who would only accept the strategy as a step to socialism, and by the defection of the party's entire left wing. Many leftists had never accepted the break with the PCI and could not tolerate the center-left. As happened so often in the past, incompatible visions of the nature of socialism led to yet another split. The left, headed by Lelio Basso and Tullio Vecchietti, formed the Partito Socialista Italiano dell'Unità Proletaria (PSIUP) on January 12, 1964. The new party cost the PSI 26 deputies and 11 senators, as well as between 70,000 and 100,000 members from the most proletarian sectors of the party. On balance, the creation of the PSIUP made the PSI less of a worker movement and more of a party of office holders and electoral opportunists. But the PSIUP itself never found sufficient political space between the Socialist and Communist parties. It became a party of political purists who could neither accommodate the neocapitalist reality, nor expand its base by initiating a dialogue with the young disaffected workers and students. As time went by, the PSIUP became an electoral adjunct of the PCI. Within the PSI, Lombardi and his group, now the left wing of a diminished party, fought a lonely and losing battle against Nenni's center-left strategy.

The first true center-left government, formed by Aldo Moro on December 4, 1963, lasted only a few months before it broke down over differences over economic issues. The socialist budget minister, Antonio Giolitti, was a prime architect of the policy of structural reforms, who firmly believed in an aggressive policy of public-sector investments. He was blocked by the Catholic party, and by the Bank of Italy, which pressed for an anti-inflationary program. These and other differences between Christian Democrats and socialists resulted in the fall of the first Moro government in June 1964.

A second coalition, put together by Moro within a month, also faced tremendous obstacles. Not only were the two socialist leaders most associated with planning and real reform, Giolitti and Lombardi, were outside the government, but the political climate in Italy began its long slide toward political violence and subversion of parliamentary institutions. In early 1964, General De Lorenzo, the head of Italy's security agency (SIFAR), developed emergency plans for a state of siege that included the arrest of key political figures and the occupation of vital communication centers. The opportunity seemed to present itself during the crisis of the first Moro government. In July, at the request of Antonio Segni, the President of the Republic, a meeting was held among De Lorenzo, Moro, and the secretary of the DC, Mariano Rumor. It was widely believed that Moro was pressured to dissolve parliament and to hold new elections that were opposed by the left. Moro then used the threat of rightist intervention to push Nenni, who had been informed of the plans for a coup, toward settling on terms favorable to the Catholic party.

The new Catholic-socialist government had almost no chance. Restrictive economic policies brought on a recession and continued to limit any significant reforms. But the summer of 1964 brought two events that again changed the context within which the left operated. On August 7, 1964, President Antonio Segni had a stroke and was forced to resign. Two weeks later, on August 21, Togliatti died. The new leadership of the PCI was immediately presented with an opportunity to coordinate its policies with the other parties of non-Catholic center and left. The elections for president in December 1964 reopened the battle between the Catholics and the lay parties. A united left once again presented Giuseppe Saragat as its candidate for the presidency. Saragat emerged victorious with communist support, and new options were presented to the PCI, which had been largely excluded from the political game after 1948.

THE PCI AND THE OPENING TO THE LEFT

After 1956 the PCI faced multiple challenges. There had been no significant threat to the party's predominance on the left since the collapse of a potential alliance between the Action party and the PSI during the resistance years. But the meeting between Nenni and Saragat in the summer of 1956, and the formal split between the PSI and PCI after Hungary, posed a new challenge. Within its own ranks the Communist party faced substantial dissidence for the first time. The abject support from the PCI to the Soviet invasion of Hungary was unpopular. The "Manifesto of the 101," a protest signed by leading communist intellectuals, called for greater liberalization of interparty debate. Membership in the party and its youth organization (FGCI) began to decline. From the 1956 high of over two-million party members in the PCI, and about 350,000 in the FGCI, membership fell to about a million-and-a-half in the PCI, and 154,400 in the FGCI by 1966. The number of factory cells dropped from over 10,000 to 4,100 in the same time period. While it still remained the predominant party of the Italian working class, the PCI was not winning the allegiance of younger workers or the new white-collar employees. While the percentage of older workers and pensioners increased in the party, a new radical youth movement was growing in the early 1960s outside of the PCI.

The Italian communists also operated in a new international context. The movement for European unification, relaunched after 1956, led to the creation of the Common Market in 1957. The initial communist reaction was relative hostility, but the European movement proved durable and successful. Yet, the party had opposed the creation of Euratom in 1957, and had been hostile to the Common Market. Despite his political tactics, Togliatti had always adhered to a rigidly orthodox view of capitalism. He never revised his belief that Italy's backwardness was the result of a semi-feudal economic system incapable of producing any real progress. This vision of limited Italian potential could not adjust to changes caused by the economic miracle or Italy's integration into the Atlantic and European economic communities. After the late 1950s and early 1960s, the changes in ordinary life were too evident to be ignored. The communists had to modify their ideology to stress the quality of development. In 1962, at a conference on the "Tendencies of Italian Capitalism" and at the party congress in December, there was much discussion of economic planning. The PCI rapidly adjusted to the new European reality by altering its position with regard to the European economic community in an effort to avoid isolation from the most dynamic aspects of Italian political and economic life.

Although relations with Tito improved after 1956, the PCI remained anchored to the USSR until after the beginning of the Sino-Soviet split in 1960. The break between China and the USSR, revealed in November 1960 at the Moscow meeting of communist parties, opened new possibilities for autonomy within the socialist camp. Such logic was attractive to the PCI.

The improvement in relations between the United States and the USSR during the Kennedy administration also favored the PCI. The Italian communists needed a relaxation of tension to develop room for maneuver within a polarized political system. They had lined up behind the USSR during the Hungarian crisis, but this would not be the case in the future. At the Soviet party Congress in October 1961, further revelations about Stalin's crimes led to a new round of criticism of the Soviet system within the PCI. During the Tenth party Congress of the PCI in December 1962, Togliatti defended the USSR in the dispute with Albania and China, but the PCI also made it clear that it opposed the excommunication of China as a violation of the notion of polycentrism.

On a trip to the USSR during the summer of 1964 to persuade Khrushchev not to break with China, Togliatti had his fatal stroke. One of his last acts was to prepare what came to be known as the "Yalta memorandum." The document revealed that, despite his acceptance of the status quo within Italy, the old communist leader had done little theoretical revision on the nature of capitalism, or on relations between the capitalist and socialist world. His most original contribution was the demand for a more equal relationship between the Soviet and the allied communist parties, based on the real diversity within the socialist camp. Togliatti insisted that the unity of the communist world could only be created on the basis of equality, and that a centralized organization as had existed under Stalin was impossible.

The death of the long-time leader of the PCI posed few problems. Luigi Longo took Togliatti's place and continued to follow the same policies. As party leader, Longo was the last of his generation. The others of the old guard—Grieco, Berti, Secchia, Scoccimarro, Li Causi, D'Onofrio—were either gone or marginal to the life of the party. Terracini was far too independent to take a leadership role. After Longo, a younger generation of communist leaders took over. Two men, Giorgio Amendola and Pietro Ingrao, had already emerged as leaders in the debate over party strategy in the rapidly changing context of the 1960s. The center-left experiment had proven to be a fragile alliance. The PCI moved from a cautious wait-and-see attitude to more open hostility, but the new parliamentary configuration opened interesting opportunities. During the December 1964 presidential election, disputes between the

Christian Democrats and lay parties resulted in a stalemate. Twenty-one ballots and a completely united left, including the PCI, were needed to elect Giuseppe Saragat.

The alternatives offered by Amendola and Ingrao were not between a hard or soft line, but rather between different accommodations to the new Italy. Giorgio Amendola, backed by a group of younger activists such as Gherardo Chiaromonte, Giorgio Napolitano, and Luciano Barca, argued that the Italian neocapitalist economic system could only be challenged by a broad coalition of political forces, interested in re-shaping the economy in the direction of greater economic and social justice. Amendola suggested two parallel initiatives. The first centered around a model of socialism that would break once and for all with Stalinism. In 1964, Amendola called for a constituent assembly of the left to forge a new united party. The opening to the left and efforts to reunite the PSI and PSDI (which, as we shall see, succeeded in 1966) offered hope that the entire left might be restructured. Unlike past overtures for a united front, Amendola now seemed to be calling for a new beginning, and his suggestions met the unremitting hostility within the PCI from old-guard leaders such as Pietro Secchia and Luigi Longo.

Amendola, however, knew that the decline in party membership demanded drastic remedies. More than any other leader, he understood the ramifications of Italy's shift to a neocapitalist consumer-service economy. Both agriculture and traditional blue collar industries were losing ground to the dynamic service sectors. Paolo Sylos Labini, the economist and sociologist, has estimated that in 1900 one million of 16 million people employed worked in white collar and commercial occupations. By 1971 that figure was five out of 19 million. The PCI faced the threat of inevitable decline if it failed to adjust. To remain competitive, the Communists had to win a larger share of this lower middle-class vote. Interclass alliances and a progressive program within the existing parliamentary system were both necessary to enter this competition. Amendola's logic directed the PCI away from total opposition to the center-left, and toward a dialogue with the Socialist and Catholic parties.

A dialogue between Catholics and communists was also part of the alternative offered by Pietro Ingrao and his followers (Alfredo Reichlin, Massimo Caprara, Lucio Magri and Achille Occhetto). However, Ingrao felt the gradualism and reformism of Amendola was unnecessary. The PCI did not have to abandon an essentially socialist program. As worker radicalism became evident in 1963 and 1964, Ingrao urged the PCI to link up with the new unionism of militant workers, who sought to alter the way the factory was organized. The dialogue between Catholics and communists would take place at the trade-union level. A worker-based interconfessional strategy could mobilize support for an alternative to neocapitalism and rampant consumerism. Ingrao, no Stalinist, also called for free debate on all levels of the party that would be based on full information from the party leadership.

Both Ingrao and Amendola challenged old party traditions. They favored more democracy at the base of the party, and agreed that the PCI had to respond to the social and economic changes within Italy. Amendola pointed to a parliamentary strategy of dialogue with Catholics and socialists to push for more rapid reforms; Ingrao's more radical program would be directed at socialist and Catholic workers outside of the parliamentary context. Moreover, Ingrao carried his dissent further. Against the wishes of almost the entire old guard, he broke an unwritten rule by making his differences public. Party elders—Longo, Giancarlo Pajetta, Umberto Terracini, Emilio Sereni, and Mario Alicata—joined younger leaders of various persuasions such as the Togliattians, Enrico Berlinguer and Ugo Pecchioli, or the neo-Stalinist Armando Cossutta, in opposing Ingrao. The more diplomatic Amendola retreated from his reform proposals at the meeting of the party's Central Committee in June 1965, and again at the party congress in January 1966; but Ingrao pressed forward and lost at the congress. He and his followers were purged from key party posts. Mario Alicata, a much more orthodox figure, took Rossanna Rossanda's place as head of the cultural section of the Central Committee. Romano Ledda was removed as editor of *Critica Marxista*, and Aniello Coppola was out of the editorship of *L'unità*. Just at the moment when youth radicalism would explode in 1968 and 1969, the PCI cut off those who advocated an understanding of the new culture of the young workers and students. The consequences of Ingrao's defeat were not long in coming. Although Ingrao remained in the PCI, many of his supporters—Lucio Magri, Rossanna Rossanda, and Massimo Caprara—broke from the PCI in 1969.

SOCIALIST UNIFICATION: AN OLD REFRAIN, ONE MORE TIME

The center-left experiment of 1964 ended the power of the maximalist tradition that dominated the PSI for so long. Almost the entire left wing was now in the PSIUP. The new leader of the opposition to Nenni, Riccardo Lombardi, never really took a hard-line leftist position, but advocated an aggressive reformist strategy. The shift of the PSI to the right coincided with the election of Giuseppe Saragat as president of the Republic with the combined votes of the entire left. What was immediately significant, however, was not the participation of the PCI in this majority, but the rapprochement of the PSI and PSDI. When the PSI abandoned much of its reformist program in the second center-left government, it accepted the tactical logic of participation that had motivated the Social Democratic party over many years. The way was finally open to resume discussions for unification that began in 1956.

The merger of the PSI and PSDI had slight chance of creating a dynamic third force in Italian politics that could draw votes from both the Catholics and communists. Those like Lombardi, who believed firmly in such a party, had little influence in the PSI. Moreover, neither the socialists nor the Social Democrats were noted for their abilities to mobilize the masses. The PSDI was merely a postal box for office holders, and the socialists now seemed headed in the same direction. As it turned out, greed rather than ideology undermined unification from the beginning. The PSI hoped that the PSDI would be totally absorbed in a new political party, while the Social Democratic office holders feared losing their leverage in such a party. Neither side wanted a truly unified and coherent party that would offer an alternative to the communists.

The off-again, on-again romance between the PSI and PSDI reached a new stage when the two parties decided to merge once again, in October 1966, into the Partito Socialista Unificato (PSU). The merger worked only from the top down and not very far down at that. The two parties continued a semi-independent existence on the provincial and local level. The *coup de grace* to unification came during the elections of 1968, when the PSU lost a third of the support that the PSI and PSDI, separately, had gained in 1963. The new PSU received 14.5 percent of the votes, but the PSI alone in 1963 had won 13.8 percent, and the PSDI 8.5 percent. Nothing could be worse for a party based on patronage. To make matters worse, the communists increased their share of the electorate from 25.3 percent to 26.9 percent.

At the first and only congress of the PSU in the fall of 1968, the alliance between the ex-leader of the PSDI, Mario Tanassi, and Nenni began to come apart. A key ally of Nenni, Francesco De Martino, who controlled the old PSI party apparatus, broke off from the majority. When he was joined by Giacomo Mancini, a powerful southern politician, a new majority, hostile to the continuation of the PSU, was created. In 1969, the PSI resumed its independent existence, with Giacomo Mancini and Francesco De Martino as leaders. Mancini hoped to identify the PSI with the student and worker protest movements that emerged a year earlier. The new leadership of the PSI also decided to use the party's pivotal position to push for an opening to the PCI. Both Mancini and De Martino were willing to press the Catholics harder for more reforms, as part of the "advanced equilibrium" strategy. Unfortunately, the communists showed little interest in the PSI as a mediator or bridge to the Catholics. Instead, the PCI sought a direct accommodation with the Catholics. Mancini and De Martino faced another obstacle. The Christian Democrats steadfastly refused to become hostage to their junior partner in the government. Thus, the De Martino-Mancini years, from 1969 to 1975, were extremely difficult and frustrating ones for the PSI. The party operated against a background of economic crisis and increasing political violence. Once again, the socialists found little political space to maneuver between the two blocs. By the mid-1970s, the party was unstable and in crisis. The PSDI emerged from the experience of merger even more crippled, when a large part of its trade-union movement, the UIL, stayed with the PSI. Thus, just at the moment when the ideology of reformism and acceptance of parliamentary democracy had become the rule in the major parties on the left, the Social Democrats became nothing more than an electoral cartel of hungry politicians.

Both the center-left experiment, from 1962 to 1969, and socialist reunification could be judged failures. The socialist-Catholic alliance certainly did not accomplish its major objective to weaken the Communist party, and it undercut those who felt that a third force between Catholics and communists might be created. The major reforms came in 1962 and 1963, when the PSI remained outside the government. After 1963, socialist participation was dictated increasingly by defensive reasons. Nenni sought merely to avoid a worse outcome. Yet the center-left in the 1960s cannot be described entirely in negative terms. It is true that planning did not succeed, and that nationalization of the electrical industry was less than satisfactory. But there was tax and school reform, a major reform of sharecropping contracts, regional government, and a statute of worker rights, designed by Giacomo Brodolini, the socialist minister of labor in the 1970 Rumor government. This last piece of legislation guaranteed job security and other benefits to millions of workers, assured union presence on the company level, granted the legal right to hold meetings, and gave workers legal recourse against unfair labor practices. Most important, it created a legal framework for future action on the part of the unions. The center-left experiment would continue on into the 1970s with much the same cast of characters, but the dynamic was to be quite different. Both De Martino and Mancini regarded the alliance with the Catholics as a short-term expedient. The Catholic party began to look beyond the PSI to the communists, and the PCI seized the opportunity to enter the majority for the first time since 1947.

CHAPTER 10

The Perils of Prosperity, 1968–1979

The late 1960s and early 1970s were spent under the shadow of an unstable and deteriorating economy. The boom years from 1958 to 1963 had seen an average growth rate of 6.6 percent that was fueled by export industries and relatively high investment in relationship to labor costs. In the process, Italy became a consumer society with a progressively rising standard of living. Official statistics for unemployment declined from 5.2 percent in 1959 to 2.5 percent in 1963, but, as this happened, wages began to rise. Then, by 1962, there were 378 million work-hours lost to strikes, and average salary increases rose from 4.4 percent in 1961 to 10.7 percent in 1962, and 14.7 percent in 1963. As labor costs jumped, profits and investments that had been extracted from low wage levels rather than efficient production declined. Imports of a broader range of goods brought worsening trade deficits.

The first center-left governments broke up in disputes over how to deal with the inflationary spiral. Orthodox economists, such as La Malfa, pressed for limits on consumption and wages at the same time that the socialists sought to protect their reform program. The problem of budget deficits became even more intractable during the 1960s and 1970s because a large part of the cost of worker benefits was shifted to the state, either directly by expanding the rights of employees in the public sector, or by picking up a larger share of private-sector obligations.

By 1964 the boom was over. The next five years were marked by slowed growth, a lower rate of investment, and higher unemployment. Higher hourly productivity in industry kept Italian goods competitive, but caused sharpened conflicts within the factories. Management was no longer as cohesive as it once had been in the past. In 1957, the major employer confederation (Confindustria) lost control of the public corporations that were grouped in a new organization, Intersind, in 1958. The state-controlled sector became far more sensitive to the political changes in the country. In 1962 Intersind broke the management front and settled a long contract dispute with the unions. The large public sector had always been a bonanza to be parceled out among the factions in the Christian Democratic party; now the PSI, an aggressive new player, joined the ranks of parties that traditionally shared Christian Democratic patronage. Subsidies and bailouts of weak firms by the government continued to be common in Italian industry, but now they became prizes in a political lottery. The state holding companies, IRI and ENI, took over Montedison, the badly managed, privately held successor to the nationalized electrical industry. Similar problems and solutions were applied to Alfa Romeo's southern production and to the Taranto steel works.

The 1960s also brought other changes. Greater discrepancies between regions appeared, as the North advanced far more rapidly than the South or the islands. The movement from South to North and from rural to urban Italy created a class of new migrants who lived in shanty towns, or in hastily constructed suburbs with inadequate social or educational services. As a class of new poor appeared, other social changes were giving new meaning to the notion of two separate nations.

Old hierarchies were being undermined and new ones established. Within the working class there was a shift from blue- to white-collar labor, which was accompanied by pressures on the educational system. When the postwar baby boom hit the schools, education, like so many other previously unattainable things, became an item of mass consumption. Distinctions between students and workers diminished as the universities became more proletarianized, and the wage gains of the blue-collar workers narrowed the gap between factory and white-collar workers. In both the universities and in the unions, political movements no longer centered on issues involving the struggle for subsistence, but also stressed the quality of life. Formerly unchallenged institutions, such as the traditional family, the church, or the political party, were now called into question by an international youth-centered culture. As family ties loosened, women assumed new roles in Italian social and political life. By 1967–68 they comprised 36 percent of the university population—a seven percent increase in five years. A new generation of feminist leaders set the agenda for the 1970s around such issues as divorce and abortion.

THE NEW LABOR MOVEMENT

As old loyalties gave way, innovative political and social combinations could emerge. Nowhere was this more apparent than in the trade unions. After fifteen years of political rivalry, the union movement began to draw together in the early 1960s. At the same time, union leaders tried to separate themselves from the political parties that were their historical sponsors. It was clear that nothing could be done to unify the worker organizations as long as political differences predominated. Again, the metalworker federations led the way. Already, by the late

1950s, they had worked together on negotiations and strikes. In 1964, at its congress, the FIOM (CGIL) forbade officials to hold public or high party posts.

The center-left governments further complicated matters. With the PSI in the government, socialist labor leaders within the CGIL now found it hard to tolerate a wholly negative role from the communist-led confederation. At the same time, socialist union leaders were not convinced that the system of planning that the PSI tried to impose on the center-left governments would succeed. By 1965 the CGIL followed the FIOM in trying to separate trade union and political offices. However, the ban on political office-holding was not immediately extended to the highest levels because many of the top leaders in the CGIL were parliamentary deputies or key figures in the PCI hierarchy. In July 1965, under socialist pressure, the CGIL disaffiliated with the international communist syndical confederation. Then, in 1969, it took the final step by forcing its leader, Luciano Lama, to resign from his post as a PCI executive and as a parliamentary deputy. Other prominent communist labor leaders, such as Bruno Trentin, a member of the PCI Central Committee, and Agostino Novella, a deputy and member of the Political Office of the PCI were forced to make similar choices.

Both the UIL and CISL progressed along parallel lines to distance themselves from the Social Democratic and Catholic parties. In 1969, the Catholic metalworkers federation cut its ties to the DC, and the CISL imposed a total veto on all party and political offices. Another important step in the process of separating both the UIL and the CGIL from political parties came when the PSI and PSDI merged in 1966. The socialist trade unionists refused to break off from the CGIL as the Social Democrats wished. Moreover, many of the Social Democratic unionists in the UIL used the merger to shift their allegiance from the PSDI to the PSI. Finally, in 1972, the three confederations formed a loose Federation CGIL-UIL-CISL which lasted until a dispute over wage indexing broke up the arrangement during the Craxi government of the early 1980s.

The process of extricating the unions from political subservience was facilitated by the new challenges that the unions faced from Italian employers and their own rank-and-file. As Italian industry sought to recover from the recession of 1964, new, more specialized assembly-line techniques were introduced that increased productivity, but also bore-dom and frustration among workers. Absenteeism and industrial sabo-tage became part of a prolonged guerrilla warfare in many factories. The discontent was unusual because it developed amidst general pros-perity and raised issues that caused the traditional unions to scramble to develop new bargaining strategies. Negotiations on the plant level replaced the old national contracts. Separate salary scales by sex, geo-graphy, and age, were ended in the 1960s and early 1970s. In 1968, for instance, the three confederations jointly organized a national campaign to revise the pension system and to end regional salary differentials. In 1969, the government conceded on the pension issue and granted up to 74 percent of the last year's wage after forty years of employment.

Many of these changes came as the result of intensified labor struggles. After the great gains of the 1960–1963 period, union power regressed in 1964 during the economic downturn. With the return of better times in 1968 and 1969, the stage was set for further confrontation. Now, however, two factors entered into the calculation. First, there was the upsurge of student radicalism, which reached its peak between 1968 and 1973. Second, different forms of union organization were in place. In early 1968, the Unitary Base Committees—a new version of factory councils—were formed to express worker grievances more directly. These base committees brought forth a new stratum of younger labor leaders, who were elected outside of the formal factory commissions and traditional unions, and often had sympathy for the broader youth-protest movement.

Only after 1972 did the three confederations regain a measure of influence, but to do so they were forced to become much more aggressive. Throughout the 1970s Italy led other nations in hours lost to strikes. New political weapons, such as the hiccup strike (short, plant-wide strikes) or the checkerboard strike (which jumped from sector to sector within a plant), were used. The objectives were not wages per se, but related issues, such as the forty-hour week, reduction of overtime, the right to hold worker assemblies in the factories, and the right to union dues check off. Many of these changes equalized fringe benefits among blue- and white-collar workers and simplified the number of job categories. By the early 1970s, backed by the extraparliamentary-left political movements, the radical workers were demanding access to company planning and a voice in investment and employment policies. Management saw many of these demands as a threat to its own control of the factory. In 1969, 520 million hours—many of them in the "hot autumn"—were lost to strikes. Settlements tended to favor the unions. Wages in industry increased by 18.3 percent in 1970 and by 9 percent in the two succeeding years. As a result, membership in the three main trade-union confederations grew. For instance, the CGIL jumped from 2,630,000 in 1969 to 3,440,000 in 1973.

THE OLD AND NEW LEFT

The impact of the worker protests was intensified by the simultaneous occurrence of the student-protest movement. University enrollment increased 117 percent between 1961 and 1968. Higher education had become an item of mass consumption, but the university system was hopelessly antiquated. Classrooms, libraries, and laboratories over-flowed with students unable to find a place to study. To make matters worse, high youth unemployment meant that a large percentage of these students would not find work commensurate with their skills, following graduation. These young people faced the negative side of the economic boom in their daily lives.

Two aspects of Italian radical thinking on the "new left" came together in the movement of disenchanted students and workers. The first was the tradition of Morandi and Raniero Panzieri, which called for au-tonomous organization of the working class at the factory level. Many of the intellectual leaders of the new-left movement after 1956 had broken with the Communist and Socialist parties, and now sought a political base by linking their protest with that of the workers. Mario Tronti, Alberto Asor Rosa, Toni Negri, and others, joined Panzieri in calling for direct contacts with the Worker Base Committees. Panzieri, Negri, and others on the "new left" were convinced that the Communist party had become merely an adjunct of an existing social order that had to be overthrown at all costs. They believed in a strategy of confrontation with the state. The capitalists would be forced to impose an authoritarian solution in the ensuing crisis that would unite the satisfied workers who voted for the Communist party with the discontented young students and radicalized proletariat of the urban slums. In short, an alliance of the socially marginal sectors of society—the young workers and poor students—might be the the force through which the entire system would be revolutionized.

The second was a generalized belief, shared by the extreme neofascist right as well, that change might be brought about by direct action. The far-right wing moved first in 1969. During the year a series of rightist bombings culminated in the explosion at Banca dell'Agricoltura, in Mi-lan's Piazza Fontana, that claimed sixteen lives and wounded ninety. Direct action by the left was initially quite different and took the form of militant action within the factories—hiccup strikes, slowdowns, rigid application of work rules, and occasional sabotage of production. Only in the early 1970s did it progress to kidnapping, kneecapping, and out-right murder of individuals connected with the state's legal and police system.

The rise of the new left most directly challenged the Italian Com-munist party. It had been an axiom of the party that no rival should arise on its left. But events in the late 1960s opened considerable political space to the left of the PCI. The communist leadership was surprised by the strength of the dissident worker and student movements, in part because attention was focused on international events. Throughout the 1960s the PCI had been distancing itself from the USSR and from the more orthodox parties in the Soviet camp. These moves were paralleled by a new dialogue with the German, English and French Socialist parties.

In the process, the PCI had considerably revised its views on European unity. Not only had it accepted the Common Market, in early 1969 it became the first Communist party to win representation at the European assembly which met at Strasbourg. Although the PCI did not yet alter its position on NATO and the western orientation of Italy's foreign policy, the stage was clearly set for such a change in the early 1970s. In short, the PCI drifted further into the political mainstream, just as many students and workers opted to act outside of it.

THE CZECH CRISIS OF 1968: THE LIMITS OF INDEPENDENCE WITHIN THE SOVIET BLOC AND THE ROLE OF THE PCI

The PCI had followed the changes that had been taking place during the spring and summer of 1968 in Czechoslovakia with great enthusiasm and had identified itself with the "socialism with a human face" that was being worked out in Prague. In May, Luigi Longo visited the Czech capital to offer full support to the reforms introduced by the new Dubcek government. Thus, when the Soviets moved into Czechoslovakia, there could be no repetition of the PCI's acquiescence to Soviet violence against Hungary. It openly and publicly rejected the use of force against the Czechs. After the invasion, the Italians pressed for changes in the relationship between the Soviet and the other communist parties. At the Twelfth party Congress in January 1969, Longo and his designated successor, Enrico Berlinguer, were blunt in their criticism of the USSR. But the lessons of worker spontaneity in Prague were quick to be applied by those within the PCI who wanted greater change in their own party. Many followers of Ingrao (Aldo Natoli, Rossanna Rossanda, and Luigi Pintor) drew on parallels between the Czech democratic organizations and Italian worker committees to call for the PCI to recognize the importance of worker and student protests.

After the party congress, the most active critics, such as Rossanna Rossanda, Luigi Pintor, Natoli, Luciana Castellina and Massimo Caprara, representatives of the "new left" within the party, began to publish *Il manifesto* to advance their radical version of Ingrao's worker-oriented strategy. They supported the development of grassroots social and economic organizations, such as the base committees, to break out of a purely consumerist and trade-union mentality. *Il Manifesto* urged the PCI to forge a new alliance with blue-collar workers, alienated white-collar employees, and students. As if this were not enough, the review called on the party to introduce more internal democracy in order to give substance to its criticism of the USSR over Czechoslovakia. A reaction from the party soon followed. The editors of *Il manifesto* were charged with factionalism and told to close the review. When they refused, Rossanda, Natoli, Pintor, Lucio Magri, and Massimo Caprara were suspended and then expelled from the party.

THE NEW LEFT BETWEEN POLITICS AND DIRECT ACTION

By the early 1970s the worker and student protest movement fragmented and polarized. To the left of the PCI, the *Manifesto* group attempted unsuccessfully to unite with the dissidents of such Communist publications and movements as *Potere Operaio, Lotta continua,* and *Avanguardia operaia* in order to run a separate slate of candidates for the elections of 1972. However the effort failed completely. The PCI then began to pick up some of those who wished to move back into the political mainstream. In 1972 and 1973 the Communist Youth Federation gained 20,000 new members to reach 112,000. In frustration, those who rejected the PCI's establishment-style politics turned to violence. Even before the 1972 electoral failure, a bulletin of October 20, 1970, announced the formation of the Red Brigades. A few years later, in 1973, the Nuclei Armati Proletari (NAP) was formed. Initially, both the Red Brigades and NAP acted on the fringe of the nonviolent extra-parliamentary left, which was primarily represented by militants who rallied around *Lotta continua* and *Il manifesto.* But, already, individual acts of political terrorism were taking place, such as the 1972 attempt to damage Milan's electrical power system, which claimed the life of the publisher Giangiacomo Feltrinelli. That year also saw the first kidnapping by the Red Brigades and the assassination of a police inspector who had been prominent in the crackdown on the left. The failure of the extra-parliamentary left in 1972 elections deepened the divisions between those who advocated nonviolent tactics and those who wanted to topple the capitalist system by any means.

By 1973 it became clear that the four or five main groups on the extra-parliamentary left (*Potere Operaio, Il Manifesto, Lotta continua, Avanguardia operaia,* and the Partitio Communista-Marxista-Leninista) had failed either to break out of political isolation or to find a common line that would unite their protest. One of them, *Potere operaio* broke up and formed *Autonomia operaia* with key leaders, Oreste Scalzone and Toni Negri, seeming to condone direct and often violent tactics. The Manifesto group, clearly the most political and intellectually creative, joined with other left dissidents to form Democrazia Proletaria, a political alliance that had some limited success in the 1976 elections.

The terrorist campaign of the 1970s included both the left and the right. Two particularly costly bombings at the Piazza della Loggia in Brescia, and on the Italicus Express train between Florence and Bologna in May and August 1974, signalled the beginning of overt rightist subversion of the Republic. This neofascist offensive culminated in the bombing of the Bologna train station in August 1980 that claimed 85 lives. In contrast, the Red Brigades concentrated on individuals connected with the antiterrorist crackdown. Typical was the kidnapping of Mario Sossi (the state prosecutor in Genoa), and the kneecapping or maiming of judges and police officials. This type of violence eventually took the lives of Carlo Casalegno, an editor of the Turinese daily *La Stampa* in 1977; the Christian Democratic leader, Aldo Moro in 1978; and Guido Rossa, a communist labor leader in 1979 before the campaign of terror and direct action subsided in the early 1980s.

SOCIAL CHANGE IN THE 1970s

While Italy never again enjoyed the growth rate of the boom years, the economy entered a cycle of expansion and recession that allowed substantial wage increases for many workers. Between 1973 and 1976 wages jumped by 25 percent and then by another 34 percent in 1976 and 1977. Most unionized workers enjoyed an unprecedented level of benefits guaranteed to them by the state. This welfare society was extremely costly. By the 1970s Italy had the highest percentage of national, regional, and local government employees of any country in western Europe. But the results were also quite tangible. The forty-hour week became standard for most workers, who also had four weeks vacation and a number of paid holidays. Job security increased and, in the case of layoffs, workers received 80 percent of their wages (the largest part of this benefit paid by the government). Health and other social insurance benefits were expanded in the 1960s and 1970s. Wages for most blue-collar workers were tied to the cost of living index in 1975, which more than kept pace with inflation. Moreover, many Italian families had two or more sources of income, as the underground economy became ever more important.

Perhaps the most striking changes came in the role of the family. Decades of rapid migration from rural and southern Italy to the urban centers of the north had modified traditional society beyond recognition. Women now composed almost 40 percent of the university population. Their monetary contribution was vital to the maintenance of a middle-class standard of living for many families. Although women still composed slightly more than a quarter of the work force—a lower percentage than in other advanced industrial economies—they received two-thirds of the new jobs created in the increasing service economy between 1977 and 1981.

Independent feminist organizations, such as the Movement for the Liberation of Women, joined older groups, such as the Union of Italian Women (Unione delle Donne Italiane—UDI) to lead successful campaigns for nursery schools in 1972, divorce legislation in 1974, family planning clinics in 1975, equal pay for equal work in 1977, and abortion in 1978. Then, when the Catholics forced referenda on divorce and abortion, the female and youth vote broke with the Church to support the existing legislation. These referenda revealed how the emergence of a new urbanized middle class society and the influx of new ideas into the heretofore conservative South had weakened a number of political organizations that had been able to guarantee a conservative vote during the first twenty years of the Republic. The most prominent casualties were the Catholic small-farmers organization, Coltivatori Diretti, and Catholic Action, whose membership declined from three million members in the 1950s to 600,000 in the 1970s.

The new independent vote, which responded to quality-of-life issues, was a tempting target for all Italian parties, but especially for the left. The stakes were extremely high because Italy had three national elections and three major referenda campaigns (divorce, public order and state financing of parties, and abortion) during the years from 1972 to 1981. As a result of those elections, the relationship among the three main political parties—Catholic, communist, and socialist—changed considerably. The years from 1972 to 1978 were marked by a favorable relationship between the Communist and Catholic parties, to the detriment of the PSI. After 1979, and continuing to 1988, the PSI under Bettino Craxi has sought to exclude the communists and make itself the focus of the progressive middle-class voter.

THE HISTORIC COMPROMISE OR CONVERGENT PARALLELS: AN OPTICAL ILLUSION?

At the Thirteenth Congress of the PCI in March 1972, Enrico Berlinguer succeeded Luigi Longo as secretary general of the Communist party. Berlinguer, the son of a politically prominent Sardinian family, began his career during the Resistance and rose to prominence in the Communist Youth Federation during the 1940s and 1950s. He represented the essence of the Togliattian vision of the party. Cultured and reserved, the very opposite of the revolutionary agitator, Berlinguer was a perfect example of the intellectual-politician which Togliatti had sought to bring into the "new party" after 1944. He was ideally suited to appeal to the white-collar voter whose support was necessary if the PCI wished to move beyond its hold over a quarter of the electorate.

Berlinguer took various policies that had been outlined by Amendola during the 1960s and applied them in the changed political context of the 1970s with spectacularly successful results. The decision to make a direct appeal to the Catholic party in what came to be known as the "Historic Compromise" was most significant and initially fruitful. Working in favor of a new relationship between Catholics and communists seemed to be politically realistic. The PCI leadership firmly believed that the Christian Democratic party's hold over the country was too firm to be shaken, and that Ingrao's hopes for an alternative majority of the left was completely unrealistic. Berlinguer, backed by Amendola, calculated that, if the PCI wished to enter the national arena once again, it would have to reach a *modus vivendi* with the Catholics. There was ample precedent for this in the party's history. Gramsci made it clear that to succeed in the long and difficult struggle for power, the proletariat would have to win both a political and cultural battle for control of the state. Only by reaching the Catholic masses could this be done. Togliatti, who came to similar conclusions during the Interwar period and after the Liberation, had sought a direct understanding with the Vatican and the Christian Democrats. Now, twenty-five years later, Berlinguer prepared to reopen this dialogue.

THE BREAKDOWN OF THE CENTER-LEFT

But other, more immediate concerns dictated the Historic Compromise. In December 1970, a war hero and prominent fascist, Valerio Borghese, attempted a coup d'état. Although it failed miserably, Borghese clearly had allies within the state security apparatus. The discredit into which parliament had fallen, as the center-left formula bogged down in recriminations between Catholics and Socialists, represented a permanent danger to the state. Many Christian Democrats had grown increasingly resentful of the PSI. They felt that the reforms of the center-left had cost the party its right-wing support, and were determined to take a much harder line toward the socialists after 1970. For instance, the PSI's nomination of Lelio Basso to the Constitutional Court was vetoed, as were a number of reforms of the health system. While this temporarily slaked the thirst for revenge, it did nothing to improve the relationships within the governing coalition.

After the unhappy experience of unification with the PSDI, the socialists showed more determination than ever to reassert their position as a major party on the left. In local elections of 1970, the PSI recovered many of the votes lost by the fusion and had high hopes for national parliamentary elections. Giacomo Mancini and Francesco De Martino defined their new policy as one seeking "a more advanced equilibrium," which could only be interpreted as a call for an opening to the PCI. Although De Martino did not fully accept Lombardi's ideas of an alternative majority, he did believe that the PSI could serve as a bridge between the communists and Catholics.

Relations between the Catholics and socialists hit a low point during the elections for president in 1972. The socialists openly tried to block the two leading Catholic candidates, Amintore Fanfani and Giovanni Leone. When Leone was elected with the help of votes from the neofascist Italian Social Movement, the old center-left was moribund. Giulio

Andreotti, Italy's man for all seasons, formed a center-right government that called for new elections. The Catholics proceeded to regain ground lost in earlier elections to the neofascists. To their dismay, the socialists did poorly, receiving 9.6 percent of the vote and hardly advancing over the disastrous results of 1968. The communists increased their vote only slightly from 26.9 percent to 27.2 percent, but the gains represented a small beachhead into the middle-class electorate. On the negative side of the PCI balance, the PSIUP, which had been allied to the communists, failed to gain a seat and dissolved.

At their congress in November, the socialists replaced Giacomo Mancini with Francesco De Martino as party secretary. De Martino, backed by an old and ailing Nenni, now party president, proposed relaunching a version of the center-left. However, subsequent attempts to revive the old Catholic-socialist coalition under Mariano Rumor, in 1973 and 1974, collapsed in conflicts over how to handle inflation, Catholic insistence on the divorce referendum, and a nasty scandal over payments by petroleum importers to prominent politicians. The issue of divorce was particularly difficult. The PSI and the small Radical Party led the fight for divorce and abortion. Loris Fortuna, a prominent socialist deputy, was the primary sponsor of the divorce law, and introduced a draft law for abortion in 1975. After the Rumor government collapsed in October 1974, the PSI abandoned efforts to revive the center-left and remained outside of the government. It did not return until a quite different version of the center-left was relaunched in 1980.

THE HISTORIC COMPROMISE AND THE LESSONS OF CHILE

Against the background of governmental impotence, bickering, and scandal, came a warning from abroad about the fragility of democracy. In 1973 an American-backed coup brought down the government of Salvador Allende in Chile. Allende, a socialist, had tried to forge a democratic, but exclusively leftist bloc in order to govern against the united opposition of the bourgeois parties. The Chilean lesson implied the necessity of negotiating with the Catholics in order to avoid a similar confrontation. In an important article, "Reflections on the Recent Events in Chile" (of September 1973 in *Rinascita*), Berlinguer formally announced the abandonment of a left alternative strategy and called for direct dialogue with the Catholic party. Still to be defined was the nature of the Historic Compromise and the role that the PCI would assume vis-à-vis a Catholic government. The options were the same as had been presented to the PSI: formal participation in a government or parliamentary support without ministerial posts. The unhappy history of socialist-Catholic collaboration argued in favor of the first option.

EUROCOMMUNISM AND THE PCI

Between the Hungarian revolt of 1956 and the Czech crisis of 1968, the PCI established three basic guidelines for its foreign policy. First, the Italians, along with the Yugoslavs and Chinese, refused to accept a single path to socialism or recognize a single center of the Communist movement: The PCI had long since restored good relations with Tito's party. And, in 1970, close ties were established with the Chinese party by Longo and Berlinguer. Second, the PCI advocated equality between all communist parties. The third guideline was the adoption of the principle of nonintervention. During the early 1970s, the PCI pushed the ideas of autonomous development further by defining a western or Eurocommunist road to socialism. By then, the Italian and Spanish parties had abandoned the idea of the dictatorship of the proletariat and denied the applicability of the Soviet model of revolutionary change to the West. The Italian communists fully agreed that change would come only through parliamentary means and by coalitions with other political forces. Little remained of the intransigent revolutionary party that had been formed at Livorno in 1921.

Just as the PCI looked to new understandings with the Christian Democrats in Italy, it also began to reach out to the Social Democratic and Communist parties of western Europe. In March 1973 Berlinguer visited London to meet with representatives of the Labour party. Further contacts with socialists came at the European parliament in Strasbourg, where the PCI was the first Communist party so represented. Simultaneously, the Italian communists sought to build a bloc of like-minded Communist parties in the West. Between 1973 and 1975, a series of encounters between Italians, French, and Spanish party leaders culminated in a July 1975 meeting between Berlinguer and Santiago Carrillo, the head of the Spanish Communist party. The stress on democracy and pluralism in their final communique led observers to introduce the term "eurocommunism" into political vocabulary. Then, a year later in June 1976, Berlinguer startled observers when he stated that the PCI might be more capable of building socialism within the western bloc.

THE PCI ADVANCES: ELECTORAL VICTORIES
OR RUNNING ON A TREADMILL

The policies of the PCI paid off handsomely. In the local elections of 1975 the communists made important gains. They now participated in one-third of local and provincial governments—most often in alliance with the socialists, who were more willing to form such alliances after the failure of their alternative alliance with the Catholics. By 1978 half the provinces, and a majority of the population of Italy's cities and towns, were under some combination of socialist-communist administration. Communist party membership also increased from 1,521,631 in 1971 to 1,657,895 in 1974 and 1,798,000 in 1976. Much of the gain was made among younger voters, who viewed the PCI as the only uncorrupt political force that was capable of forcing change upon a stagnant system. The percentage of party members under the age of 25 rose from 6.4 percent to 11.3 percent in 1976. While the backbone of the PCI was still in the working class, young middle-class voters were clearly attracted to the new image of the party. In the June 1975 regional elections, which saw 18 year olds vote, the PCI reached 33.4 percent of the vote, a dramatic jump of 5.1 percent over the last regional elections in 1972, while the PSI gained a disappointing 2 percent and the Christian Democrats lost 3.1 percent of the vote and sank to 35.3 percent.

The national elections of 1976 were the highpoint for the PCI's historic compromise campaign. The communists advanced from 27.2 percent to 34.4 percent of the vote, while the Catholic party remained stationary at 38.7 percent and the PSI at 9.6 percent. The PSDI was reduced to a bare shadow with only 3.4 percent. The electoral power of the PCI could no longer be ignored. All of the leading Catholic political figures sought to bring the PCI into some relationship with the government in order to pass austerity legislation that would stabilize the fragile economy. The problem was that the left, backed by the unions, had just won indexing of salaries in 1975. Now, if limits were to be imposed on wages and public spending, the PCI would have to join the parliamentary majority. The PCI used its new bargaining power to elect Pietro Ingrao as Speaker of the Chamber of Deputies and to win a number of committee chairmanships in the Chamber and in the Senate. In return, the Communist party went from opposition to limited support of a "great coalition," which ruled Italy from 1976 to 1978. Never, since 1947, had the communists seemed so secure. They had blunted the extra-parliamentary challenge on their left and seemed on the brink of entering the Italian government.

BETTINO CRAXI AND THE REMAKING
OF THE PSI

If the communists rejoiced, the socialists were in despair. For the PSI nothing seemed to work. The communists gained credit for wage indexing, the radicals for divorce reform. The PSI's attempts to tap the youth vote in 1972 and 1976 were total fiascos. The effort to mediate between Catholics and communists had been rejected by both sides between 1970 and 1976, and now, with its reduced electoral strength, the PSI had no leverage at all. Once again, the PSI had been out-maneuvered by the communists.

During the summer of 1976 De Martino was ousted from the leadership of the party by a coalition of left and right socialists. Bettino Craxi, an obscure leader of the Milanese federation and protegé of Pietro Nenni, was named as secretary of the party. He won his position by compromising with old-line leaders such as Giacomo Mancini, and young leftist allies of Riccardo Lombardi, such as Claudio Signorile. Few observers gave him a serious chance of changing a party that had resisted reform for eighty years, but the old generation of socialists, who had come of age either in the struggle against fascism or during the resistance, now passed away. In their place emerged an extremely pragmatic and nonideological generation of socialists—Craxi, Rino Formica, Enrico Manca, Gianni De Michelis, Claudio Signorile, and Claudio Martelli. For most of them the old factional fighting over reform or revolution had little meaning. One by one, the old symbols of the party were thrown overboard. The red carnation replaced the old rising sun and hammer and sickle. Marx gave way to the Harvard Business School's management theories, as the PSI cast away the heritage of the past to compete for an entirely new electorate of middle-class professionals and bureaucrats in the public and private sector. The socialists were willing to gamble that economic prosperity had produced a large independent vote that cared little about radical change. They wanted competent managers of the existing system who responded more to quality-of-life issues than demands for redistribution of wealth and power. The problem with the socialist strategy was that the communists were making similar calculations.

Craxi believed that the old PSI had reached a dead end with the election of 1976, which reduced the party to its bedrock support. If it did not wish to become a party of patronage workers like the PSDI, the PSI had to be remade with new men and objectives. Craxi rejected out of hand the left alternative as it had been proposed by Lombardi since 1963 because it implied permanent acceptance of communist hegemony over the left. Not only had the PSI been consistently out-maneuvered by the communists, but a case could be made that the PSI and PCI could never conquer a majority as long as the communists continued to be the largest party. Thus, little could be gained by moving further to the left. Only by defining the PSI more sharply from the communists could the socialists hope to reemerge as a serious political force. Craxi's new Socialist party would also compete with the Christian Democrats for the centrist electorate. It was a risky strategy for a weak and small party. The PSI secretary seemed confident that he could create political space where none had existed by pushing the Catholic party further to the right and blocking the movement of the PCI toward the center. But, for Craxi's gamble to succeed, voters would have to be ready to abandon the traditional mass parties and the PCI and DC would have to tolerate passively such an assault on their power.

In short, Craxi was about to move the PSI into what had been, since 1945, a small, secular and democratic third camp between the rival Catholic and communist blocs. The Socialist party now took the leadership of this democratic center which was composed of the Republican, Social Democratic, Radical, and, possibly, the Liberal parties. This bloc of small parties had rarely been strong enough to exert decisive influence, but Craxi was determined to challenge political wisdom. Even within this centrist formation resistance to socialist domination could be expected from the Republican Party which would produce its own contender in Giovanni Spadolini, soon to be Italy's first non-Christian Democratic prime minister since the Parri government of 1945.

THE PCI AND THE PERILS OF POWER

Berlinguer's leadership of the Communist Party in the 1976–1978 period seemed to have already preempted a part of Craxi's strategy. The communists were willing, even overeager, to stabilize the economic and political system. Like Craxi's socialists, they sought to project the image of competent managers who asked only to be given a chance. The model was that of the German Social Democrats who joined the Great Coalition government with the Christian Democrats in order to reassure German voters that socialism meant only a reformist variant of the existing system. Any talk of a leftist alternative was brushed aside. The communists believed that they could hold both their working-class constituency and compete for the new independent middle-class voter. They gambled that sharing power with the Catholics would not tarnish the party's image as an uncorrupted political force. Given the experiences of the PSI during the 1960s, this expectation was extraordinarily optimistic. It was even more so because the Catholics wanted communist support to impose truly unpopular economic policies. In July 1977 the PCI joined the Christian Democrats, Socialists, Social Democrats, Republicans and Liberals on a program of antiterrorism and austerity. For all intents the PCI accepted the position of relatively orthodox policy makers like Ugo La Malfa who crusaded against waste in the public sector and for control of inflation, so that Italy might reestablish its international export position.

THE LABOR MOVEMENT AND THE PCI,
1975–1978

When the PCI sacrificed its short-term interest for longer-term political objectives, it never expected an immediate backlash of unpopularity. But the communists could no longer deliver the labor movement as they had done in the 1940s and 1950s. Reunification of the three labor confederations met with partial success on July 24, 1972, when an accord was signed creating the Federation of the CGIL-CISL-UIL. To achieve this limited unity all the labor confederations, but especially the CGIL, had to loosen ties to political parties. The CGIL also accepted the principle of parity with the smaller UIL and CISL. In compensation, unity brought immediate success as wages continued to advance, and indexing in 1975 insured the workers against the ravages of inflation. It was, however, uncertain how these same workers would respond to calls by the PCI to limit future gains in the interests of a capitalist economic system.

The influence of the PCI in the political system grew during 1976 and 1977, and peaked in early 1978. In February 1978, at the congress of the three union confederations, the majority of delegates backed the PCI's program of linking wage containment with reforms of housing, health, transportation, and taxation. Soon after, the government in power, headed by Giulio Andreotti, resigned. Both Andreotti and Aldo Moro, now president of the Christian Democratic party, maneuvered to bring the PCI into even closer collaboration with the next government. Then, on March 16, 1978, Moro was kidnapped by the Red Brigades and murdered on May 9. During these long weeks the hopes of the PCI to play a larger role all but vanished.

THE PCI BETWEEN THE USA AND THE USSR

In fact, the communist position had already begun to decline even before the Moro kidnapping and murder. The PCI had arrived at a measure of political power, but at a steep price. The PCI no longer appeared to be the only uncompromised political force. Communist control of major local governments, such as Naples and Turin, proved frustrating. Communist-led cooperatives had long been part of the business and governmental structure of central and northern Italy, but now the party itself was receiving large subsidies from the state as a result of public financing of political campaigns. The PCI found itself in the new position of representing both the majority in parliament and the discontented. At first, the Communist party took a leading role as advocate of public order. The party backed the suppression of the Red Brigades in 1977 and 1978. Radical groups like Autonomia operaia struck back at the PCI. In February 1977, Luciano Lama, the communist head of the CGIL, was jeered at the University of Rome. Then the Red Brigades attacked communist labor and political leaders. During the Moro kidnapping, the PCI, which opposed the campaign of left-wing violence on political and ideological grounds, took an extremely hard line in opposing negotiations with the terrorists.

Part of the PCI's mystique was derived from the extraordinary image that the party had created for itself in international affairs. The great advance of the PCI coincided with the arrival in power of the more liberal Carter administration in 1977, and opened the possibility of the modification of the American veto against the Italian communists. The PCI had been interested in contacts with the United States as part of its policy shift since 1973. Those most associated with Eurocommunism, such as Giorgio Napolitano and Sergio Segre, made overtures to the American embassy, and the party took a favorable stand on NATO during the 1976 elections. But these efforts were rebuffed by the Americans in 1977 and 1978, when Carter made it clear that he was as firm as his predecessors in rejecting communist participation in the Italian government.

The PCI also had difficulty making its Eurocommunist alternative acceptable in the face of growing Soviet resistance. On March 2 and 3, 1977, the leaders of the Italian, French, and Spanish Communist parties met in Madrid and called for a democratic and pluralistic road to socialism. Then, when Moscow hardened its position, the French Communists wavered and returned to pro-Soviet orthodoxy, while the Spanish moved further than the PCI in defiance of Moscow. By mid-1978, the PCI had failed to persuade either the United States or the USSR. The American veto still stood, and the Eurocommunist initiative stalled. Even more important, the death of Moro removed the foremost advocate of cooperation between Catholics and communists. The Historic Compromise was in a shambles.

After 1976, membership in the party leveled off and the PCI faced losses in the local elections of 1977 and 1978, and they suffered a national setback in 1979. Clearly, little more could be gained by remaining within the parliamentary majority. In January 1979, citing the government's failure to reform the public television system and the universities, the PCI withdrew its support. In the national elections that followed in June, the party dropped from 34.4 percent to 30.4 percent of the vote, while the Catholics and socialists remained stable. The small, nonconformist Radical party made the most significant gains by picking up the vote of those who were disaffected by the PCI's entry into the political establishment.

CRAXI'S SOCIALIST ALTERNATIVE
REVIVED: A SOULLESS SOCIALISM?

By 1978 Craxi had begun to trace a new role for the PSI. At the party congress in March 1978, the PSI jettisoned what remained of its marxist heritage in favor of a social democratic program modeled after the German SPD of Willy Brandt and Helmut Schmidt. The new party policy or "Project for a Socialist Alternative" included such economic and institutional reforms as the strengthening of the executive, and creation of a more presidential style of leadership. This renewal was carried further in 1981 when the PSI congress changed its statute to make the party secretary (Craxi) removable by congress and not by the central committee. Then, in 1984, the central committee itself was abolished and replaced by a large party assembly of almost 500 members, a body unlikely to challenge the party leader. Little remained of the old guard except a residue of bitterness that was revealed by the cold and formal relationship, from 1983 to 1985, of Craxi and the socialist president of the Republic, Sandro Pertini.

The socialists mobilized prominent intellectuals, such as Norberto Bobbio and Massimo Salvadori, behind their new program, and aggressively used their control over part of the public television network, and over a series of well-financed periodicals, to challenge both the Catholics and communists. To further distinguish PSI's image from the others, Craxi was the sole major political leader who urged giving priority to saving Moro.

As soon as it became apparent that the PCI had failed to achieve its objectives, Craxi realized that the PSI could once again emerge as a pivotal political force, and moved to take advantage of the new situation. After bringing down a government headed by the Christian Democrat Francesco Cossiga, in March 1980, the PSI joined the first pure center-left cabinet since the mid-1970s. But much had changed since 1964. The Catholic party, exhausted after thirty-five years in power, was badly divided and incapable of producing another generation of political leadership. The defeat in the referendum on abortion and the outbreak of the P-2 scandal in May 1981—a major case of political corruption that reached the highest levels of power—left the Catholic party thoroughly demoralized. In July, Giovanni Spadolini of the Republican party formed the first non-Christian-Democratic-led government since that of Ferruccio Parri in 1945. Two years later, in August 1983, Bettino Craxi realized his ambition of becoming the first socialist prime minister of Italy. The strategy of building a third force in Italian politics seemed to have paid extraordinary dividends in a short time.

This analysis concludes, in 1979, with the exhaustion of both the original 1964 center-left and the communist alternatives. It is still uncertain whether Craxi, who recently resigned after three-and-a-half years as prime minister, has forged a viable Socialist party between the Catholics and the communists, or whether his personal popularity has translated into votes. The success of the PSI and the decline of the communists in the June 1987 elections might be the first indication of a breakthrough for the socialists. This trend has been confirmed by local and regional elections in May and June 1988, which saw major gains for the PSI and a sharp decline for the PCI. However, Craxi must still face a Christian Democratic party that has stabilized its electoral position and appears determined to reclaim the leadership of the government. Thus far, Craxi has succeeded in gaining power but not the institutional reforms— such as direct election of the president—that might allow the PSI to emerge as a substantial political force. His prolonged term as prime minister has translated into a tenuous triumph for the PSI, although, with persistence, he could still emerge at the head of a government dedicated to realizing major constitutional changes.

The Communist party never fully recovered from the collapse of Berlinguer's strategy in 1978 and 1979 and then from his untimely death in 1984. Since 1979 the PCI alternated between policies of cooperation and hostility. In 1984 the Federation CGIL-UIL-CISL broke up over the PCI's and CGIL's determination to protect wage indexing against the equal determination of the Craxi government to control inflation. That same year, the PCI suffered a severe defeat when it lost a referendum on the wage escalator. The return to East-West confrontation in the early 1980s further limited the options of the Italian communists. The waning Brezhnev years were certainly not auspicious ones for new initiatives, and the attitude of the Reagan administration in the United States has been unremittingly hostile. Alessandro Natta, Berlinguer's successor, has been unable to offer any serious alternative to a resurgent PSI. Until the elections of June 1987, an unusually passive PCI appeared willing to await the outcome of Craxi's attempt at power before formulating a new strategy. Now, however, the decline of the party to just over 26 percent of the vote, from a high of 34 percent in 1978, has precipitated another change of leadership from Natta to the younger Achille Occhetto. Political developments in France and Spain offer little consolation for the Italian communists. Even the party's cultural and political supremacy, so clear throughout the 1970s, is no longer assured.

Italian politics in the 1980s has followed trends in other countries by becoming less ideological but more subject to special-interest and quality-of-life pressure groups. These are no longer reliable allies of political parties and often operate on the local level. It is unclear how any of the major parties will adapt to this new reality, although early indications are that competition for this new electorate will accentuate the rivalry between the Socialist and Communist parties to the advantage of the PSI.

Conclusion

Stalin, the Big Moustache, never came. The weapons, so carefully concealed by the communist partisan forces after World War II, rusted from disuse. The communists take out the red flag of revolution on ceremonial occasions, although the socialists now prefer the more benign red carnation. The maximalist tradition died with Rodolfo Morandi in 1955 and was buried under the wheels of Soviet tanks as they marched into Hungary a year later. The communists, accused of playing the double game of accepting parliamentary democracy after 1944 in order to destroy it, were indeed engaged in an elaborate hoax, but not on the capitalists. Rather, Togliatti and his successors played their double game against their own membership in calling for revolution but following reformist policies. The transformation of socialist and communist revolutionaries into reformists took place while the classic reformist tradition—represented by the Social Democratic party—degenerated into mere political opportunism and corruption.

All of this was far from the intentions of most left-wing leaders. A balance sheet on the long and complex history of the Italian working-class movement must start with the fate of the three traditions that we discussed earlier. Each of these traditions—reformism, maximalism, and communism—has, as we have seen, undergone drastic changes during the more than ninety years since 1892.

The underlying assumption of this study is that some version of reformism was the only practical policy for the Italian worker movement. A second assumption is that the basis for a successful reformist movement existed only for brief periods in Italy from 1892 to 1960. Extreme poverty, great disparities of wealth, and an alienated rural and urban proletariat rendered problematical any prolonged and consistent reformist strategy. Reformism, as an organized political force, played a major role in the history of the working class only during the years before World War I. Thereafter it was reduced to a marginal movement unable to affect the outcome of the political struggle directly.

The tragedy was that the Italian reformists failed, during the Giolittian era from 1903 to 1914, to build an institutional basis for future political action. But this failure can only in part be attributed to the policies of the PSI. In fact, most bourgeois politicians, starting with Giovanni Giolitti, never envisaged the PSI as an equal partner within a modern party system. The Italian political class preferred traditional methods of personalized politics and parliamentary deals. Moreover, as long as the middle class was organized politically on the basis of old-fashioned municipal-based, liberal-monarchical or constitutionalist associations—feeding off the prestige of local elites—there could be no question of accepting the challenge laid down by the reformist socialists. This muted and weak challenge, however, demanded that the middle-class parties negotiate with the PSI on the basis of equality and eventual power sharing. The middle class simply had no counterpart to the national organization of the PSI. When it developed one in the Fascist party, it was designed to crush the socialist movement rather than negotiate with it.

The reformists, however, weakened their position by being politically timid. They declined in 1903, and again in 1911, to accept Giolitti's offer to enter the government. While this refusal might have been correct from the point of view of doctrinal orthodoxy, the reformists had no real alternative but to continue to bargain with Giolitti for concessions from a much less advantageous position. When the Italian economy soured after 1907, the basis for reformism was gradually eroded. The outbreak of the Libyan war ensured that the major electoral reform of 1912, which allowed most males to vote, would not benefit the reformists. The entry of the masses on the political stage during the elections of 1913 only reinforced the polarization of political life.

The reformists were never able to control the PSI after they lost the struggle for the leadership to the maximalists in 1912. Their one chance to regain the party during World War I slipped from their grasp in 1917 and 1918, when, under the sway of the Bolshevik Revolution, the PSI leadership opted for an ultra-revolutionary program. For the most part, from 1912 until 1922, when Turati, Treves, and Matteotti split off to form the Partito Socialista Unitario, the reformists merely sought to avoid the disastrous consequences of the headlong plunge into the search for an Italian version of bolshevism.

Defeat at the hands of the fascists offered the reformists one last chance to regain control over the movement, but again this effort was frustrated after 1934 when the PSI signed the Unity of Action pact with the Communist Party. That accord, and the leftist orientation adopted by Pietro Nenni between 1934 and 1956, crippled the reformists. Unable to influence party policy during the years of transition to a republic from 1944 to 1946, the reformists, led now by Giuseppe Saragat, withdrew from the Socialist Party to form their overtly social-democratic Partito Socialista dei Lavoratori Italiani. But the conditions of the split in 1947 were radically different from those of 1922. Turati and Matteotti took with them the leadership of the CGL and the cooperatives when they left the PSI. This was not the case with Saragat's PSLI, which lacked union support and soon lost almost all of its working-class constituency. No more fitting example of Marx's idea—that history comes first as tragedy and then as farce—could be imagined. In one of the ironic twists of history—just as all the parties of the Italian left moved to an essentially reformist position after 1960—the Italian Social Democratic Party lost its function in the political system. The heirs of Bordiga, Gramsci, and Serrati celebrated the ideological victory of Turati. Togliatti and Nenni, two former revolutionaries, and their successors, Berlinguer and Craxi, led their parties to a substantial acceptance of parliamentary democracy as it had been advocated by reformists from Turati and Bissolati to Matteotti and Saragat.

Maximalism figured as the major casualty of the troubled politics of the Italian left. This variant of socialism had always been more of an attitude toward politics than a coherent ideology. It expressed the unwillingness of the majority of socialists to come to a compromise with the bourgeois order or to accept the rigid discipline of the Communist International. The maximalists were emotionally unprepared to accept the legitimacy of parliamentary democracy. When they took control of the PSI in 1912, the maximalists had no coherent program. They won the victory by default because the reformists were politically exhausted by divisions over participation in the government and over the Libyan war. During their long domination of the PSI, the maximalists led the party into dramatic confrontations with Italian governments. Nearly all of these battles were lost from the start. Tragically, with their eye on the greater prize of revolution, the maximalists rejected lesser but tangible gains that might have transformed Italy into a more democratic system.

One of the great defects of maximalism was the belief that the unity of the PSI could be maintained either by ignoring real differences between right and left factions or by refusing to define a coherent socialist position. Serrati and Lazzari, true maximalists, could not decide whether to opt for the reformists or for the communists when it counted most. Pietro Nenni was, for most of his career, the quintessential maximalist. He began his career in the PSI as a protegé of Serrati. In 1923 he joined Arturo Vella in blocking Serrati's belated efforts to fuse the PSI and PCI. For a time, Nenni seemed to draw closer to the reformist camp. Between 1926 and 1930 he was one of the proponents of reunification between the PSI and the reformist party. Then, when that was accomplished, Nenni proceeded to undermine it by veering once again to the left after 1934. In that year he signed a Unity of Action pact with the PCI, which became the cornerstone of socialist politics until 1956. Then from 1956 until the mid-1970s he urged the PSI to move back toward a policy of collaboration and reform.

Nenni's zig-zag course often involved a series of tactical maneuvers, dictated by external events, that obscured any clear sense of what made the socialist movement different from communism. Without a clear idea of the mission of his own party, the unity of action alliance with the PCI sapped the intellectual and political vitality of the PSI and drove the socialists to their hopeless and self-destructive split in 1947. By that time, the socialists no longer believed in their own party. Awed by the superior organization and militancy of the communists, they embarked under Morandi on a second-rate version of Stalinism in a moribund party. Only after 1953 was there a slow reassertion of autonomy and a gradual recovery from the debacle of the united front, when the PSI all but disappeared in the electoral defeat of 1948.

The entire basis of maximalism collapsed with the boom of the late 1950s and early 1960s. This current within the PSI, which had rested on the alienation of the great majority of peasants and workers, now became a fringe phenomenon of old-line militants, discontented students, intellectuals, and worker radicals who could not abide the new gradualism of the PSI and PCI or the preference of workers for a more comfortable present over the future revolutionary utopia. The new-left movement of the post-1968 period fancied itself as a return to Leninist virtue, but it was the end of a longer national tradition. Maximalism, which had been the mainstream of Italian socialism, now became a cult.

The final tradition on the left that remains to be examined is communism. At first glance, its evolution seems the most surprising. The Italian Communist Party was organized by Bordiga on the most sectarian and extremist program. Its early history gave little indication that it would become the most flexible and innovative communist party in Europe. Three things redirected the course of the PCI. First, the emergence of Antonio Gramsci and Palmiro Togliatti, leaders of extremely high intellectual and political stature, gave the party a rich cultural heritage that firmly implanted the party in the national tradition. The PCI never abandoned its sense of the complexity of Italian economic and social reality, even during the Stalinist era. Second, the PCI maintained continuity within its leadership group after the terrible purges of the 1929–1931 period. The party's defeat at the hands of Mussolini, which rendered it politically ineffectual after 1922, also made it less important in the eyes of Stalin. Togliatti abjectly accepted Stalin's most brutal dictates, but he preserved the essence of the party structure. Fortunately, most of the key party leaders were in exile in Paris rather than Moscow, and were out of the reach of the Soviet dictator.

Finally, Togliatti drew extremely intelligent conclusions from the triumph of fascism and its long domination of Italy. These lessons formed the basis of the "new party" that Togliatti forged after 1944. He concluded that the political and cultural hegemony of the Italian ruling class could never be destroyed by a frontal assault. Moreover, he saw that the fascist regime was based in part on mass organizations and that the Catholic Church could and would create a similar popular mass movement during the postfascist era. After 1944, Togliatti was determined to avoid the extremist policies that marked the Red Years of 1919 and 1920. Coalition politics became the order of the day in order to insert the PCI into the institutions of republican and postfascist Italy. To succeed, Togliatti had to buy time at an extremely high price. The leader of the PCI was willing to sacrifice opportunities for profound but risky change in favor of his long-term goal of building a mass political movement that could not be ignored by bourgeois Italy.

The communists under Togliatti succeeded only in part. The party gained control of the union and cooperative movement and undermined the Socialist party. But the consolidation of its working-class base and the partial destruction of its only ally did not advance the PCI closer to political power. In fact, after 1947, the PCI found itself relegated to the margin of political life. Two factors seemed to reopen the doors for the Communist party. First, the economic boom allowed the communists formally to abandon their revolutionary heritage in favor of overt reformism. They quickly realized that the new Italy that had been created by the "economic miracle" would never respond to a traditional revolutionary appeal. Second, the Christian Democrats, unable to govern on the basis of center-right coalitions, were forced to reopen the dialogue with the newly independent Socialist party and eventually with the PCI.

Economic prosperity finally allowed Italy to create its own version of the neocapitalist welfare state. The vast array of social and economic benefits, currently available to Italian workers, resulted from the pressures exerted on the political system by the socialists and communists from 1960 to 1979 and beyond. Both of the major parties of the Italian left openly operated within the parliamentary system. Each put forward a version of social democracy, but, in the end, their programs differed in degree, not in essence. In fact, until the emergence of Bettino Craxi in 1976, it was the communists who assured voters that their management style, proven countless times on the local level, would make the Italian welfare state function more smoothly.

Yet, once again, the PCI could not find a strategy that would take it to power. From 1973 to 1979 Berlinguer hoped that the alliance with the Catholics—the so-called Historic Compromise—would succeed in bringing the communists, first, a share of political power, and then a parliamentary majority. But the Catholics never needed the PCI's support badly enough to offer more than a temporary alliance that would benefit the Christian Democrats more than the communists in 1977 and 1978. By 1979 the PSI had once again emerged as a possible and, in the short term, a less dangerous partner for the Catholics.

The socialists under Craxi, badly burned by earlier center-left experiments, have recaptured a central role in a parliamentary system that offered only two options: a Catholic-socialist alliance, or a broader coalition that would include the PCI. Craxi, a new, nonideological Social Democrat, took advantage of the total demoralization within the leadership cadre of the Christian Democratic party after more than thirty-five years of continuous power to transform his party's 11 percent parliamentary base into the leadership of the government. He openly used the prime ministership to undermine his communist rival on the left and divide the Christian Democrats on his right. But the socialists have only begun to translate Craxi's personal success into durable gains for the party. The differences over tactics that have grown between the socialists and communists have foreclosed for the immediate future any left alternative. The socialists now risk doing to the PCI what the communists almost accomplished in their policies toward the socialists from 1944 to 1956. They wish to relegate the PCI to the fate of the French communists who have become almost marginal to the Fifth Republic's parliamentary system. But the Italian Communist party, with its hold over a quarter of the electorate, still has many cards to play. To undermine systematically either of the two main parties on the Italian left will benefit neither. Short of a major change in the institutional framework of Italy, such as the direct election of the president, which Craxi would like very much, there is little that either the PSI or PCI can do to alter the balance between them or to win a majority single-handedly.

In the end, this is a book written by a historian, not a political scientist. Our terminal point in 1979 is already perilously close to current events and political prediction. The account presented here offers a background for understanding the evolution of the left and its role in the political system. Despite bitter defeats, the achievement of the Italian left has been considerable. In a land where, historically, things change only to remain the same, the revolution that would bring about a socially and economically modern Italy did occur—but in a totally unexpected form. Perhaps in the context of this new Italy a united left will also emerge that can blend the moral idealism of the revolutionary past with a pragmatic sense of the possibilities for the present.

BIBLIOGRAPHICAL ESSAY

This brief essay does not presume to do justice to the growing body of literature about the history of Italian socialism and communism. The criteria for inclusion are somewhat subjective. These are the works that have proved most useful in the composition of this study. My appreciation of and debt to these scholars is enormous.

THE ITALIAN SOCIALIST PARTY

There are two or three general histories of the Italian Socialist Party from its origins to the present. Giorgio Galli's *Storia del socialismo italiano* (Bari: Laterza, 1980) is a good introduction, but the collective work, edited by Stefano Caretti, Zeffiro Ciuffoletti, and Maurizio Degl'Innocenti, *Lezioni di storia del Partito Socialista Italiano, 1892–1976* (Florence: Cooperativa Editrice Universitaria, 1977) is better, and contains essays by socialist scholars on various periods of the movement. Also useful, if somewhat dated, are *Il movimento operaio e socialista: Bilancio storiografica e problemi storici* (Milan: Edizioni del Gallo, 1965), and Carlo Cartiglia, *Il Partito Socialista Italiano, 1892–1962* (Turin: Loescher, 1978). A multivolume history of the PSI has been projected under the editorship of Giovanni Sabbatucci. Volume 4, which deals with the 1926–1943 period, has appeared: *Storia del socialismo italiano*, vol. 4 *Gli anni del fascismo* (Rome: Il Poligono, 1981). It contains two excellent sections by Bruno Tobia ("I socialisti nell'emigrazione della Concentrazione antifascista ai fronti popolari") and by Leonardo Rapone ("L'età dei Fronti popolari e la guerra").

Most works cover limited periods in the history of the PSI. The classic survey of the literature, with analysis of the early history of the party, is Leo Valiani, *Questioni di storia del socialismo* (Turin: Einaudi, 1958). The prehistory of the movement has been traced by Richard Hostetter, *The Italian Socialist Movement: Origins, 1860–1882* (Princeton: Van Nostrand Company, 1958). Unfortunately, Professor Hostetter never completed the volume that would have carried the history to the founding of the PSI. Aldo Romano's *L'egemonia borghese e la rivolta liberaria, 1871–1882* (Bari: Laterza, 1966) concentrates on the rise and decline of anarchism. Ernesto Ragionieri's *Socialdemocrazia tedesca e socialisti italiani, 1875–1895* (Milan: Feltrinelli, 1961) fills the gap by introducing the development of marxism in Italy. Paul Piccone's *Italian Marxism* (Berkeley: University of California Press, 1983) is insightful, but demands a solid grounding in Italian history and politics.

There are two brief general histories of the PSI from 1892 to the post-World War I period: Gaetano Arfè, *Storia del socialismo italiano, 1892–1926* (Turin: Einaudi, 1965) and Alceo Riosa, *Il Partito socialista italiano dal 1892 al 1918* (Rocca San Casciano: Cappelli, 1969). The ideological conflicts of the 1903–1914 period have been covered in great detail. Giuseppe Mammarella's *Riformisti e rivoluzionari nel Partito socialista italiano, 1900–1912* (Padua: Marsilio, 1968) is a clear and concise summary of the conflicts between reformists and syndicalists. A good study in English of Turati's politics is Spencer Di Scala, *Dilemmas of Italian Socialism: The Politics of Filippo Turati* (Amherst: University of Massachusetts Press, 1980). Franco Livorsi has edited a collection of Turati's writings (*Socialismo e riformismo nella storia d'Italia: Scritti politici, 1878–1932* [Milan: Feltrinelli, 1979]).

An essential source for anyone working on the history of the PSI is the Filippo Turati-Anna Kuliscioff correspondence, which has been edited by Alessandro Schiavi in several volumes beginning with the letters during the crisis of 1898 and continuing to the fascist period: Filippo Turati-Anna Kuliscioff, *Carteggio* (Turin: Einaudi, 1949). This correspondence has been analyzed with additional unpublished material by Brunello Vigezzi in *Giolitti e Turati: un incontro mancato,* 2 vols. (Naples: Ricciardi, 1976) and in *Il PSI, le riforme e la rivoluzione: Filippo Turati e Anna Kuliscioff dai fatti del 1898 alla prima guerra mondiale* (Florence: Sansoni, 1981). There is a collection of essays, *Anna Kuliscioff e l'età del riformismo* (Rome: Mondo Operaio-Edizioni Avanti, 1978), which gives some indication of the impact of the great Russian exile on the movement. Bissolati's career is treated in the biography by Ugoberto Alfassio Grimaldi and Gherardo Bozzetti, *Bissolati* (Milan: Rizzoli, 1983).

For the syndicalist and maximalist side, see Alceo Riosa's *Il sindacalismo rivoluzionario in Italia* (Bari: De Donati, 1976); Enzo Sanatarelli's *La revisione del marxismo in Italia* (Milan: Feltrinelli, 1964); and Renzo De Felice's first volume of his multivolume work on Mussolini, *Mussolini il rivoluzionario* (Turin: Einaudi, 1965), which not only traces the rise of the future Duce within the socialist movement, but also presents a comprehensive picture of Italian maximalism before the Great War. For those syndicalists and socialists who followed Mussolini to fascism, see David D. Roberts, *The Syndicalist Tradition and Italian Fascism* (Chapel Hill: University of North Carolina Press, 1979).

On the rise of the labor movement, see Idomeno Barbadoro, *Storia del sindacalismo italiano: Dalla nascita al fascismo,* 2 vols. (Florence: La Nuova Italia, 1973). Maurizio Degl'Innocenti has provided an important study of the structures of the early PSI in *Geografia e istituzioni del socialismo italiano* (Naples: Guida, 1983).

A special edition of the *Rivista Storica del Socialismo* was dedicated to the history of the PSI during World War I and has been republished as Luigi Cortesi, ed., *Il PSI e la Grande guerra* (Florence: La Nuova Italia, n.d.). On the same subject, but from a local perspective, see *Torino operaia nella Grande guerra* (Turin: Einaudi, 1960).

The tragic history of the PSI from 1918 to 1922 has formed part of the chronicle to the rise of fascism. Both Roberto Vivarelli's *Il dopoguerra in Italia e l'avvento del fascismo,* vol. 1, *Dalla fine della guerra all'impresa del Fiume* (Naples: Istituto Italiano per gli Studi Storici, 1967) and Renzo De Felice's *Mussolini il fascista: La conquista del potere* (Turin: Einaudi, 1966) contain much information about the PSI. Angelo Tasca's *Nascista e avvento del fascismo* (Florence: Nuova Italia, 1950) is merciless toward the maximalists but remains the best analysis of the events leading to the rise of fascism. Giuseppe Maione's *Il biennio rosso* (Bologna: Il Mulino, 1975) is by far the best work dealing with the activities of the PSI during the revolutionary years after World War I. Paolo Spriano has chronicled the most famous of the revolutionary events in *L'occupazione delle fabbriche, settembre 1920* (Turin: Einaudi, 1964). Finally, Tommaso Detti's *Serrati e la formazione del Partito Communista d'Italia* (Rome: Riuniti, 1972) attempts to understand the complicated politics of Giacinto Menotti Serrati.

In addition to the already-cited essays by Tobia and Rapone, the history of the PSI during the years of defeat and exile have been covered in the recent collective work, edited by Francesca Taddei, *L'emigrazione socialista nella lotta contro il fascismo, 1926–1939* (Florence: Sansoni, 1982) and in the essay by Giuseppe Berti to the diaries of Angelo Tasca, *Problemi del movimento operaio: Scritti critici e storici inediti di Angelo Tasca* in *Annali della Fondazione Giangiacomo Feltrinelli 1968* (Milan: Feltrinelli, 1969). Stefano Merli has used some of the Tasca archive for his study of PSI-PCI relations during the 1930s. See *Fronte antifascista e politica di classe: Socialisti e comunisti in Italia, 1923–1939* (Bari: De Donato, 1975). The internal debates in the PSI have been treated extremely well in Simona Colarizzi's *Classe operaia e ceti medi* (Venice: Marsilio, 1976). Jane Slaughter traced the stormy career of Angelica Balabanoff in her essay "Humanism and Feminism in the Socialist Movement: The Life of Angelica Balabanoff" in Jane Slaughter and Robert Kern, *European Women of the Left: Socialism and Feminism and the Problem Faced by Political Women 1890 to the Present* (Westport, Conn.: Greenwood Press, 1981). Aldo Agosti has provided a good intellectual biography of Rodolfo Morandi, one of the key figures in the Internal Center of the PSI: see *Rodolfo Morandi: il pensiero e l'azione politica* (Bari: Laterza, 1971). See also L. Solari, *Eugenio Colorni* (Venice: Marsilio, 1980) and M. Panzanelli, "L'attività politica di Eugenio Curiel," *Storia Contemporanea* 2 (1979). The history of Giustizia e Libertà is treated in Elena Aga Rossi, *Il movimento repubblicano: Giustizia e Libertà, il Partito d'Azione* (Bologna: Cappelli, 1969) and Aldo Garosci, *Vita di Carlo Rosselli* (Florence: Vallecchi, 1973).

The effort to rebuild the PSI during the resistance and in the postwar years is treated in Stefano Merli, *Il 'partito nuovo' di Lelio Basso* (Venice: Marsilio, 1981); in Elio Giovannini, *Lelio Basso e la rifondazione socialista del 1947* (Cosenza: Lerici, 1980); Francesca Taddei, *Il socialismo italiano del dopoguerra: Correnti ideologiche e scelte politiche, 1943–1947* (Milan: Angeli, 1984). The socialists are treated in the larger postwar political context in Piergiovanni Permoli, *La Costituente e i partiti politici italiani* (Bologna: Cappelli, 1966); in Pietro Scoppola, *Gli anni della Costituente fra politica e storia* (Bologna: Il Mulino, 1980); and in Antonio Gambino, *Storia del dopoguerra: Dalla liberazione al potere DC* (Bari: Laterza, 1975). The frustrating experience of the Action Party is given in Giovanni De Luna, *Storia del Partito d'Azione* (Milan: Feltrinelli, 1982).

There are several general histories of postwar Italy. The best is by Norman Kogan, *A Political History of Italy* (New York: Praeger, 1983). An excellent survey of recent events is Frederic Spotts and Theodor Wieser, *Italy: A Difficult Democracy* (London: Cambridge, 1986). Peter Lange and Sidney Tarrow have edited a useful series of essays on the contemporary political system. See *Italy in Transition: Conflict and Consensus* (London: Frank Cass, 1980).

The basic work on the history of the PSI during the postwar period is by Alberto Benzoni and Viva Tedesco, *Il movimento socialista nel dopoguerra* (Padua: Marsilio, 1968). Also useful are *Trent'anni di politica socialista: Atti del Convegno di Studi Storici, Parma 1977* (Rome: Mondo Operaio-Edizioni Avanti, 1977); Ivano Granata, *Il socialismo italiano nella storiografia del secondo dopoguerra* (Bari: Laterza, 1980); Giuseppe Tamburrano, *Storia e cronaca del centro-sinistra* (Milan: Feltrinelli, 1971); Paolo Moretti, *I due socialismi: La scissione di Palazzo Barberini e la nascita della socialdemocrazia* (Milan: Musia, 1975); Antonio Landolfi *Il socialismo italiano: Strutture, comportamenti valori* (Rome: Lerici, 1968); Pasquale Amato, *Il PSI tra frontismo e autonomia* (Cosenza: Lerici, 1978); Valerio Stronati, *Politica e cultura nel Partito Socialista Italiano, 1945–1979* (Naples: Liguori, 1980); and Giancarlo Lupi, *Il crollo della Grande coalizione: La strategia delle elites dei partiti, 1976– 1979* (Milan: SugarCo, 1982). Biographies of the major figures of post-World War II Italian socialism are lacking except for Pietro Nenni, whose diaries have recently been published. See Pietro Nenni, *Tempo di Guerra Fredda: Diari 1943–1956* (Milan: SugarCo, 1981) and *Gli anni del Centro sinistra* (Milan: SugarCo, 1982). Giuseppe Tamburrano has recently published a comprehensive biography of Nenni that uses his diaries and letters. See Giuseppe Tamburrano, *Pietro Nenni* (Bari: Laterza, 1986) and Pietro Nenni, *Intervista sul socialismo italiano* (Bari: Laterza, 1977). Spencer D. Scala's new book, *Renewing Italian Socialism: Nenni to Craxi* (Oxford University Press, 1988), combines interviews with some of the important leaders of Craxi's new PSI with analysis of the future prospects of the Socialist party by a leading American student of socialist politics.

THE ITALIAN COMMUNIST PARTY

The fundamental work on the history of the PCI from its origins to 1945 is Paolo Spriano, *Storia del Partito Comunista Italiano*, 5 vols (Turin: Einaudi, 1967–1975). A brief history, written by a leading intellectual of the PCI, is Giorgio Amendola, *Storia del Partito Comunista Italiano, 1921–1943* (Rome: Riuniti, 1978). If Spriano and Amendola have written the history of the PCI from within, Giorgio Galli has provided a brief, critical history of the party in his *Storia del Partito Comunista Italiano* (Milan: Edizioni il Formichiere, 1976).

On the formation of the PCI, the following are extremely useful: Giovanni Gozzini, *Alle origini del comunismo italiano: Storia della Federazione Giovanile Socialista, 1907–1921* (Bari: Dedalo, 1979); Paolo Spriano, ed., *La cultura italiana del '900 attraverso le riviste*, vol. 6, *L'Ordine nuovo, 1919–1920* (Turin: Einaudi, 1963); Renzo Martinelli, *Il Partito comunista d'Italia, 1921–1926* (Rome: Riuniti, 1977); Palmiro Togliatti, *La formazione del gruppo dirigente del Partito Comunista Italiano nel 1923–24* (Rome: Riuniti, 1974); Paolo Sprinao, *L'Ordine nuovo e i consigli di fabbrica* (Turin: Einaudi, 1971); Claudio Natoli, *La Terza Internationale e il fascismo* (Rome: Riuniti, 1982). The largest collection of documents on the history of the PCI in the early years was published with an extremely important introductory essay by Giuseppe Berti, as *I primi dieci anni di vita del Partito Comunista Italiano: Annali della Fondazione Giangiacomo Feltrinelli 1966* (Milan: Feltrinelli, 1966). Giulio Sapelli's *L'analisi economica dei comunisti italiani durante il fascismo* (Milan: Feltrinelli, 1978) and Franco Sbarberi's *I comunisti italiani e lo stato, 1929–1945* (Milan: Feltrinelli, 1980) cover very well the political and economic thinking that the PCI developed during these years. Ferdinando Ormea's *Le origini dello stalinismo nel PCI* (Milan: Feltrinelli 1978) and Umberto Terracini's memoir, *Sulla svolta* (Milan: La Pietra, 1975) cover the Stalinization of the PCI.

There are several biographies of the founding generation of the PCI. On Bordiga, see Franco Livorsi, *Amadeo Bordiga* (Rome: Riuniti, 1976) and Andreina De Clementi, *Amadeo Bordiga* (Turin: Einaudi, 1971). On Angelo Tasca, see Alceo Riosa, *Angelo Tasca socialista* (Venice: Marsilio, 1979) and A. De Grand, *In Stalin's Shadow: Angelo Tasca and the Crisis of the Left in Italy and France* (De Kalb: Northern Illinois University Press, 1986). Umberto Terracini wrote an overview of his years in the party in *Intervista sul comunismo difficile* (Bari: Laterza, 1978) and Camilla Ravera published her *Diario di trent'anni, 1913–1943* (Rome: Riuniti, 1973).

The publishing of works on Antonio Gramsci is practically an industry, with new titles coming out every year. The classic work is by John Cammett, *Antonio Gramsci and the Origins of Italian Communism* (California: Stanford University Press, 1967), covers the career of Gramsci to the creation of the PCI. A complete biography is by Giuseppe Fiori, *Vita di Antonio Gramsci* (Bari: Laterza, 1966). Good recent treatments of Gramsci's political thought are by Leonardo Paggi, *Gramsci e il moderno principe* (Rome: Riuniti, 1971) and Walter Adamson, *Hegemony and Revolution: Antonio Gramsci's Political and Cultural Theory* (Berkeley: University of California Press, 1980). The best biography of Palmiro Togliatti is by Giorgio Bocca, *Palmiro Togliatti* (Bari: Laterza, 1973), but Ernesto Ragionieri, the editor of Togliatti's collected works, has given us a much more orthodox interpretation of Togliatti's early years in *Palmiro Togliatti* (Rome: Riuniti, 1976).

In addition to these broader studies on Italy's post-1945 politics, there are several works that deal with the recent history of the PCI: Giuseppe Mammarella,

Il Partito Comunista Italiano, 1945–1975: Dalla liberazione al compromesso storico (Florence: Vallecchi, 1976); Sergio Bertelli, *Il gruppo: La formazione del gruppo dirigente del PCI, 1936–1948* (Milan: Rizzoli, 1980); Nello Ajello, *Intellettuali e PCI, 1944–1958* (Bari: Laterza, 1979); Leo Valiani, Gianfranco Bianchi, and Ernesto Ragionieri, *Azionisti, cattolici, comunisti nella Resistenza* (Milan: Franco Angeli, 1971); Mario Margiocco, *Stati uniti e PCI, 1943–1980* (Bari: Laterza, 1981); Santi Fedele, *Fronte popolare: La sinistra e le elezioni del 18 aprile 1948* (Milan: Bompiani, 1978); Grant Amyot, *The Italian Communist Party: The Crisis of the Popular Front Strategy* (New York: St. Martin's Press, 1981); Sidney G. Tarrow, *Peasant Communism in Southern Italy* (New Haven: Yale University Press, 1967); *The Italian Communist Party in International, Comparative and Ideological Perspectives*, special edition of *Studies in Comparative Communism*, 13 (Summer–Autumn 1980); and, finally, the excellent study by Joan Barth Urban, *Moscow and the Italian Communist Party: From Togliatti to Berlinguer* (Ithaca: Cornell University Press, 1986). For the PCI's views on Eurocommunism, see Eric Hobsbawn and Giorgio Napolitano, *The Italian Road to Socialism* (Westport, Conn.: Lawrence Hill, 1977). A broad study of Eurocommunism is contained in Wolfgang Leonhard, *Eurocommunism: Challenge for East and West* (New York: Holt Rinehart and Winston, 1978).

On the extreme-left movements of the 1960s and 1970s, see Mino Monicelli, *L'ultrasinistra in Italia* (Bari: Laterza, 1978). Richard Drake's work on political terrorism in Italy to be published by Indiana University Press will deal with this subject in a more comprehensive way. Joan Barkan's *Visions of Emancipation: The Italian Workers' Movement since 1945* (New York: Praeger Special Studies, 1984) covers some of the history of the post-1945 labor movement, but Sergio Turone's *Storia del sindacato in Italia, 1943–1969* (Bari: Laterza, 1973) is more complete, if somewhat dated. The role of women in the PSI and in the PCI is the subject of Mirella Allioso's and Marta Ajo's, *La donna nel socialismo italiano tra cronaca e storia, 1892–1978* (Cosenza: Lerici, 1978); see also Maria Michetti, Margherita Repetto, and Luciana Viviani, *UDI: laboratorio di politica delle donne* (Rome: Cooperativa Libera Stampa, 1984).

Finally, no bibliography would be complete without mentioning the extremely useful biographical dictionary of the worker movement, edited by Franco Andreucci and Tommaso Detti, *Il movimento operaio italiano*, 5 vols. (Rome: Riuniti, 1975–1978).

Index